SECOND EDITION

VISUAL
WORKPLACE

VISUAL THINKING

VISUAL WORKPLACE

VISUAL THINKING

CREATING ENTERPRISE EXCELLENCE
THROUGH THE TECHNOLOGIES
OF THE VISUAL WORKPLACE

GWENDOLYN D. GALSWORTH

SECOND EDITION

CRC Press
Taylor & Francis Group
Boca Raton London New York

CRC Press is an imprint of the
Taylor & Francis Group, an **informa** business

A PRODUCTIVITY PRESS BOOK

Visual Office®, Visual Machine®, and Visual-Lean®, are federally registered service marks, globally licensed to Visual Thinking Inc.

All photographs in this book are the property of Gwendolyn Galsworth or used and cited by permission of the person and/or company represented in the associated photograph.

Book Design: William Stanton
Cover Design: Iwan Sujono, eOne Design, Sydney, Australia
Editor: Aurelia Navarro

CRC Press
Taylor & Francis Group
6000 Broken Sound Parkway NW, Suite 300
Boca Raton, FL 33487-2742

First issued in paperback 2019

© 2017 by Gwendolyn D. Galsworth
CRC Press is an imprint of Taylor & Francis Group, an Informa business

No claim to original U.S. Government works

ISBN-13: 978-1-138-50214-7 (hbk)
ISBN-13: 978-1-138-68468-3 (pbk)

Visit the Taylor & Francis Web site at
http://www.taylorandfrancis.com

and the CRC Press Web site at
http://www.crcpress.com

Printed and bound in Great Britain by
TJ Books Limited, Padstow, Cornwall

To the millions of supervisors, managers, change agents, trainers, and executives around the world who contribute their work lives to their companies.

AS KINGFISHERS CATCH FIRE

As kingfishers catch fire, dragonflies draw flame;
As tumbled over rim in roundie wells
Stones ring; like each tucked string tells, each hung bell's
Bow swung finds tongue to fling out broad its name.
Each mortal thing does one thing and the same:
Deals out that being indoors each one dwells;
Selves—goes itself; *myself* it speaks and spells,
Crying *What I do is me: for that I came.*

—Gerard Manley Hopkins

C O N T E N T S

List of Photos, Albums, Figures & Insets

Section 2
Chapter 3: Leadership and the Power Inversion

Chapter 4: The I-Driven Culture

Section 3
Chapter 5: Visual Order: Visuality's Foundation

Chapter 6: Visual Standards and Visual Scheduling/Visual Displays

Chapter 7: Visual Leadership: Metrics, Problem-Solving & Hoshin

Chapter 8: Visual Controls, Visual Pull Systems, and Visual Guarantees

Chapter 9: Visual Machine, Visual-Lean Office & the Visual Macro Environment

ABOUT GWENDOLYN GALSWORTH

Gwendolyn D. Galsworth, PhD, is president and founder of Visual Thinking Inc. and The Visual-Lean® Institute, where in-house trainers and external consultants are trained and certified in her nine core visual workplace courses. Dr. Galsworth's career in operational excellence began as the head of training and development at Productivity Inc. in the early 1980s. There she worked closely with Dr. Ryuji Fukuda to adapt, among many things, the CEDAC® method for western audiences—and with Dr. Shigeo Shingo on poka-yoke for the West. She was also principal developer and implementer of Visual Factory, TEIAN (associate-based suggestion systems), and Hoshin Kanri/X-Type Matrix Planning (policy deployment).

A former Baldrige and Shingo Prize Examiner, Dr. Galsworth helps companies all over the world accelerate their rate of transformation, build leaders, strengthen cultural alignment, and achieve long-term, sustainable bottom-line outcomes through the technologies of the visual workplace. She is author of seven books, including *Work That Makes Sense: Operator-Led Visuality* and *Visual Workplace-Visual Thinking*, both of which are recipients of the prestigious Shingo Prize. All of Galsworth's books are available globally on Amazon, Kindle, and Print-On-Demand.

When not onsite with clients or teaching at the Institute, Gwendolyn can be found hiking or working on her next book. She can be reached through *visualworkplace.com*.

Thanks

Acknowledgements

Writing the second edition of *Visual Workplace-Visual Thinking* brought wonderful new people into my orbit—and a renewed opportunity to work with many of the remarkable people who already participate in my professional community. For that alone, this book has brought a bounty.

First—always first—amongst them, is my editor, Aurelia Navarro. She has long been a part of my life and my work, having been editor for every book I have written and for practically every word. She understands my voice. Her skill, though, goes far beyond watchdogging the shape and sense of my books. Ms. Navarro brings an unerring understanding of what the reader will understand and wants to understand. She is a master of the arc. I shall never succeed in thanking you enough, Aurelia.

Great thanks as well goes to Iwan Sujono of eOne Design in Sydney, Australia for the splendid new front cover design for this book's second edition.

Another new contributor is art designer, Ethan Parker Wright. Though much of the original book design by William Stanton was retained for this second edition, Ethan agreed to take on a tough deadline and tricky challenges—and delivered meticulous work, flawlessly, and with unfailing good cheer. Thank you.

Cindy Lyndin, VP of Communications at my company, Visual Thinking Inc., helped on so many aspects of this second edition. Though not an editor by title, Ms. Lyndin has an exceptional ear for the well-turned phrase as well as for ones that go thud. She is a fastidious proof-reader. Cindy, your willing participation was instrumental in achieving the book's fine quality and meeting our deadline. Thank you.

Derek Neuts, our IT/website/marketing guru, is an Air Force veteran whose skill, professionalism, steadfastness, and good heart are unsurpassed. We are so honored to have you on our team. Your special gift to this book is the website you built while I wrote. Both your project and mine reached completion within a week of each other, giving me twice as much to celebrate. Thank you.

Steven Li, of Visual Workplace/China, fearless educator and intrepid translator of this book's first edition. China and I thank you and David Cao.

Michael Sinocchi and Alexandria Gryder of Productivity Press. Thank you for your courtesy, expertise, and care in launching this book's second edition.

I am a very lucky person. I work in a field I love and every day I encounter brilliant visual thinkers who share with me (and you) their dazzling inventions. Huge thanks to the many hundreds of individuals who contributed their creativity to this book in the form of their own visual solutions and inventions (some of them used in this book, some in books to come)—and to companies supporting them in this.

Because this book is written for managers, supervisors, and executives, I express a special thanks to you. You are the stewards of the future of your company and the custodians of its current efforts. Your leadership makes a difference every day in the work lives of the people who depend on you—your employees, customers, suppliers, shareholders, and communities. For all that and more, I thank you.

To you who have allowed us to enter your companies and assist you on the journey to workplace visuality, thank you for your vision, and for your pursuit of excellence before we arrived and after we had completed our work with you.

My special thanks to: Joseph Linehan, Ken Theiss, Steve Harvey, Paul Baker, Larry Moore, Bill Cornell, Jim Looney, Rick Ell, Dorothy Wall, Sheila Bowersmith, Michael Church, James Justice, Ron and Judy Lake, Dave Dobbins, Gerald Holland, and the entire production team at Parker Dennison (formerly Dennison Hydraulics); Curt Williams, Matt Furlan, Troy Gerard, and the entire production team at Parker Hannifin; Larry Pike, Mark Swisher, Marty Harnish, Margie Herrara, John Casey, Robert Boykin and the entire production team at Lockheed-Martin; Peter Dobbs, Stephen Pollard, Michael Kern, and Robin Tannenburg at Rolls-Royce Aerospace/UK.

Also to: Rick Keller, Donald Van Pelt, Jr., Steve Renforth, and the team at Plymouth Tube; Henk Nooteboom, Marc De Leeuw, Henk Hop, Frank Bogels, Jan Peters, Coby Hermens, Max Janssen, Victor Geertruida, and the entire production team at Royal Nooteboom Trailers/Holland; Lars Stenqvist, Henk Heijden, and the entire production team at Scania Trucks/Holland; Tom Wiseman, April Love, and Jason Morin, and the entire production team at Trailmobile/Canada.

Beverly Nichols, Rich Mini, John Barrett, Dave Martin, Joyce Clark, and the entire production team at Seton Identification Products; Ronn Page, Carleton Hitchcock, Jonathan Hitchcock, Cindy Krejcha, Mike Suchy, Melanie Haggard, Tim Auelt, Wes Gustafson, Ron Halliday, Adam Koronka, Mike Robbins, Ken Trottier, Troy Zuelzke, and the entire production team at Hitchcock Industries; Dave Reiss, Paul Plant, Bill Antunes, Cindy Barter, Luis Catatao, Bob Comeau, the incomparable John Pacheco, and the entire production team at United Electric Controls.

Carol Lepper, Georgia Brown, and Carol Labanco of Midwest Regional Medical Center, Cancer Treatment Centers of America; Armando Botti, Socorro Garza, Mark Brown, and the entire production team at Delphi Deltronicos; Florencia Martinez, and the entire production team at Delphi Rimir; Annie Yu, Kenny Bushmich, George LeVan, Paulette Benedictus, and the entire production team at Skyworks Solutions (formerly Alpha Industries); Angie Alvarado, Frank Lopuzinski, Georgeann Georges, Marv Thaxton, and the entire site and technical team at Sears Home Repair Services.

Dr. Shigeo Shingo, Kenneth Snyder, Robert Miller, Jake Raymer, Shaun Barker, and Mary Price of the Shingo Institute; Sherrie Ford and Steve Hollis of Power Partners; Wes Eklund, Brett Balkema, and the entire production team at Fleet Engineers; Barry Landon, Mark Metzger, Joseph Wilson, and the entire production team at Schlumberger; John Saathoff, Sue Osier, Janet Jones, Carolyn Rabe, Pat Humke, Larry Penn, Deanna Butler, Beverly Sparks, Buzz Harlan, Melody Sparrow, and the entire production team at Harris Corporation; Jerry Hall, Junior Oliver, Francis Davis, and the entire production team at Delphi Automotive/Plant 20/Indiana; Jeff Madsen of Wiremold; and Jeff Ellis of Freudenberg-NOK,

Cleveland, Georgia.

For their brilliant insights and steadfast support over the years in the tricky business of business, my heartfelt thanks to Dr. Ryuji Fukuda; Dr. Carol Shaw and Jeanne Steele; Dr. Richard Schonberger; Marley Lunt; Norman Bodek; Tom Duffy; Don Guild; Dr. Robert "Doc" Hall; and Tricia Moody.

To the VTI Team, in addition to those already mentioned, my sincere appreciation goes to Jessica Russell, Harald Hope, Beth Ann Bennett, and Merlin the Cat.

For the gifts of friendship and care, I send great thanks to Mataare, Dawn Bothie, Carolyn Hawkins, Kathryn and Andrew Kimball, Jacqueline and Robert Miessen, Wally Chapman, Marilynn Considine, Diana Brynes, Sarah Fahey, Camilla England, Judy Barry, Linda Caso, Debaura Shantzek, Jan Caviness, Sara Kane, Robert Zubik, Marcy Roban, Sarah Sporn, Howard Boster, Sharon Ward, and Claude Kennedy.

And to my remarkable teacher and guide, Swami Chetanananda, a lifetime of gratitude.

To my family, for all that you are to me: my brother, Gary Galsworth, my nieces, Ondine Galsworth, Stacy Joyce, and Karen Cathcart; my nephew, Daniel Spencer Galsworth. And to those who have passed on: my parents, Geraldine and Daniel Galsworth, Robert, my brother, and Mimi Breen—I send you all such love.

And, finally, my eternal gratitude to Philip Hylos, Samuel Bear, and Anderson Merlin for their wildly creative participation in my life and their flawless, unwavering guidance. It is your song I sing.

VISUAL
WORKPLACE

VISUAL THINKING

Introduction to
the Second Edition

I am so pleased to welcome you to the second edition of *Visual Workplace/Visual Thinking*. A lot has happened in the twelve years since the book was first published; nearly every page had to be re-constructed or re-written—and many, many pages added.

My continued work helping companies convert to visuality has uncovered elegant new formulations of visual workplace theory and practice, with faster results, wider impact, and increasingly more stable outcomes. Some of these outcomes stack nicely in the business-benefit column. Others support cultural alignment and the more complete development of improvement infrastructure. I am delighted to share these with you in this new edition.

We start with Chapter 7, a full chapter on Doorway 4, newly titled *Visual Leadership*. Previously, Doorway 4 covered only metrics and problem-solving. In working with corporate and site executives, however, it was clear to me that visuality had a great deal to contribute to their effectiveness as leaders and as people. Chapter 7 maps that out for you and reveals how structure can induce skill, clarity, and even courageousness. Visual leadership principles and practices has become a field of continuing research and application for me; and I will have more to say about this in my forthcoming book of the same name.

The relevance and usefulness of the Ten-Doorway Model has only increased over the past decade. It remains the organizing principle of this edition and of my client work, which now always begins with an assessment of the client site against a Ten-Doorway reference.

Chapter 10 addresses another new piece of the conceptual puzzle: the connection between workplace visuality and the commonly (and, in my view, wrongly) used term "visual management." They are neither the same nor equal. Visual management (VM) is a *subset* of the visual workplace and though it is important, it does not stand alone. The central diagram in this chapter spells that out by placing VM along the a continuum of visual function. Words matter and I think you will find this discussion an important addition to your understanding.

And finally, because the relationship between visuality and lean remains largely misunderstood, we visit this theme in both Chapters 1 and 11. Since its introduction some 30 years ago, "lean" as a concept has become diluted and stretched thin. Here, I return to the more traditional description of lean—with its intense focus on time—and contrast that with visuality's focus on building a robust informational landscape in support of excellence. They are different but equal, like two wings of a bird, and ideally work in parallel.

Visuality builds the informational details of work into the physical environment. As a result, people can adhere to those details and work precisely and with increasing, soul-satisfying self-regulation. Lean defines, extends, accelerates, and controls the flow of work that visual spells out, dramatically reducing lead-time and flow distance. Visual embeds lean gains into the physical workplace and creates self-leadership and alignment on every level of the organization. Visual and lean work hand-in-hand; they are of equal importance.

There is understandable confusion on this point because nearly every early training session on lean has a built-in module under the "5S" rubric that teaches the importance of orderliness, supported with any number of lines and labels. This, in turn, leads people to mistakenly assume that the lean approach incorporates visual. It does not.

In fact, as you move through the chapters of this book, you will see that applying 5S solely within the context of lean not only gives us a false impression that we are implementing workplace visuality, it also vastly reduces the impact that 5S can contribute to the company's journey to excellence.

In over 35 years of research and hands-on implementation, I have never found an approach more powerful than workplace visuality in liberating, empowering, and aligning the workforce—not just value-add employees but all employees, including managers and executives. And it almost always triggers double-digit productivity gains, often as high as 30%. Because organizations have an incomplete understanding of the visual approach, however, they under-implement and therefore under-use the remarkable set of principles, concepts, methods, tools, and practices that constitute the technologies of the visual workplace.

A New Understanding

This greatly amplified second edition invites you to consider a wholesale upgrade of your vision and understanding of visuality—and how and why it is capable of populating the operational landscape with hundreds, even thousands, of visual devices and mini-systems that redefine, the way: work gets done, waste is reduced, employees are involved, customers are served, and profit is made in your organization.

Embedded in this invitation is the promise of a new enterprise, one that reaches for and gains excellence as a way of doing business, as part of daily work. That excellence is founded upon the emergence of a new core competency in the enterprise, one that I call *visual thinking*.

> *Visual thinking is the ability of each employee to recognize motion and the information deficits that trigger it—and then to eliminate both through solutions that are visual.*

Visual thinking, which fits hand-in-glove with lean principles and outcomes, is the doorway to the tomorrow you have been seeking, whatever the industry, whatever the venue: manufacturing site, continuous process flow facility, office, agency, hospital, oil rig, utilities system, construction site, hospital, retail store or open-pit mine. There is no work setting the visual workplace cannot transform.

How to Use this Book

Ultimately, this is a book about thinking—visual thinking—and how to create a workforce of visual thinkers. It is written for executives, managers, supervisors, team leaders, and union leadership in its entirety—in short, for anyone and everyone who must work through others to achieve their own objectives and those of the organization they serve.

The second book in this series, *Work That Makes Sense*, focuses on the visual contribution of operators and line employees—the value-add level of the enterprise.

This book is most emphatically not an implementation manual, even though it provides many details on the previously misunderstood field of workplace visuality. While it explains what each visual workplace technology is, implementation requires much more detail. The improvement workscape is already littered with too many failed implementations—failed because either the initiative caused more harm than good and/or because improvements did not last.

Primarily, then, this is a book about knowledge and a new way of thinking. The first of its four sections focuses on basic concepts and principles, with Chapter 1 discussing enterprise excellence and the pure power of visual information-sharing. Chapter 2 presents the eight building blocks of visual thinking and is as close to a methods primer as you will find in this volume.

The second section focuses on the culture of work, beginning with the discussion in Chapter 3 of the role of executives in discovering and developing new facets of leadership—including initiating the empowerment conversion that results in a deeply engaged, spirited, inventive, and aligned workforce. Chapter 4 discusses the evolution of individual employees into visual thinkers, capable of creating a genuinely visual work environment.

The five chapters in the book's third section detail the technologies of the visual workplace, what they are, why they are important, and who takes the lead in implementing them. In the process, the reader walks through the ten doorways that lead into a fully-functioning visual workplace, one that includes such categories of visual functions as: visual order, visual standards, visual displays/visual scheduling, visual metrics, visual problem-solving, visual leadership, visual controls, visual pull systems, and visual guarantees—plus the visual machine®, and the visual-lean® office. Also presented is the role and importance of the visual macro team in the company and an enterprise-wide audit process, focused on the extent to which visual principles are in place—not just visual tasks.

The final book section contains two chapters. The first defines visual management as a sub-set of the visual workplace, describing its important but narrow contribution to operational excellence. The final chapter of the book explains how the Ten-Doorway Model can be used as an assessment tool and then supports that with a mini-case study of a company that opened seven of the ten doorways as it underwent a complete visual conversion—a transformation of everything.

 Graphics, illustrations, and charts anchor your understanding, along with 25 photo albums of actual examples. Other visual solutions populate the text. I hope these visual devices and visual systems knock your socks off, much as they knocked off mine when I first watched them being developed.

As you turn the last page, it is my sincere wish that you will have gained a deeper and more complete understanding of why workplace visuality is crucial to your company's journey to excellence and your own.

If all goes well, by book's end, you will be well on your own way to becoming a visual thinker in your own right—and interested in helping others become visual thinkers as well. Let the visual transformation begin.

Section | **One**

VISUAL BASICS

This is a time of great change for all aspects of work, across all industries, on every possible organizational level. The patterns and paradigms of the past no longer serve. Those of the future are not yet in place. We are in a time of transition.

Part of that transition requires a redefinition of what prosperity means and a reformulation of how excellence is achieved in the workplace. A powerful part of that new formula is workplace visuality.

In this section's first chapter, *The Visual Workplace and the Excellent Enterprise*, we will:

- Make broad-stroke distinctions between visual's approach to improvement and that of lean;

- Paint a picture of a fully-functioning visual workplace;

- Name *information deficits* as the enemy and *motion* (moving without working) as its footprint;

- Describe the remarkable bottom-line and work

culture conversion the visual approach creates, when effectively implemented; and

- Show the importance of launching a visual initiative, even for companies that cannot or have no immediate plans to implement lean.

Chapter 2, *The Building Blocks of Visual Thinking*, focuses entirely on the set of principles and tools fundamental to installing workplace visuality as a new core competency. These conceptual elements may appear to be discrete and sequential. It would be more accurate, however, to describe them as a *system of elements* because of the way they interact and impact each other. In this regard, the eight building blocks represent more of a mindset (a cycle of thinking) than a step-by-step prescription for improvement action.

We are what we repeatedly do.
Excellence, then, is not an act
but a habit.

Aristotle

CHAPTER | **1**

The Visual Workplace and the Excellent Enterprise

The entire world of work—factories, hospitals, banks, airports, stores, and government agencies—is striving for operational excellence. They want to make work safer, simpler, more logical, uniform, fluid, linked, and far less costly. Companies now commit to this conversion to excellence, both as a destination and a journey.

The journey is one of building stability and growth in the organization and creating prosperity for shareholders, executives, and the workforce itself—as well as for the communities where the organization resides, and the environment which supports it.

Some call this the *journey to lean*. But are they correct? Are lean and excellence in operations really the same? Or is lean, like visuality, a co-contributor to operational excellence? This is my premise: that the technology of lean and the technology of the visual workplace work hand-in-hand to build outcomes that are foundational. They are co-creators of excellence in operations.

What is Lean?

A great deal has transpired in the field of operations since the term "lean" appeared at the end of the 1990s. My own history in this field started over a decade earlier when western companies searched for the secrets of the so-called Japanese Miracle, best exemplified by the automotive giant, Toyota.

Exhilarated by Toyota's success, companies in the West imported cultural formulas like quality circles and employee suggestion systems. On the technical side, they investigated JIT/pull, kanban, quick changeover, and load leveling. They made good use of all of them.

In the 25 years since, however, the cultural and technical sides of Toyota's success have become fused in the minds of many of these companies, turning a field of exquisitely-defined improvement methodologies into a murky alphabet soup of good-enoughs, including the vast catch-all—CI, continuous improvement.

When I define lean, I shy away from this "all-things-to-all people" array and cling steadfastly to the precise application that ties lean to improving the critical path—the route that material, information, and people follow as they move through the company and either add or gain value. That path is comprised of both macro flows of value and hundreds, even thousands, of micro flows. It is, in short, the value stream.

I hold to this as lean's abiding purpose: to identify and eliminate barriers in the critical path—repeatedly and relentlessly, cycle after cycle, in its uncompromising war on waste. Lean's macro metric is time and its corollary, speed. The goal of lean is to make work happen more quickly. Drive the time out. Shrink the footprint/shrink time. Shrink time/shrink cost.

Time as lean's driver powers that side of operational excellence. When a company launches a lean conversion, it deploys a core set of time-based methods: standard work, cellular design, quick changeover, and pull systems (that can culminate in the high-speed scheduling system called *heijunka*). This—in the playbook that Shigeo Shingo gave me in 1985—is how lean is achieved in operations.

Naturally, there are mindset changes that accompany this, especially on the management level. Yes, lean has a significant impact on your work culture. But the cultivation of an improved work culture is not, in his play-book or mine, a part of lean's mandate (however much that definition may have morphed in its popular usage).

Lean is a pre-set engineering change in which many participate. And a handsome bit of work it is, too. The gains are equally impressive, as seen in these representative results from lean's success in manufacturing:

- Product flow distance and flow time shrink by 60%–80%
- Product defects decline by 60%–90%
- Finished goods inventories all but vanish
- WIP levels are cut from days (or even weeks) to hours
- Productivity levels double or even triple, using half the square footage or less
- Batches (and, with them, lead times) are slashed to a cycle of one
- All at a dramatically lower cost and produced in a radically safer environment

Liberated from its former burdens, the company is free to innovate and grow. This is the promise and reality of a lean conversion. What enterprise would not be overjoyed to achieve it?

Those improvements, impressive though they are, do not represent the sum and substance of operational excellence. Operational excellence is a far more comprehensive outcome. To qualify, you must not only achieve excellence in operations, you must have a system that is fully capable of sustaining that excellence. That is because lean gains, left on their own, can and do routinely erode—often quickly. Sustainability, then, is the differentiator.

The Visual Workplace

The self-same companies that achieve the dazzling lean outcomes cited above often do not realize—and therefore do not prepare for—the erosion of those gains. Yes, unless specific other steps are systematically undertaken during the lean conversion, those hard-won results will deteriorate. It may take a while. Since it usually takes three to five years to convert an operation over to lean, it can take about that long for the gains to evaporate. But it could take less, even as short as a year. Either way, evaporate they will. The heart aches and the pocketbook weeps to see it all go away.

Companies are stunned when this begins to happen. At first, they may attribute the weakening of results to a bad crop of managers or a distraction in the corporate plan. Only after months does the corporation understand that in its rush to lean, it neglected one crucial building block of success, the one that would ensure that it lasted: *the visual workplace.*

The purpose of a visual workplace is to embed the details of your operations into the living landscape of work through visual devices and visual systems. These devices and systems not only stabilize your lean gains, they build entirely new levels of performance and improvement capability into the enterprise: precision, sustainability, and self-leadership.

Visuality is not about buckets and brooms or posters and signs. It is a compelling operational imperative, central to your war on waste, and crucial to meeting daily performance goals, impeccable safety, vastly reduced lead times, dramatically improved quality, and an accelerated flow that you control at will.

Lean addresses the time-driven facets of your operations. Visuality addresses the informational landscape. If you ask which is more important, it is of course the wrong question.

The same world of work that is rightly committed to lean has begun to recognize the importance of visual information-sharing and the visual workplace. Yet many people still underestimate visuality's tremendous power, thinking of it as an add-on to—or enabler of—lean. In this they are mistaken.

The technologies of the visual workplace are, in their sum, a comprehensive methodology for transforming the entire physical work environment and making work safer, simpler, more logical, uniform, fluid, linked, and far less costly—*while ensuring that operational outcomes are not just repeatable but sustainable* (including in low-volume/high-mix work sites). As a result, the enterprise becomes increasingly capable of creating value at less cost and building prosperity for employees, stakeholders, and the community.

Yes, visuality is not lean; nor is it lean's little helper. The two are, instead, equal and powerful partners in operational excellence—a partnership I call, for the purposes of this book, *The Visual-Lean® Alliance.*

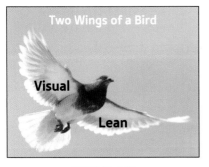

FIGURE 1.1:
EQUAL PARTNERS

The Visual-Lean® Alliance

The correct relationship between *visuality* and *lean* is more in keeping with the way wings work on a bird. Both wings are required if the bird is to fly—and yet they are separate (Figure 1.1).

One of the bird's wings represents lean. The other wing is for workplace visuality. The first wing is about the critical path, time, and pull. The second wing is about information, meaning, and adherence. Which one is more important? The critical path without information? Pull without adherence? Or how about information without time? Ask a bird which of its two wings is more important—and it will answer by flying away. A one-winged bird, no matter which wing remains, is no better than a turkey and not nearly as tasty.

The enterprise needs both visual and lean if it is to get off the ground, sustain flight, and reach its destination. This is the visual-lean journey to operational excellence.

You would be mistaken, however, to think only lean organizations are ready for workplace visuality. And just as mistaken to assume the principles and practices of the visual workplace are best deployed in companies that have not yet launched lean—those with high-inventory levels, long lead times, quality problems, large batch production, fire-fighting management, and a demoralized workforce. In fact, visuality builds dramatic business and people results in both scenarios.

What happens when you bring the power of visuality to a company that has not yet started lean? Our experience with such companies is extensive. A favorite example is a stamping plant in Michigan that had stacks of inventory when we arrived—and stacks when we left 18 months later. Yet, in the interim, productivity (which in this company was a roll-up of lead time, quality, and on-time delivery) had improved from 15% to 30% in each department and across the facility as a whole. As for employee morale—well, let's just say the company finally had some; and it was sparkling (Photo Album 1).

Should that company have waited until it had implemented lean before launching workplace visuality? Based on three decades in the field, my answer is absolutely not. In many organizations, a strong visual workplace initiative is easier and much more effective *prior* to lean. Done first, visuality grooms the work environment as well as the work culture and paves the way for a resounding lean success.

Why wait? Understand where workplace visuality fits in, what it can do for you and your company—and why. Understand its power to transform and inspire even as it builds and secures performance. Start where you are. Start now.

Photo Album 1

The Visual Where
at Fleet Engineers

Implementing Workplace Visuality First

Fleet Engineers in Flint, Michigan is a high volume/low mix manufacturer of mud flaps for the trucking industry. Fleet began its journey to excellence by implementing workplace visuality. When the company was ready to tackle the macro flow, the site had a rich application of visuals already in place and a workforce of visual thinkers, poised to take on the challenge. Here is a sample of only one of hundreds of pockets of visual transformation.

The Pre-Visual-Lean® Workplace ▶

This snapshot of the FB-27 cell was typical of the overall state of the company's production floor before the launch—piles of WIP and stacks of finished goods inventory.

◀ WIP on Wheels

Fleet's FB-27 Cell was its first visual workplace showcase. With floor borders in place, the team realized it could put bins of WIP on wheels and do its own material handling—instead of waiting for the shift's single forklift. This small innovation, in the midst of many, reduced material handling inside the cell by 100%.

Double-Function Borders ▶

This double-border function lets the FB-27 team tell at-a-glance which product was being worked on—straight on for Product A; slanted for Product B. Such local and particular needs-to-know keep a visual implementation vital and build ever more refined information into the process of work itself.

The Solution: Visual Meaning—Visual Performance

What precisely is a visual workplace? Here is the definition I developed many years ago and use throughout this book:

> A *visual workplace is a self-ordering, self-explaining, self-regulating, and self-improving work environment—where what is* supposed *to happen* does *happen, on time, every time, day or night, because of visual solutions.*

This definition has not changed over more than three decades of implementations. It is worth a closer look. The first half of the definition describes the outcome in terms of functionality:

- The environment will keep itself orderly

- It can and will explain itself to us

- Because the work environment can explain itself, it will regulate itself

- And because these are in place, over time, the workplace acquires the ability to correct itself—to become self-improving.

The second half of the definition describes a broader outcome: the ability of a visual workplace to reliably and predictably assure the execution of *what is supposed to happen*: your standards—your technical and procedural standards. Why is that important? Your standards are the means by which the enterprise translates perceived value (what the customer wants) into received value (what the customer buys). Your standards ensure that both happen repeatedly and reliably as part of the work itself.

In its entirety, the definition at the top of this section positions workplace visuality as a strategy that translates the thousands of informational transactions that transpire every day in the life of the enterprise into *visible meaning*. This visible meaning doesn't just impact performance; it creates performance.

That's right, the visual workplace is a gigantic adherence mechanism that ensures that what is supposed to happen does happen—on time, every time, day or night—because of visual devices and visual mini-systems.

> *Management means getting people to do ordinary things extraordinarily well.* —Ryuji Fukuda

INSET 1.1: WE ARE VISUAL BEINGS

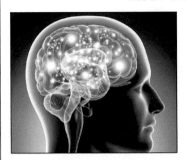

OUR BRAIN CONSTANTLY
SEEKS VISUAL INFORMATION

We are visual beings, therefore we live in a visual world, and not the other way around. The world—with all its useful wayfinding devices and self-regulating people systems—did not teach us to be visual. These devices did not teach us the value of visual information-sharing for safety and the quality of our lives. We, as sense-based beings, require that of our world.

Walk through an airport and you see all sort of signs with all sorts of information on them: at the airline counters; as you approach security, are processed, and leave; as you walk to your gate. From the moment we enter an airport, visual information-sharing is helping us get precisely where we need to go, on time, and safely. Yes, we live in a world full of visual devices. Are they important? Take a moment and erase them in your mind's eye and you will understand that they are indispensable. Without them, not only would we struggle but our very economy would not be possible.

But the world did not teach us to get visual so we would not struggle. The world is populated with visual devices because we need it to be so. Fully 50% of human brain function is dedicated to finding and interpreting visual information. This function is built into our brain. We do not instruct our brain to seek out visible information. It simply does—just as our hearts beat without any decision on our part. From the dawn of humankind, we used our sense of sight to protect ourselves from danger and the unknown. When we left our primitive dwellings and built civilizations, our reliance on sight-based information did not just persist—it grew stronger. Our world is visual because we need it to be so.

We are beings of our senses, all five of them—sound, touch, taste, hearing, and sight. But our sense of sight dominates. What we see with our eyes gives us pleasure, fires our imagination, rallies our resources, makes us feel deeply—and can make us laugh.

The combination of our senses and our mind creates an understanding within us of something that is at once vast and personal, crucial and appealing: relationship—relationship between ourselves and others and between ourselves and the things of the world.

WHAT WE SEE WITH OUR EYES GIVES US PLEASURE, FIRES OUR IMAGINATION, RALLIES OUR RESOURCES, MAKES US FEEL DEEPLY—AND CAN MAKE US LAUGH.

We send messages with our eyes—and we receive them, naturally. Not just with our eyes but with all our senses. Our senses connect us with others and enrich the enjoyment of our lives. A freshly-baked loaf of bread, for example, is a delight to our senses: beautiful to behold in its golden roundness, filling the room with its fragrant aroma, crispy to the touch as we reach for it, with a sharp crunchy sound when we bite into it—and then, yum, what a taste! Our senses envelop us and we enjoy the

THE PRE-VISUAL WORKPLACE CAN SEEM LIKE A DESERT

bread, on a largely unconscious, involuntary basis. The messages come. They just happen.

And in that black box we call mind, these messages are translated into meaning—and meaning into action, naturally. Why not also at work?

Yes, our senses support our lives and our understanding of our lives. We want to experience our world, to understand it, to know it. We don't need to be motivated in doing this. The compelling vitality of our senses makes this unavoidable and exhilarating. Why not also at work?

We are visual beings—sight-dominant beings. Without an effective deployment of visuality at work, we are quite literally lost—as though dropped in the center of the Sahara Desert. We have no navigational anchor.

Without a visual workplace, we find ourselves in a state of risk—physically, psychologically, and emotionally.

Without visual information-sharing, we don't know what to do, which way to go, or how to move forward. The only thing we can do is to ask questions, that is, if we can find anyone

WITHOUT VISUALITY, WE ARE AT RISK

to ask them of. How likely, then, is it that we can do our work? How do we orient? How do we find our way, move forward safely, with confidence and purpose without a workplace that shares information with us, at-a-glance? Without a workplace that speaks?

Without a work environment populated with visual devices, our questions can rapidly surpass our ability to keep track of them—and we go numb or ballistic. Visuality is fundamental to our ability to conceptualize, connect, and contribute.

Human-based environments are flooded with visual devices—cinemas, parking lots, sports stadiums, retail stores, supermarkets, and our roads and highways. We are visual beings. We need our workplaces to be visual.

This must be music to the ears of executives, managers, and supervisors whose primary job it is to make sure that people perform—to make sure that people do what they are supposed to do, time after time after time. That is the central role of the manager. Or, as my sensei, Dr. Ryuji Fukuda used to say: "Management means getting people to do ordinary things extraordinarily well." There is another reason the visual workplace is so important: human brain function. See Inset 1.1 for more.

Visual Information—Visual Functionality

In a visual workplace, information is converted into simple, universally under-stood visual devices and installed in the process of work itself, as close to the point-of-use as possible. The result is the transformation of a formerly mute work environment into one that speaks, eloquently and precisely, about how to use it effectively and efficiently.

What happens when the workplace speaks, when formerly voiceless work stations, equipment, tools, machines, and material can communicate freely with those who use them? What happens when employees can know vital informa-tion—the details of work—at-a-glance, without speaking a word, without asking a single question?

When a work environment becomes a fully-functioning visual workplace, each employee has instant on-demand access to the information needed to do high quality, low cost, timely, and safe work. The workplace is infused with intelligence, visual intelligence, that illuminates and drives the corporate intent.

Every section of the floor, every bench, work surface, hand tool, part, machine, rack, cabinet, and bin is equipped to make a contribution to the collective purpose that is beyond its mere existence—because it now can visually communicate vital information to anyone and everyone who needs it, as they need it. There are no exceptions.

In a visual workplace, floors do not exist simply to walk on—or to hold you and me up. When they are given a visual voice, such as through borders and addresses, floors help us do our work, repeatedly and with precision. Benches are not merely surfaces on which to place the implements of work, or shelves merely storage places. Through *visual order* and the subsequent installation of the *visual where*, floors and benches provide precise visual location information for all the "things" of work. They become performance partners.

Through *visual standards* and *visual controls*, tools are not restricted to merely helping us convert material. Given a "visual" voice, they tell us how to use them properly, when they need to be calibrated, where they belong when not in use, and when they are unsafe. They become even more vocal partners in the production process through the technology of *Visual Machine®*—the same visuality that enables equipment to assist in its own quick changeovers. (See *The Four Power Levels of Visual Devices* in Photo Album 2.)

Cells are not merely a collection of functions, things, and people. They are given a voice through *customer-driven visuality, visual displays*, and *visual metrics*—and become allies that manage themselves and people who work in them.

Senior leaders and their direct reports use the visual formats of effective leadership to decide, deploy, and drive. They become better leaders as a result—and they and the enterprise benefit.

In a fully-functioning visual workplace, people and the things of the physical workplace and the workplace itself contribute to the making of profit in ways that go far beyond their mere presence. They become active visual partners in the process of work, in the process of improvement, and in the process of sustaining the gains.

The Problem: Information Deficits

As every company knows, workplace information can change quickly and often: production schedules, customer requirements, engineering specifications, operational methods, tooling and fixtures, material procurement, work-in-process, and the thousand other details on which the daily life of the enterprise depends. In any single day, literally hundreds of precise data points (information) are required to keep work going. And these data points can and often do change dozens of times every shift. The multiples of these are enormous.

In an information-scarce workplace, people ask lots of questions and lots of the same questions, repeatedly—or don't and make stuff up instead. Either way, the company pays in long lead times, late deliveries, poor quality, accidents, low operator and managerial morale, and runaway costs.

Looking across any organization, if workplace visuality is not firmly in place, then these occurrences are not rare. They are chronic and unrelieved. They happen "all the time"—day in/day out, week in/week out, year in/year out. It is a way of life in far too many companies.

Photo Album 2

Building Adherence through Visuality

Four Power Levels—Types of Visual Devices

A visual device is an apparatus, mechanism, or thing that influences, directs, limits or controls behavior by making information vital to the task at hand available at-a-glance, without speaking a word.

SPEED LIMIT INDICATOR   USEFUL 3-D ADDRESS TABS

Visual Indicator—No Power ▶

A *Visual Indicator* tells only; it has no power to make us do anything. The 40 mph speed limit sign has no power to make us slow down, any more than these excellent 3-D tabs can make us find the resistors. Both are elective; the choice is ours.

Visual Signal—Some Power ▶

A *Visual Signal* first catches our attention, then delivers the message. This rumble strip sends a kinetic signal that keeps us from going into the ditch. The andon/stacked lights alert us to shortages and other abnormalities.

RUMBLE STRIP   STACKED OR ANDON LIGHTS

VISUALLY-CONTROLLED TOOL BOXES DESIGNED-TO-TASK

◀ Visual Control—Significant Power

A *Visual Control* structures in behavior through size or number. Its power is considerable, as you see in tool delivery system and kanban squares.

VISUAL PULL SYSTEM: KANBAN ▶

Visual Guarantee—Absolute Power ▶

A *Visual Guarantee* allows the correct response only by embedding exact information into the design of the process itself. These stairs boat-side make us start climbing with our right leg (the stronger one) and prevent us from skipping steps. Interestingly, the Navy invented this device during World War II to get sailors topside and fast during an attack.

BOAT-SIDE STAIRWAY

In the pre-visual workplace, everything and everyone is forced to exist within a narrow definition of their capability. The physical work environment is bereft of meaning. Attempts to improve the process of work invariably fail because even the smallest gains disappear overnight. A pre-visual workplace has no means to sustain them, however hard-won.

This unhappy state of affairs devolves into a single problem: deficits in information. Calculating the level of information deficits in your company is the quickest way for you to diagnose the extent to which a visual work environment is both lacking and needed.

Information deficits are both chronic and everywhere. Offices are flooded with them. The production floor is saturated with questions asked and unasked. And the unasked question is even worse—because when a question exists but never gets asked, people make stuff up. We simply make stuff up. Sometimes that works to the benefit of the company, but all too often it works against it. People make stuff up and accidents happen, material is lost, defects are produced, delivery times are missed, customers flee. Working in an environment without visual information-sharing is like trying to reach a destination by driving a hundred miles on a road with no signs, no signals, and no lines down the center of the road. You can probably make it, but you are likely to pay a terrible price.

If yours is already an excellent work environment, you may be tempted to dismiss this scenario as irrelevant to your purposes because companies such as those just described will be out of business soon enough, and good riddance.

I am glad your organization is doing well. Just be aware that the costs and burdens of organizations that suffer in the face of conditions they have yet to address are your costs as well. These enterprises are your suppliers, your hospital, your motor vehicle department, your trucking company, your schools, and your grocery and department stores. The change must happen with them as well. Until it does, the benefits you reap are limited, at best. We live and work in one world.

Information Is Not Performance

From sales to design, procurement to planning, fabrication to assembly, receiving to pack and ship, and at all points in between, information is the lifeblood of work and all the activities and functions that support work.

In the vast majority of companies, accurate, complete, timely, relevant information is unattainable or simply too hard to come by—and the truth is even harder to locate. That is not to say there aren't plenty of data. Data abound. Data can be found everywhere—in quality reports, SPC graphs, management briefings, in team meetings, and weekly and annual reports. Data flood the workplace.

But compiling data is a fruitless activity if the data are not translated into information and the information is not translated into meaning.

It is *meaning* that we are after. Without understanding the meaning of the data, we cannot make sound decisions and move the company and the people who work there forward. We cannot *perform*.

The purpose of the visual workplace is to convert data into information, information into visual meaning, and visual meaning into safe, aligned, and sustainable performance. If the enterprise is to improve, stabilize, and grow, this must happen on both tactical and strategic levels. It must happen in operations where value is added; and it must happen on leadership levels that ensure the company benefits from that value, stabilizes, and grows.

In their totality, visual workplace technologies contain over a dozen discrete methods for reducing motion and increasing visual competency in an organization. Implementing these technologies improves virtually every performance function in the enterprise. Indeed, the continuum of principles and practices contained in these technologies can (and should) be implemented across the company, in all functions, departments, and areas. Once that is firmly in place, move on to your sister companies and down your supply chain. Let all workplaces speak.

Visuality Aligns the Culture

Thinking about your company's visual conversion merely in terms of increased productivity and profits, however, is not enough. A visual conversion produces a change that changes everything, including your work culture.

Yes, achieving a workplace that speaks triggers an inevitable transformation of your work culture. When we implement workplace visuality, we lib-

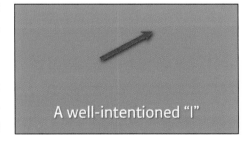

A well-intentioned "I"

FIGURE I.2: A HARD-WORKING INDIVIDUAL

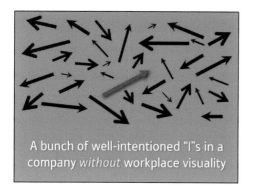

A bunch of well-intentioned "I"s in a company *without* workplace visuality

FIGURE I.3: A BUNCH OF INDIVIDUALS

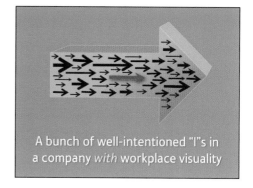

A bunch of well-intentioned "I"s in a company *with* workplace visuality

FIGURE I.4: INDIVIDUALS ALIGN

erate information—and when we liberate information, we liberate the human will.

Nearly every employee goes to work to make a contribution—to do good. The red arrow in Figure 1.2 represents such an employee, working in a company that is not yet visual; he works hard, believing he is going in a direction that supports the corporate intent. Figure 1.3 shows what his co-workers and bosses are doing—those other arrows. They too work hard in the belief that they are contributing to the same corporate good. Yet many are going in other directions, some of them opposite. This is a snapshot of the *pre-visual* workplace.

The image in Figure 1.4 is very different. It shows the same employees, working in a visual enterprise. They have a clear understanding of both their work and their contribution within the larger good—the big-arrow encasement. All the inside arrows are aligned, moving purposefully in the same direction, supported in intent, behavior, and outcome by a fully-functioning visual workplace.

They achieved this by converting information into visible, at-a-glance devices for all who need them, information that was formerly imprisoned in the binders, reports, books, computer files, and data systems of the company—and in the hearts and minds of its employees. (See the visual thinkers in Photo Album 3.)

Information is power. People come to understand this more than ever before when they work in a fully-functioning visual workplace. Work there and we cannot help but feel powerful. The availability of information makes it so. When we liberate information, we liberate the human will.

Does this relate to a company's work culture? The answer is plainly and indisputably *yes*. When you have the words *information* and *power* in the same

Photo Album 3

Creating a Workforce of Visual Thinkers at RNT/Holland

The Visual-Lean® Journey of Royal Nooteboom Trailers

Founded in 1881, Royal Nooteboom Trailers (RNT) specializes in premium-built specialty trailers, produced by a workforce of 300 strongly-motivated, customer-oriented employees. Company owner/president Henk Nooteboom launched RNT's journey to excellence with workplace visuality. Eighteen months later, RNT was ready to tackle the challenges of lean and the macro-flow. RNT's visual-lean journey continues to this day.

THE FIRST RNT TRAINING AND IMPLEMENTATION GROUP

RNT PRODUCTION FLOOR

THE EURO TRAILER (MULTI-AXLE/LOW LOADER)

DOUBLE-BORDER FUNCTION AT RNT

alle wartels vast !
waterlussen gelegd !

Rolling Red Tool Box 🔺

RNT assembler Berry Voogt raised a simple tool box to a high-level of visuality. He welded it to a pedestal on wheels and put SOPs in a plastic sleeve on the lid—everything he needs handy and at point-of-use, designed-to-task.

Victor Invents 🔺

With a simple but marvelous inventiveness, Victor Geertruida re-constructed this wrench, making it easier for him to reach tight places. He went on to create many highly-inventive visual solutions.

Kanban Tubes 🔺

Max Janssen, assembler and all-associate Steering Team member, combined his knowledge of visuality and pull to invent the tube holder above. The green/red markings let him know when more is needed.

sentence, you cannot avoid talking about culture. Culture reflects and structures beliefs about them both: power and how it is used and distributed in the enterprise; and identity—who I think I am and who I think the other is. The work culture becomes aligned when I know that I am you.

The New Enterprise

The new enterprise is an inclusionary entity. It is holistic. As such, it functions on multiple levels, not just meeting the company's daily production goals but also addressing its need for clarity, imagination, community, and alignment. Any effort to make the new enterprise about just one thing, whether production or culture, is a failed concept, unless that concept is unity itself.

The new enterprise, like the human body, must support and express various forms of health—mental, physical, emotional, and, yes, spiritual. It must perform on these multiple levels if it is to remain viable in today's world.

We are on a tremendously accelerated and accelerating journey to a transformation that we can hardly imagine. There is no way to draw the line from where we are now to our future. While there will certainly be familiar signposts, there will also be much that startles and even confounds.

If you haven't noticed it by now, we are in a revolution, not just in manufacturing, not just in offices, not just in hospitals, and not just in the USA. This revolution is taking place in every aspect of lives and livelihood on this planet. It is a revolution in consciousness—and no industry, country, company or person is exempt.

CHAPTER | **2**

The Building Blocks of Visual Thinking

A visual workplace is populated by hundreds, even thousands, of visual devices and mini-systems, invented by a workforce that knows how to think visually—a workforce of visual thinkers. What is a *Visual Thinker?*

A visual thinker is a person who recognizes motion and the information deficits that cause it—and knows how to eliminate both through solutions that are visual.

One of the main by-products of effectively implementing the technologies of the visual workplace is the emergence of a new core competency in the enterprise: employees who know how to think visually. Such thinkers see problems in the workplace and solve them from the vantage point of the discrete set of principles called the *Eight Building Blocks of Visual Thinking* (Figure 2.1). This chapter explains each building block and puts it in context.

Building Block 1: I-Driven Change

There is one simple reason why a visual workplace is needed: People have too many questions. Some of these questions are asked. Most of them remain unasked. When people don't ask the questions, one of two things happens. Either they live without the answers they need and do nothing—or they make stuff up.

Some of what people make up can be useful and does the job. Some of it can be irrelevant or half-wrong, all wrong or, even worse, dangerous. And all this is a problem.

You may wonder why people don't just ask when they don't know. The answer lies in the mysteries of the human heart. Some people don't ask because they don't want to appear uninformed—or worse, "dumb." Others don't ask because they know that nobody knows the answer anyway—so why bother? Still others have been given wrong answers so often (intentionally or otherwise) that they don't trust any answer anymore from anyone.

Still others refuse to ask because:

a. The question is simple but the answer is hidden (such as, "What do I do next?") and that person refuses to ask such plain questions over and over again; or

b. The person would have to ask someone younger (or someone new to the company) who just happens to have the answer. That "someone" is almost always in a position of authority over the person with the question—and the questioner flatly refuses to suffer the indignity of asking a "youngster" or newcomer.

These are not uncommon choices for people to make. Sometimes these conditions combine so that you are asking the same simple question over and over again of a person half your age. In the face of any of the above, some people simply refuse to go after the answers they need—or, as mentioned, just make stuff up.

The fact is, many people feel disempowered when asking questions—while others feel far too powerful when answering them. One way or the other, asking/answering questions can become a form of power play.

Whatever the motivation or reason, workplace questions that are left unasked and therefore unanswered can and do cause problems—in safety, quality, cost, on-time delivery, and the great bucket for them all, overall lead time. In a moment, we will study some examples.

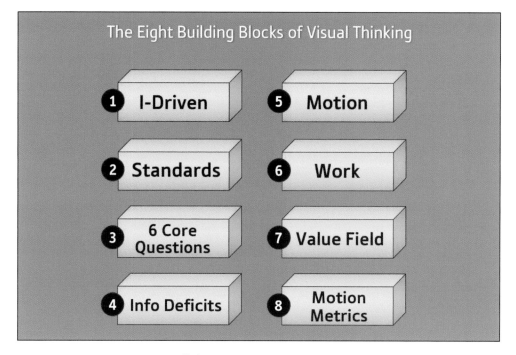

FIGURE 2.1: THE EIGHT BUILDING BLOCKS

The Two Driving Questions

Look again at our definition of the visual workplace:

> A *self-ordering, self-explaining, self-regulating, and self-improving work environment, where what is* **supposed** *to happen* **does** *happen, on time, every time, day or night—because of* **visual solutions**.

The visual workplace is about answering all the questions that anyone has related to work: questions about what is known as well as unknown; questions spoken out loud as well as those on a sub-vocal level; questions that are commonplace as well as those so specialized that only a few people think to ask them.

To the uninitiated, this sounds a daunting task. To a visual thinker, it is business as usual. The visual thinker knows that all questions devolve into only two:

Question One: "*What do I need to know?*" What do I need to know that I do not know right now in order to do my work—or do it better, more safely or more on time? *What do I need to know?*

FIGURE 2.2: THE TWO QUESTIONS THAT DRIVE A VISUAL WORKPLACE

Question Two: *"What do I need to share?"* What do I know that others need to know in order for them to do their own work—or do it better, more safely, more on time? *What do I need to share?* (Figure 2.2)

These two questions drive workplace visuality and fuel its development. While they cannot replace visuality's step-by-step methodology, they can help us start to understand and appreciate the power of a fully-functioning visual workplace.

The Need-to-Know

Begin with the need-to-know question: "What do I need to know?" I am always surprised at how plain these "Need-to-Know" questions can be (Inset 2.1). Hank taught me that many years ago. Here's his story.

Hank worked as an assembler for an electronics manufacturer in the Midwest called, shall we say, Acme Corp. I met Hank along with 35 other operators at the first training session I conducted for the Acme visual workplace rollout. As usual, early in the session, we discussed the two driving questions; I asked everyone to list out their need-to-know questions. Then I asked for volunteers to share their lists.

Hank, who was sitting in the back of the room, responded first. He didn't bother to raise his hand. He simply started standing up. And as he rose, he repeated the question over and over—*"What do I need to know? What do I need to know?"*—his face getting steadily redder and his voice getting lower and tighter. At full height, Hank leaned forward, rolled his knuckles under, and snarled, "What do I need to know?"

INSET 2.1: THE NEED TO KNOW

Here is a sample of need-to-know questions from various organizational functions. Notice how plain they are, pointing squarely at the absence of the most fundamental workplace information.

Value-Add Employees

- What am I supposed to run next?
- Where is the mold for my changeover?
- When is this claims report due?
- Who runs the blitz this week?
- How many rooms need to be made up?
- How do I do this changeover?

Supervisors/Managers

- What is the quota for today?
- Where is the material we're waiting for?
- When will the sub-assemblies be ready?
- Who is out today?
- How many X-ray plates are left?
- How do I calculate OEE?

Yes, these are plain questions that deserve plain and speedy answers—visual answers.

"Yikes! What's going on with this guy?" I thought. Hank looked as if he would blow at any moment. As the instructor, I ventured forth and drew the fire, "Hey Hank, what do you need to know?" He growled: *"I need to know where my pliers are!"* and brought his hand down on the table hard.

My mouth dropped open; my mind raced: All that upset-ness over a pair of pliers!? I asked for detail. Hank provided it, without missing a beat.

"Listen, I punched in this morning at 6:25 to try to get some stinkin' work done before I had to spend the whole stinkin' morning in this stinkin' class. But I couldn't find my pliers, see! I looked everywhere! *I still don't know where they are!*"

Aaah, that explained things! As with the vast majority of a workforce, people come to work *to work*—to make a contribution. That was Hank's intention when he punched in. But to work or even begin to work, Hank needed his pliers. And until he had them in hand, he was stymied.

Hank's work requirement was plain and unadorned. He did not need to know the blueprint to the Death Star or the company's secret acquisition plans. Hank simply needed to know the location of his pliers so he could get about his work. When I saw Hank's actual list later that morning, the pliers question was the only one on it; his vision stopped there; and he would have no further questions until that one got answered.

But there was more to come. As the group and I discussed the need-to-know further, we talked about ways of securing the answers and turning them into visual devices. "In that way," I said, "you never have to ask or answer those particular questions again." Since we were at the very first stage of the journey to visuality, we then talked about *visual order* (amplified 5S)—borders, addresses, and ID labels—the elements required to achieve the *visual where*. The session ended.

A month later I was back on site at Acme and Hank found me. "Hey, Gwendolyn, guess what happened after you left. I tried that border thing you talked about. I decided to put a border on my bench for my pliers (yes, I did eventually find them). And just as I was doing that, Suzie came over. You remember Suzie...."

Yes, I remembered Suzie: A very pretty woman with a very large mouth. Suzie had a lot of energy that she sometimes used as a weapon to throw a damper on things she didn't like or understand. She was a handful.

Hank went on. "So Suzie came over and said, 'Hey, what are you doing, Hank?' I told her I was trying out what you talked about in class. And then Suzie just let it rip. 'You have got to be kidding! You are not actually going to try that, are you? Put lines around your pliers? You can't be serious! That'll never help! Anyway, we tried that a few years ago and it didn't work. Don't you remember?'"

"She went on and on, Gwendolyn. She just wouldn't let up."

Hank took a deep breath. "So I took a deep breath and said, 'Suzie, I'm gonna do it anyway! I'm gonna give my pliers a home—right now!' Suzie shot back, 'Well, you just go right ahead, Hank. You do that. But your pliers won't be there in the morning. Oh, I won't touch them! I swear I won't! But they are NOT gonna be there—not in this company! Mark my words!' And she stomped off."

"The next morning, as per usual, I punched in at 6:25, went to my bench, and you know what? My pliers weren't there! But guess who was? Yep, Suzie! She was standing there with hands folded across her chest. Before I could say anything, she started in: 'I didn't touch them! I never laid my hands on your pliers! I swear! But I don't see them, do you? I mean I told you they wouldn't be here, right! Right?'"

Hank hung his head in front of me, but his eyes were still sparkling. "Gwendolyn, the pliers were not there. I knew she had me," he said. "Well, I don't know what possessed me to say what I said next, but I said to her, 'Suzie, you are wrong!' That's what I said."

"Suzie blinked at me a couple of times, put her hands on her hips, leaned in real close to my face, and blasted: 'I'm wrong, Hank? How am I wrong, Hank? I mean I don't see your pliers on your bench! Do you? Hank, do you see your pliers? Because I don't! So how am I wrong?'"

Hank continued. "She had me again. And she knew it! But I didn't want to give in. Then BINGO! I got this idea and shot back: 'Suzie, I will tell you why you are wrong. Yesterday it took me 30 minutes to get that my pliers were gone, really gone. *Today I knew it right away—instantly!*' Then the both of us just stood there. I think I was as surprised as she was."

BINGO again! In that short exchange, Hank not only named the true outcome of the process called the *visual order*—installing the *visual where*—he also demonstrated how the question *"What do I need to know?"* drives workplace visuality.

Workplace Visuality: An I-Driven Approach

Note that the question Hank answered reads: "What do *I* need to know?" It does *not* read: "What do *WE* need to know?"

If it did, Hank would have to meet with the area team (Suzie plus other operators) to discuss what needs to be visually "known." Probably the team ("we") would then agree to make the answers to some workplace questions visual—maybe the ones with a direct cost benefit. So there would be a pretty good chance that the team might dismiss Hank's worries about his pliers as trivial or not their problem or showing no concrete cost benefit. The "we" of the team would rule and Hank's need might be rejected, if not scorned: "You mean to tell us that you don't know where your pliers are, Hank!? No wonder you are always behind schedule."

In visual thinking, we deliberately look for ways to make each person independent and singular in his or her actions—an independent and unencumbered visual thinker. I call this the *I-driven* approach to improvement. To many, this may seem counter-intuitive, the antithesis of creating a unified, team-based work culture. In fact, it is a powerful step in exactly that direction.

In this first part of the journey to a visual workplace, people are asked to find and follow their own internal improvement goals, their own improvement vision. Although the I-driven approach applies to every employee in the organization, it is most powerfully active with employees on the value-add level (hourly associates, operators, producers or, as Rolls-Royce refers to them, experts) since that is, by and large, the weakest level in the enterprise for genuine involvement. There, the need for self-referenced thinking is immediate and urgent.

I-driven, this first building block of visual thinking, presses each area associate to take charge of his/her own area of control and apply the need-to-know question as a prod and trigger for populating the work area with visual devices and mini-sys-

FIGURE 2.3:
WHAT DO I NEED TO KNOW

The yellow concentric circles show repeat of the question/answer process as associates apply and re-apply the need-to-know to their own individual work. This creates a widening circle of visual devices that capture answers in ever more specific detail. The result is: Visual thinkers gain increasing control over their corners of the world.

tems that answer that first question repeatedly—iteratively—question after question after question (Figure 2.3).

The I-driven approach to continuous improvement can impact enterprise excellence in a number of ways. In our current discussion, I-driven refers to a reliance on and confidence in the individual's need-to-know, on a local level, as the trigger of high-impact/low-cost visual devices.

Among its many other benefits, an I-driven approach to improvement removes the need for outside approval or authorization that in the early stages of an initiative can often delay or discourage individual resourcefulness.

Instead of second-guessing outside factors or relying on someone else to do an analysis, visual thinkers-in-the-making learn to notice their individual motion (moving without working) and use it to identify the missing answers that caused that motion. Then they create visual devices to hold the answers. When that happens, information deficits disappear, along with the motion they caused. This is the *I-driven* need-to-know in action.

In the end, every employee has a deep desire to be in charge of something. In I-driven visuality, individuals can declare: "I am in charge of my corner of the world" because they have made it so.

There is no way to overemphasize the importance of the I-driven dynamic in creating and sustaining workplace visuality—and, ultimately, excellence in the enterprise. Indeed, "I-driven" surfaces as a theme again and again in the pages of this book. We have only begun to lay out the reasons.

The Need-to-Share

When first hearing about the I-driven approach and the first two driving questions, some people envision an improvement free-for-all or anarchy. Others comment that too much emphasis on the individual could make people selfish. Where do other people come in? And what about teams? Where do they fit? Where is the "we"?

When a visual workplace gets created, other people and teams—and "we"—enter the picture with the second question that drives visuality in the workplace: "What do I need to share?"

That is, *"What do I know that others need to know in order for them to do their work—or do it better? What information do I need to share?"*

Notice the question is still formed around the "I"—the individual. It is still I-driven. The focus, however, is now turned outwards to others (Figure 2.4). Reaching out a hand in service, we ask: "How may I help you?" Can you hear the *team* in that? Can you hear the *we*? The need-to-share is a deeply team-minded question (Inset 2.2).

Each of us has knowledge and know-how that could help others if only we shared it. Visuality's second-driving question puts a premium on developing visual devices that do just that.

FIGURE 2.4:
WHAT DO I NEED TO SHARE?

The purple circles show how the need-to-share travels outwards beyond local info deficits (yellow circles) as visual thinkers find opportunities to create visual devices that help others do their work better, more safely, and more completely,

---

INSET 2.2: THE NEED TO SHARE

The need-to-share exists on every organizational level. Used iteratively (repeatedly), its application completes the need for visual answers enterprise-wide. Here are examples.

Value-Add Employees	Supervisors/Managers
• Where I put the parts that I just ran	• Where I will be this afternoon
• What I am working on next	• What parts get worked on next
• When that report will be ready	• When the new parts will arrive
• Who is my backup if I'm called away	• What revisions were made
• How many beds are available	• How the new metric gets collected
• How many bottles I used	• How many pallets are safe to stack

The technical process is identical to the one tied to the need-to-know but flipped. With the need-to-share, the visual thinker is still on the alert—but for someone else's information deficits. The visual thinker notices the motion of others—then invents a visual device that removes the other person's info deficit and the motion it caused. See Sheila Bowersmith's need-to-share device in Photo 2.1.

PHOTO 2.1: NEED TO SHARE IN ACTION

When Sheila Bowersmith, master machinist, saw the new planner wandering around, she asked to help. The planner said he could not figure out what she was running *now*. Sheila told him. Next day, she put a yellow border on her machine, welded on a clip, and posted her current order—so she never had to answer that question again and no one had to ask it.

When a workforce begins to create visual devices and mini-systems, they start with their individual need-to-know. This is the foundation of the process.

As they achieve control over their corners of the world by applying the first driving question, visual thinkers grow in enough skill, confidence, and command over their local situation to turn to others and begin to share another type of information—the information they know others need ("What do I need to share?").

In this way, workplace visuality shifts from a solo to a collaborative process, even as people retain their individuality—the "I."

Deployed cycle after cycle, the need-to-share connects up the work area and then the entire enterprise. Need-to-share in visuality creates unity, one of the most highly-prized and difficult to achieve organizational outcomes. See Figure 2.5 for an image of this process.

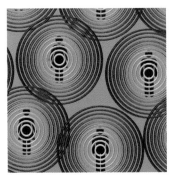

FIGURE 2.5: UNITY

When people create need-to-share devices, the area—and soon the entire company—gets visually linked.

Building Block 2: Standards

Our definition of a visual workplace states that, in such a work environment, what *is* supposed to happen *does* happen (Inset 2.3). So we must ask ourselves: What is supposed to happen? What is that thing that *does* happen in a visual workplace?

The answer is: your standards. *A company's*

INSET 2.3: DEFINITION OF A VISUAL WORKPLACE

A visual workplace is a self-ordering, self-explaining, self-regulating, and self-improving work environment where what is *supposed* to happen *does* happen, on time, every time, day or night—because of visual solutions.

---

standards are supposed to happen, on time, every time, day or night—and in a visual workplace they do.

What *Is* Supposed to Happen: Standards

What do I mean by *standards*? When I speak of standards, I am not referring to the time or accounting standards used in bids and contracts. I refer, instead, to the crucial technical and procedural information that defines precisely what value means in the company—and how it is added.

In line with that and for the purposes of our discussion, there are two categories of workplace standards.

1. Technical Standards: Technical standards are the dimensions and tolerances of the customer's product and process specifications. These are the values or attributes captured in engineering drawings (Inset 2.4).

Every single object and function in your enterprise is there to meet or support these crucial attributes. Technical standards trigger the full value stream. In fact, they individually and in their aggregate demonstrate what is meant by value in the organization.

INSET 2.4: WHAT IS A TECHNICAL STANDARD?

A *technical standard* refers to the exact tolerance, dimension, specification, or value needed to meet the customer's expectation.

Examples: *outer diameter (O.D.); inner diameter (I.D.); pressure sensitivity; coil resistance level; cut length; heat-treat temperature; gloss level; torque; required response time on a fire claim; exact degree of radiation for this patient site; dilution level for Taxotere (chemotherapy drug).*

In other words, technical standards describe the precise values of form, fit, and function your customers ordered. They are your product and process attributes.

INSET 2.5: WHAT IS A PROCEDURAL STANDARD?

A *procedural standard* refers to the way in which tasks must be done—methods, standard operating procedures (SOPs). In other words, the sequence of steps we have to follow in order to achieve a specific tolerance, dimension or value (a specific technical standard).

Examples: *How to rivet a bolt; how to achieve a feed rate; how to program the CNC; how to weld; how to tighten a wheel; how to changeover a machine (in less than nine minutes); how to close the monthly books; how to mix and verify a chemotherapy regimen.*

In other words, a procedural standard defines *how* to achieve or deliver a specific technical standard. SOPs create outcomes.

They are the bedrock, the absolute foundation, of all processes in the corporation—from sales to ordering and procurement; from patient intake to surgery; from incoming deliveries to assembly; from marketing plans to the provision of services. Technical standards (and their execution) form the core of all profit in the enterprise.

2. Procedural Standards: Procedural standards are the pre-determined sequences of steps that ensure that technical specifications are met or achieved (as in *standard operating procedures* or SOPs).

Procedural standards partner with technical standards to create outputs you can sell. Procedural standards refer to exactly how you will achieve your technical standards—those values, dimensions, attributes or specifications (Inset 2.5).

Procedural standards are the step-by-step road map by which you form that 12-inch aluminum ingot into a .50 millimeter thick coil. It is the precise procedure for inserting an I.V. into a patient's arm, and the exact method for programming that CNC machine in the radial department.

The link between technical and procedural standards is as tight as it is detailed, constituting the precision in what is supposed to happen and how. Your standards are at the heart of operational excellence and reliable, repeatable, cost-effective, high-quality work.

Making the details of your technical and procedural standards *visual* is one of the core tasks of workplace visuality. In so doing, the visual workplace becomes a

---

INSET 2.6: ISO AND WORKPLACE VISUALITY—WHEN & WHY

A major benefits of ISO certification is the requirement that a company identify and document its technical and procedural standards—every single one of them.

This is tough for any company, even those with stable and consistent standards. For a company with no such base, the task can be daunting, requiring years to complete.

I am often asked if ISO comes first or a visual workplace. Company differences may persuade you to begin with ISO, especially if the company is seeking a global market. But given a choice, I recommend the company begin with visual order/visual where (Chapter 5), the indispensable first step on your journey to a visual workplace—and ISO.

There is no shortage of information in a company—but how much of it is correct, timely, accurate, complete, and relevant? Can employees access it easily, when and as needed?

Begin your ISO process with a rollout of workplace visuality and visually sort the true from the false or the blurry—and provide an ISO research platform. Doing so can reduce the usual time required for ISO certification by 30% to 60%.

Only advanced sites have the groundwork in place that allows employees to know and use technical and procedural standards in detail. Get visual—then tackle ISO.

---

gigantic adherence mechanism that helps us do the right thing, on-time, and safely. It helps us adhere. As a result, we can execute our standards with exactness.

The absence of clear and complete standards (technical, procedural or both) is a costly deficiency that impacts every single aspect of the organization. Yet a good many companies have difficulty in identifying and capturing their standards, despite the great importance this has in operational success (Inset 2.6). In the face of this unhappy soup, the technologies of the visual workplace can be of tremendous help.

Time and again, companies without documented standards have launched workplace visuality and made vast strides in stabilizing specifications and processes simply through the application of visual principles and practices. One of the beauties of a visual approach is that a company can launch a visual rollout in the absence of known operational standards and, in the process of implementing visuality, put them in place—along with an adherence to them that is both deep-rooted and reliable.

The visual workplace is about information. That is its focus, and visual information sharing is its outcome. When we visually share the precise details of what value gets added and how, we are sharing our technical and procedural standards—the *what* in "what is supposed to happen."

Photo Album 4

The Six Core Questions Made Visual

The Six Core Questions: A Leg Up

Applying the Six Core Questions is a plain way to start finding visual answers to common questions. But, without motion as a lever, they won't take you far. They cannot create a conversion. Still, look at these examples and imagine them in your company.

The Visual Where (floor) ▶

A border with an address—such a plain answer to an incredibly debili-tating question when it is not visually answered for everything that casts a shadow. That is why it is visuality's foun-dation. (Fleet Engineers, Flint, MI)

The Visual Where (shelf) ▶

Visual evidence of excellence is every-where at Delphi Deltronicos (Matamoras, Mexico), including inside this HazMat cabinet where the address element of the *visual where* is on a driver-license level—common name, part number, and photo of the thing itself—all the informa-tion you need to take value-add action.

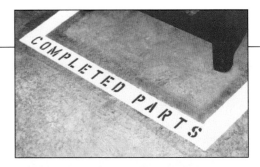

◀ **The Visual What**

This binder of critical assembly operations was compiled by Luis Catatao of United Electric Controls (Watertown, MA). He wanted to help newcomers with visual answers to *what* was difficult in building switches and controls in his area. He listed all specs, adding photos for the "tricky" parts.

◀ **The Visual When**

Camilla prepared a daily report for Nate, her boss. Anxious, he would hover around her desk and slow her work. Fine visual thinkers, the two decided to answer the *when* question (*When will the report be ready?*) with a visual device—a red clothes pin on the blue paperwork bin.

Imagination Can Go Only So Far

Too often, a company tries to "get visual" by asking employees to *imagine* visual devices that support their work. Without first learning the frameworks of visual thinking, however, people can run out of "ideas" fast. The Six Core Questions is one of several tools that help people dig into information deficits and start to become visual thinkers.

The Visual Who

Cindy Barter, a buyer at United Electric Controls (Watertown, MA), developed this splendid double-sided, laminated, airborne address so everyone knew exactly *who* she was, including what she purchased.

The Visual How Many ▶

You can tell *how many* at-a-glance at this storage grid at Seton Identification Products (CT). It visually limits the quantity that fits there: 3 deep X 5 long X 1 high. Ahh, I got it! 15 units!

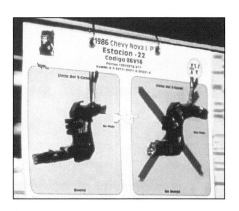

The Visual How

This visual standard—*how* to correctly tape this harness sub-assembly—hung in the mid-1980s in Rio Bravo IV, the first Packard-Electric transplant in Mexico. The company had just begun its march to excellence. Later named Delphi, it became a giant in the car industry—and in the field of workplace visuality as well.

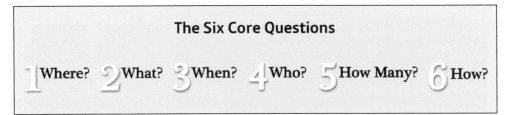

FIGURE 2.6: THE SIX CORE QUESTIONS

Building Block 3: The Six Core Questions

Look closely at your technical and procedural standards and notice that they consist of answers to the same set of six questions. I call these the *Six Core Questions*. They are: Where? What? When? Who? How many? and How? (Figure 2.6).

Their answers are the details of your technical and procedural standards. After all, that is what standards are: the answers to the six core questions in precise detail, over and over again. Answer these questions *visually*—translate them into visual devices—and you build your standards into the very process of work and into the environment that supports that process.

The set of six core questions—our next visual building block—expresses the synergy between standards, information, and visuality. Focus on making the answers to these six core questions visible, available at-a-glance. Install them as close to the point-of-use as possible. When you do, the workplace begins to speak, able to tell you where things are, what needs to be done, by when (or for how long), by whom (or by which machine or tool), in what quantity, and precisely how. See Photo Album 4 for examples of visual answers to the six core questions.

With the six core questions in hand, the task becomes simple: Identify the missing answers and install them visually as close to the point of their use as possible. Another term for missing answers is: *Information Deficits*.

Building Block 4: Information Deficits

An information deficit occurs when information vital to the task-at-hand is missing, wrong, late, incomplete, unavailable or unknown.

Deficits in information have a vast and disastrous impact on all performance indicators: from quality metrics such as defect and scrap rate, to machine repair

---

INSET 2.7: THE FIRST-QUESTION-IS-FREE RULE

Here are the five simple steps of my *First-Question-Is-Free Rule.*

Whenever someone approaches you with a question, answer it politely, truthfully, and as completely as possible. For example:

1. *Diana finds you every day, several times a day, and asks, "Hey, Boss, what am I supposed to do (or make) now?"*

2. *When she does, answer her politely and clearly; and, as she walks away, note inside your head, "That's one."*

3. *Then wait until you are asked the same question again, by Diana or anyone.*

4. *Again answer the question politely and clearly; and, as the person walks away, note inside your head: "That's two!"*

5. *The first question is free; the second time you hear that same question (from the same person or anybody else), it's time for you to create a visual device—so you never have to answer that question again and no one ever has to ask it.*

Require this of yourself and your direct reports. Become leaders of improvement, instead of managers of fires and other daily calamities. (This practice is perfect for value-add associates as well, especially in offices.) Launch a direct frontal assault on every company's enemy: information deficits.

---

and changeover times, to inspection and material handling costs, to accidents and safety-related issues, to cycle time and overall manufacturing lead time. That means that information deficits, by extension, impact the entire business cycle, including scheduling, sales forecasts and collection activities. Their power is in their absence—the absence of answers.

Questions are a virulent form of information deficits, especially among employees in salaried positions who can sometimes entertain the mistaken notion that their actual job is to answer questions—day in and day out, all the time.

Executives, supervisors, managers unite! You can trigger tremendous benefits for yourself and the entire enterprise by simply requiring, or even mandating, that your direct reports implement my *First Question-Is-Free Rule* in their own work and throughout their own value fields. You too. See Inset 2.7 for the five lethal steps of this powerful attack on the enemy.

Information deficits in the workplace trigger costs on every level and, as such, are major profit eaters. When companies speak of the war on waste, they tend to over-look the disastrous impact that missing bits of meaning can produce. Information is the context in which all work happens. If that fabric is full of holes, lots of work escapes—lots of value.

Most of the time these deficits are so chronic and commonplace, the depth to which they affect organizational performance is nearly impossible to determine. To find them, we must look for their symptom.

Forms of Motion	
Searching	Counting
Looking for	Counting again
Wandering	Asking
Wondering	Answering
Guessing	Interrupting
Checking	Waiting
Re-checking	Re-working
Handling	Re-testing
Re-handling	Stopping again
	& again & again

FIGURE 2.7: FORMS OF MOTION

Building Block 5: Motion

The range and extent of information deficits in the workplace are nearly impossible to gauge. We know that they are chronic and widespread—but how do we find them? The answer is to track what they trigger: *motion*.

In workplace visuality, information deficits are Corporate Enemy #1—and motion is their footprint. Motion is: *moving without working*. It can take a thousand forms. The easiest way to spot motion is to notice when you are wan-dering about or wondering, searching, asking or answering questions—or any combination of these (Figure 2.7). Doing anything again is another quick way to recognize when you are in motion.

When first learning about motion, people may say, "Yes, but I am wandering about because I need to find my pliers so I can do my work. How can that be motion? How can that be a bad thing? Why is that a problem?"

The answer lies in the fact that, when you are looking for your pliers *in order to* do your work, by definition, you are not yet working. And that needs to be exam-ined. (See Inset 2.8 for what motion is *not*.)

In short, motion is anything you *have to do*—anything you are compelled to do—or you *cannot* do your work. Motion is not elective. You do it *in order to* do your work or to get back to your work. You have no choice.

INSET 2.8: WHAT MOTION IS NOT

Here is what motion is *not*:

- Taking a break
- Going to lunch
- Calling home
- Going to the restroom
- Chatting with a friend

If you and the workforce do not understand this, people will feel watched and over-regulated; and they will be. One operator said it like this, "I'd feel like a robot, chained to my work bench!"

The activities bulleted above as "not motion" help to create a sense of community, safety, and personal comfort in the workplace, qualifying it as a location for human endeavor.

Dependent on the company, some of the above activities may be regulated, others discretionary. Whatever the case, for the purposes of workplace visuality, none of these are considered forms of motion.

- Hank had to find his pliers or he could not assemble the unit.

- Mary was compelled to find the new materials or she could not run the job.

- Victoria, the supervisor, had to re-verify the spec or the job might turn out wrong.

- Ishmael had to count the units again, otherwise he took the chance of shipping the wrong quantity.

- Nurse Betty had to go to the pharmacy to retrieve a pain medication that was late in arriving.

Motion is the plague you don't even see. Tied so intimately and inextricably to unanswered questions (information deficits), motion almost always looks like *business as usual*.

At the outset, only a well-trained pair of improvement eyes can spot the many forms of motion in the workplace. These activities seem so ordinary and so necessary. They are not. Motion eats up the life of the enterprise in the minutia of the micro-transactions we are forced to engage just to get to the starting line of our work—or just to get back to the work itself. It is a numbing experience.

In the chronic absence of fundamental information, employees everywhere—in offices, hospitals, banks, in the field, engineering offices, and on the production floor—become immune to a sense of urgency at work. People become desperate for the simple answers they require to work or continue to work. No one wants to wander around all day, chasing down teeny tiny informational tidbits. It is hard to imagine a more degrading experience or an activity that is more a waste of time. And should these tidbits be held by a select few but withheld from the many, insult gets added to injury. (See Inset 2.9 for more on this, *Information Hoarders*.)

This is not what most people signed up for when they agreed to work for your company. It is not how most people want to earn their daily bread. Simply put, most people want to earn their daily bread in a rightful way. They want to express excellence. In the face of insanity by tidbits, some people go numb; others go ballistic.

The internal dialogue, eyes turned up to Heaven, goes something like this: "Is this what You made me for, dear Lord? This? Chasing down answers to the same old questions, the same ones I asked yesterday, and the day before that, and the day before that? O dear Lord, give me strength!"

For those less religiously-inclined, the inner protest sounds something like: "What the heck is this? Chasing down the same stinkin' answers, day in and day out! I've had it! I'm outta this stinkin' place!"

Neither person may quit. Employees have families to support, bills to pay, mouths to feed, and limited alternatives to the job they are doing for you. But make no mistake: They do leave, if only in their minds, if only in their hearts. They make their bodies stay as they consent to a form of modern-day, soul-bending servitude.

I see this everywhere when I walk the production floors and offices of the enterprise. People stay. Yet, they and we both know that more is possible and wonder why it cannot happen.

That is the destructive power of information deficits (missing information) in the workplace. Motion is merely their symptom.

Motion as the Lever

Visual thinking is your ability *to recognize motion and the information deficits that cause it—and then to eliminate both through solutions that are visual.*

Every improvement method looks for ways to build a high sense of problem ownership in people. Because information deficits can populate a work environment like grains of sand on a beach, it is easy to make them management's problem on a systems level. When this occurs, however, people can quietly disconnect from the problem and any responsibility for its solution. They disassociate and either stop seeing the problem at all; or if they do see it, they expect management to solve it; or they blame management for causing it—or all three. The problem and its

INSET 2.9: INFORMATION HOARDERS—INFORMATION CZARS: A DAMAGING ALTERNATIVE

In far too many companies, information deficits are chronic and widespread. In some, these deficits can become so extreme and persistent that we rightfully ask how the company can stay in business. Part of that answer goes back to the natural resourcefulness of humans and our ability to figure things out and make stuff up, however thin the data stream and confusing the circumstances. The other part attests to our willingness to summon up courage and take our best shot. In this, we are both self-serving and heroic.

The stuff we make up often works—maybe not as well as actual answers, but we get by. When we do, we add weight to the claim that *people are a company's most important resource.*

In such companies, information deficits can become so habitual that chasing down answers is an expected part of the workday. Some call these *chronic abnormalities.* Perversely, such a workplace tends to stockpile or even withhold information. This, in turn, gives rise to *information hoarding*—always a double-edged sword.

Whether formalized into an actual position (e.g., expediter) or simply the informal *go-to person* (the one in the know), information hoarders erode the culture of the enterprise. They represent an unofficial system, put in place to make the official systems work, or work better. In such organizations, no decision is final until informal (and more reliable) sources have validated its wisdom. Information-based fiefdoms emerge that a company can come to depend on as the only reliable source, giving rise to information czars.

Information hoarders represent a damaging alternative when information vital to work and sound decision-making is scarce, wrong, unavailable, irrelevant, incomplete, unreliable, late or just plain unknowable. This is a work environment that tells lies—lies to itself and others. Info hoarders are the people we go to in order to learn the truth—what's really happening, really going on, really required, really the forecast. Being the single trustee of the truth is simply too much power for any to hold. When this power resides in one special person or group, whatever their intentions, the rest of us become disempowered.

Information hoarders in the enterprise are almost always a sign of trouble—but they are not the trouble itself. The trouble itself is the existence of information deficits. Such an environment (and I find them everywhere) is destructive to a fundamental requirement of the workplace: our need for the truth and our need to trust the information we are given as the truth. The upshot is an incapable, unstable enterprise with a damaged operational system that creates value at the highest possible cost.

When the time comes to initiate a change, the task becomes doubly difficult and doubly important if information hoarders are already deeply entrenched in the fabric of the workplace.

solution are someone else's job. "That's what managers are for," people say. This is especially so in paternalistic, traditionally-run companies: low or no problem ownership. This is a huge problem.

Let me say that another way: One of the great challenges in building an organizational improvement mindset is getting people to own workplace problems—and then getting *enough* people to own them.

In a visual workplace, motion is the leverage point for making the problem of information deficits detectable. (See Inset 2.10 for more on the choice of *motion* as a term.)

When missing information is named as the enemy, I suddenly have a compelling culprit to target; and it is everywhere. But I can succeed only if I find a way to *see* that which is, by definition, invisible—missing. Motion (moving without working) is the hidden enemy's footprint. Motion allows me to I-dentify with the problem of information deficits because it is my legs that carry me away from my value field, my hands that stretch for what is not there, and my mouth that asks (or answers) questions. Once I own the motion, I use it to stalk the unseen foe down the causal chain, find it, and destroy it by implementing a solution that is visual. I then claim the championship title: I am a scientist of motion. I am a visual thinker.

As you read the above, did you think that the words were a bit overblown—"stalking," "destroy," "championship," "scientist"? I assure you the language is exact, not inflated. Visuality is a system of thinking first, not just for operators—although it is revolutionary there—but for every organizational function, as you will see for yourself in the later chapters of this book. There could be no system if there were no way to go deeper, continually deeper. Motion is that way. Motion is the lever.

We have several more building blocks to understand, however, before we truly appreciate the role of motion in driving workplace visuality. Let's continue.

Building Block 6: Work

We cannot adopt the definition of motion as *moving without working* without also specifying what is meant by "working." Without that detail, the definition of motion is unclear and incomplete.

Working means *moving **and** adding value*. That is, we must move in order to add value, in order to work. Value does not get added by magic. This isn't the

Starship Enterprise where Captain Jean-Luc Picard simply speaks into a replicator and instantly gets a cup of "Tea. Earl Grey. Hot."—Wedgwood china and all. In our world, we must move in order to create—in order to add value. We have to move our muscles and engage the material world in order to build a sub-assembly, grind a housing, load the cable, check a part, administer a medication or produce a proposal.

We must move in order to add value. We must work.

Work is the polar opposite of motion. If work is *moving and adding value*, then motion can be defined as *moving and **not** adding value*. Motion becomes anything we are compelled to do or we cannot do our work.

Building Block 7: Value Field

When and where do people add value? When—*and only when*—they are in their *Value Field*. Their value field is where they add value. It's as simple as that. A person's value field is a specific location. It is where work happens.

This, the seventh building block of visual thinking, is a remarkable aide in helping people use motion as a diagnostic. The same crisp logic dictates that when individuals are not in their respective value field, they are not working—because they are not in a location where they can add value. They are somewhere else. *They are in motion.*

Conversely, when people are in motion, they are moving without working and, therefore, they cannot be in their value field.

Naming the Value Field

Realizing where one's primary value field is actually located is an evolving understanding. At first, people tend to think of their department as their value field; and they measure their motion in relationship to that. This notion, however, gets refined and redefined over time as people begin to notice their motion in detail.

My favorite story about this happened at Skyworks Solutions (formerly Alpha Industries), a Boston-area semi-conductor plant. I was working with a group of 12 associates to develop a visual workplace demonstration area (a *visual showcase*). The department in question was responsible for a wafer bonding process in which electronic microscopes were a key operational tool. (See Photo 2.2 for a look at the

INSET 2.10: THE CHOICE OF THE TERM *MOTION*

Are you wondering why I use the word *motion* and not other more widely-used terms, such as waste, *muda* or non-value-adding activity? My decision to do so was made many years ago. Read on and I believe you will understand why.

1. Waste: The term "waste" is very broad and is used for that reason: to generalize the problem into single, homogenized clusters (see the Wheel in this inset). It speaks of problems in terms of outcomes, not causes as motion does.

   Besides, my childhood home was surrounded by weeping willow trees, with long-reaching roots. The term "waste" still triggers unpleasant memories of boots, shovels, and buckets—and a burning desire to run away, run away, run away. If you don't have a clue of what I mean, count yourself lucky!

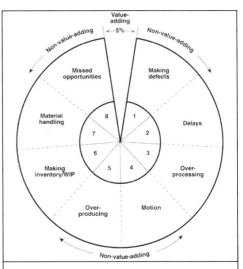

2. Muda: *Muda* is not an English word; it has no meaning except in its translation. Given a choice, I prefer English equivalents to foreign language terms. Plus, since muda is the Japanese word for waste, all the reasons in Item 1 also apply.

WHEEL OF THE EIGHT WASTES
First used in the 1950's, Toyota's waste wheel reduces operational problems into the above eight categories of waste. I selected *motion* as the perfect metric for waste triggered by information deficits.

3. Non-Value-Adding Activity. Using the term "non-value-adding" is a genuine problem for me and the relationship I seek to build with hourly or line employees.

For far too many years, I would discuss the concept of non-value-adding activity (NVA) to a room full of inspectors, expediters, rework operators, etc. By the end of the session, they thought I meant that *they* were non-value-adding. That was the moment I lost them as potential warriors in the war on waste—the attack on NVA.

Though their bodies continued to show up for sessions, the hearts, minds, and hopes of these fine individuals remained outside the room. They refused to identify with the NVA problem—and it became increasingly difficult to engage them in solving it.

Yes, language matters—a lot! Why chance throwing away the possibility of ownership and engagement just to parade around expert language that may well alienate the very people you are trying to win over? I find using the term *motion* solves all that and much more.

Bonding Department before workplace visuality.)

As the team moved through the steps of visual order (further explained in Chapter 5) and began to notice their motion, I asked: "Where is your value field?" To a person, the group responded: "This department, Bonding." Accordingly, people began to notice their motion—all the times that they left the Bonding Department in order to be able to continue to work. They kept track of these times and of the reasons they had to leave; they tracked cause.

The causes were many and, for the moment, understandable. For example:

- Looking for parts
- Getting a missing tool
- Going to get a work order clarified
- Washing off parts in a vented sink in a neighboring work area
- Finding the supervisor in order to ask a question, and so on

Next, the associates brought as many of those activities as possible inside their value field (the Bonding Department) and made them visual. They succeeded in every case but one: They still had to leave the department to wash parts in the vented sink next door.

With that, I again asked the question about the location of the value field. "Are we done? Is there any other motion that would force you to leave your value field, this department?" The group was quiet. Then Bernice Santos, a bonding specialist, spoke: "I've been thinking. I'm not certain that my real value field is this department. I think it might be my workbench. That's really where I add value."

BINGO! Other team members nodded in agreement: the benches were the newly-defined value field. They took on their next step: Track all the times you had to leave your workbench; track the reasons or causes; then see how many of those causes you could get visually installed on or near your bench, your new value field. The results were excellent. (See photos in Photo Album 5.)

When we reconvened to admire the splendid improvements, it was my turn to ask again: "Are we done? Has all bench-related motion been eliminated?" Nods all around. "Shall we check by videotape?" A few minutes later, a video camera was set up, focused on Paulette Benedictus, a veteran bonder who had volunteered to be the subject of the video (Photo 2.3). The tape ran for 45 minutes, long enough

Photo Album 5

Making the Value Field Visual

Visually Ordering the Value Fields

Under the improvement leadership of Kenny Bushmich and Annie Yu, workplace visuality at Skyworks Solutions in Boston (formerly Alpha Industries) turned the company into one of the best visual facilities in New England. This album shows the *visual where* on the benches of the Bonding Department and nearby areas.

Note: Because of anti-static process requirements, red electro-static discharge tape was used for all borders on work surfaces.

◀ The simple metal tray on the left of the value field is for small work implements, placed on a slant to ease pick/put. Each of the tray's small compartments has a photo-copied border taped to the bottom, doing double-duty as the address for what resides there. ▼

◀ A plastic tray bought at the local office supply store provides another excellent storage space for small work items. The address for each compartment is under the thing that resides there.

Visual is in the Details

Operators at Skyworks implemented visual order thoroughly, especially on work surfaces, putting many key visual details in place for the benefit of the company, newcomers, and themselves.

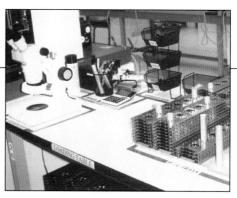

Research shows that bold black letters on a dense yellow background is the most readable color combination. We see this applied throughout Skyworks. ➡ ▶

Doors (and drawers) are automatic motion-makers because they require us to do something (open them) before we can get to what we really want. Visual workplace practices tell us to get rid of as many doors (and drawers) as possible. But when a process requires doors, as this one at Skyworks does, consider using plastic or Plexiglas. ▶

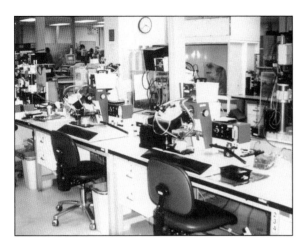

PHOTO 2.2: BONDING DEPARTMENT BEFORE (SKYWORKS SOLUTIONS, WOBURN, MA)

to answer the question of whether all motion had been eliminated—or not.

Later that day, the full team (including the supervisor) gathered in a darkened room and watched the video. All eyes were on the screen, looking to see if Paulette would leave her value field, her bench—if she would engage in motion.

As we watched the tape, something truly remarkable happened—the entire group gasped in unison and loudly at the exact same second. We gasped because we had all seen the same thing, at the same moment. What did we see? This:

1. Paulette peering into her microscope, working

2. Paulette reaching for a Q-tip

3. Paulette stretching out her arm but unable to reach the Q-tip

4. Paulette looking up—GASP!

We had all seen Paulette in motion. Suddenly, motion was no longer leaving the department. Motion was not even leaving the workbench. Suddenly motion had become: *looking up*. That's right. In a single moment in that darkened room, 14 pairs of eyes trained on the screen, every single person understood what they had not known before:

That the real value field in the Bonding Department was the postage-stamp size square platform at the base of the microscope.

All motion in the Bonding Department had to be measured from there.

Finding and defining your true value field may take several iterations, whether you are a value-add associate, supervisor, or CEO. Each time you cycle through, you gain a better understanding of what true work is for you and the information deficits that keep you from that work. This is the mandate of a visual thinker.

PHOTO 2.3:
PAULETTE BENEDICTUS

Building Block 8: Motion Metrics

The final of our eight building blocks is *Motion Metrics* (the term "metric" is identical to the term "measure."). A motion metric is a mechanism or yardstick that a person uses to track or measure his/her motion. Each person tracks his/her own motion—and no one else's—typically using one or more of the following tools: stop watch, pedometer, and/or frequency check sheet.

When individuals track their own motion, they each get rock-solid data that bear witness to the struggle in a pre-visual workplace. A cable assembler at Harris Corp. watched her pedometer rack up 5.5 miles in walking in a week, without her ever leaving the department. Her colleague, who was confined to a wheelchair, used a frequency check sheet that showed she left her value field 42 times in three days. She said she had never before thought about that as a problem.

Down the aisle, in Final Test, a 27-year veteran operator saw his stopwatch record 2 hours and 35 minutes of time he spent outside his cell during a single shift. "No wonder I can't get any work done," he flashed. The supervisor of the area simply kept track of all the questions she asked and was asked, and soon understood her own motion and what was eating up all her time.

Motion metrics give people a concrete way to see for themselves why they cannot get a full day of work done—and what they do instead. They track their struggle and back it out into the information deficits that trigger that struggle. What a fine education!

The beauty of measuring motion is that it can be done so simply and can motivate such high levels of ownership. The key is to make sure to let people measure *their own motion.* This is crucial. It is not just unnecessary for a supervisor or technician to track another person's motion, it is counterproductive, working against the very outcomes that motion metrics are designed to generate.

One of the greatest challenges of any improvement initiative is to get people on board. In this day and age, nearly everything seems elective, with many individuals expressing a tremendous sense of entitlement and prerogative over the simplest choices. Some simply refuse to cooperate. You may call it resistance; but they see it as their right. If you are a manager or supervisor, you may be tempted to threaten those who will not get on board. Not only does that no longer work, doing so will almost always kill an improvement activity because others are watching. We discuss this matter at length in the next two chapters; in fact, it is their entire focus.

Asking people to track their own motion (to collect their own motion metrics) cuts through the cultural miasma that many enterprises have created. From there, creating visual devices is only a step away, and with them, all the attendant benefits of a highly competent visual workplace.

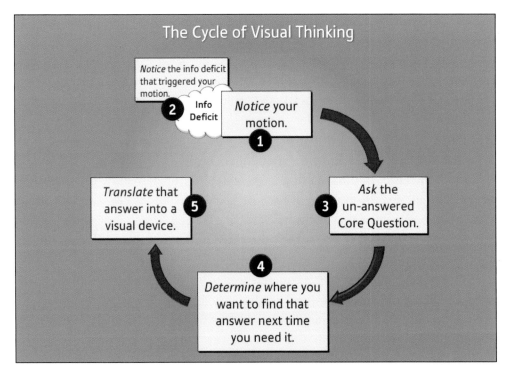

FIGURE 2.8: THE CYCLE OF VISUAL THINKING

Putting It All Together

You have just learned about the eight building blocks of visual thinking. Now let's look at how they work together to help the workforce eliminate motion and the information deficits that cause it by inventing visual solutions. It is called the *Cycle of Visual Thinking* (Figure 2.8).

Step 1: Notice the motion.
> Look! I just left my value field. That means I'm not working anymore. I must be in motion.

Step 2: Name the information deficit.
> Hmmm, if I am in motion, there must be an information deficit—a missing answer. What is it?

Step 3: Ask the un-answered core question.
> Which of the six core questions needs to be answered?

Step 4: Decide where to physically install the missing answer so it is right at hand.
> How close can I get the answer to the actual point-of-use?

Step 5: Translate that answer into a visual device.
> Now I'll turn that answer into a visual solution—and I won't ever have to ask or answer that question again because the answer will be firmly installed as close to the point-of-use as possible.

Excellent! Now at the least sign of more motion, the visual thinker starts the cycle again.

Person after person, cycle after cycle, this is exactly how the people who work in your company (on each organizational level) populate the work environment with dozens, hundreds, even thousands, of visual devices and mini-systems that result in an enterprise of splendid visual transparency.

Section | Two

THE CULTURE CONVERSION

How change gets implemented is precisely as important as what that change is. The most successful transformations are a perfect blending of the two—a perfect balance of the how and the what.

As will become increasingly clear throughout this book, the technologies of the visual workplace represent a proven protocol for embedding informational transparency in the company, on all levels. From the value-add level to the executive board room, from maintenance to engineering, from quality to finance, the result is enterprise-wide visuality.

Yet a proven implementation protocol cannot merely be dropped down from the outside into an existing work culture. However detailed and elegant that pre-built improvement framework might be, of itself it will not survive, let alone thrive. Models and frameworks are nothing without the people—people are the glue, with all their strength, imagination, skill, and goals as well as their suitcases of disappointments, bad habits, and fears about change.

Before we can consider "yet another improvement process," we must first understand the people-level of the workplace—the work culture of the organization.

The two chapters in this section address the cultural dimension of a company's journey to excellence. This dimension is engaged and amplified early in the process of implementing workplace visuality. It usually happens first as the visual where is installed—what I now call *work that makes sense: operator-led visuality*. There at the outset of the journey, the enterprise has a unique opportunity to create a robust and aligned improvement work culture, if one is not yet in place—or to strengthen it if it already is.

Chapter 3 shows us that logic from the perspective of the company's executive leadership. Chapter 4 looks at it from the vantage point of the value-add employee.

Nothing changes if nothing changes.

Hindu Proverb

CHAPTER | **3**

Leadership and the Power Inversion

A company's work culture is that combination of corporate purpose, values, beliefs, goals, and behaviors—in short, the corporate intent—that defines and reflects what winning means in the organization and how the game is played.

Work culture has the power to inspire or dishearten. It can be as powerful in the absence of a coherent corporate purpose as it is when that is fully in place and active. In fact, in many companies, work culture is more of an accident than a clear, well-designed achievement.

It doesn't have to be that way. An effective implementation of workplace visuality can and has resuscitated many a gloomy, dispirited workforce and turned it into one that is spirited, engaged, contributing, creative—and aligned. Aligned with what? Aligned with the corporate intent.

When we implement the technologies of the visual workplace, we don't just change the physical operational environment and accelerate the flow of products and services, information, and people in and through the facility. We align the work culture with the improvement vision of the enterprise. In some cases, we completely recast that culture, giving it a new set of premises, requirements, and goals. It is transformed.

This chapter starts by describing a company culture where a great deal has to change and even more needs to be removed from the mind and heart of the organization. In short, it needs a full overhaul. Let's call this a *traditional* work culture as compared to its opposite—a spirited, engaged, unified and aligned work culture—which I will call *new*.

The Challenge: Need for a New Paradigm

The vast majority of organizations around this country and around the world are just beginning their journey to excellence. Such companies are faced with a mighty challenge. They have to exchange outdated operational principles: adopting batch-size-of-one in lieu of large batches; designing layouts based on flow instead of function; building quality *in* instead of inspecting it *out*. And they must also rethink and reformulate the habits, assumptions, and preferences of nearly every member of the workforce, including those of management itself.

Most companies do not grasp the scope and scale of the change that is required when they first decide to transform their operations. If a factory, people are likely to say that changing lot size is challenge enough. How could there be more? Yet there is more, a great deal more. That "more" may be set to the side, temporarily— but it cannot be ignored.

The fabric of a work culture is the sum total of each and every action, trans-action, and informational exchange that occurs within a given shift, day, week, month, and year—for the life of the company. Work culture is not an isolated event. It exists across the life of the company, and it expresses the quality of that work life. It is the context of operations and of performance.

In a manner of speaking, work culture represents the personality as well as the consciousness of the enterprise. It mirrors its soul. Work culture describes, explains, and defines who the enterprise is, what it is about, what it values, and, accordingly, how it conducts itself. All of that is available for the world to see. Every company ships its work culture.

Every part made, every patient served, every report written, every deadline met or missed, every piece of information shared or lost, every truth, every lie, every promise made or broken—impacts the culture of work and re-shapes it, however minutely. No detail is immune. The conversion of operations to lean—installing a pull system and accelerating the flow—requires a parallel transformation in the work culture. Though changing your operational approach certainly impacts the culture of work in your organization, it does not and cannot align your culture sufficiently to make that change sustainable.

Even companies with well-oiled paternalistic frameworks of governance are faced with a challenge in this change. The genie is out of the bottle. If you had to land on one word that captured the substance of that change, that word would be *empowerment*. This revolution in consciousness was triggered sixty years ago, and the world is still unraveling its implications and applications. In business and industry, much of that activity is trained on the conversion of the work culture into one of greater balance and greater power as we seek a new governance paradigm —and a new way to define and distribute power.

The Big Picture: The Two Pyramids of Power

The old paradigm has many names: the top-down pyramid, command-and-control approach, the military model, paternalist governance—or my own personal favorite: The Thumb, as in your thumb on my head.

Whatever its name, obedience is at the heart of the top-down approach: *I say and you do. I order and you obey. I know and you don't.*

In command-and-control, the general/CEO/site manager sits at the top of the heap, at the apex of the pyramid—and the foot soldiers (line employees/operators/ value-add associates)—line the base (Figure 3.1). Command-and-control is the way fathers raised their children at the turn-of-the-century (and before). Three generations later, that was how my Swiss-born father raised me—with a heavy hand and zero tolerance for my opinion. It was a very popular model at the time, widely accepted as the only way: the Boss (or Pop) at the top of the heap; the child (*moi*) at the bottom. Thus was the tree bent.

From many perspectives, this approach was an undisputed success. It helped industrialize nations, win wars, and colonize the world. Rules, regulations, protocols, requirements, standards, decorum, structure—these were the forces that helped pull a disparate population of immigrants that once were the 13 colonies

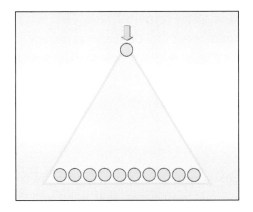

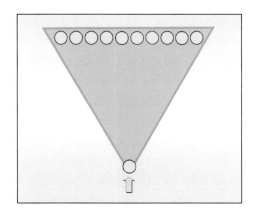

FIGURE 3.1:
THE TOP-DOWN PARADIGM

FIGURE 3.2:
THE BOTTOM-UP PARADIGM

into a viable society and thriving economy that would become the United States of America. Who would argue with that? This was the approach that got things done; and they stayed done. It was the paradigm of task.

If personal preferences or independent thinking took a back seat to orders from the boss, it was a small sacrifice to pay for stability, predictability, and control. Only recently have we discovered that the top-down model is out of balance; and we discovered why: It represents only half of the equation. There is another half—and it is the mirror opposite of the paternalistic approach.

That opposite, the bottom-up approach, is command-and-control inverted (Figure 3.2). The foot soldiers now line the uppermost edge, with the general/CEO/ site manager occupying the bottom. The notion of leadership is literally turned on its head. The supreme commander now becomes the servant-leader. And whom does that leader serve? The foot soldier, value-add associate, and hourly employee.

The message is clear: The leader's role in this new paradigm of power is to help value-add associates become more effective in their work and more engaged. The new leader supports, attunes, and listens to the needs of those whom he serves. This is his job.

The bottom-up pyramid represents the empowerment model. Its goal is transformation: greater employee participation, greater employee effectiveness, and the sharing of power. Because the pyramid is inverted, the power and authority of the enterprise flows upwards into the line of value. The focus of leadership has shifted to promoting and tangibly supporting others so that process, flow, quality, safety, and cost improve (that's long-hand for the improvement of *overall lead time*). The emphasis is not on the leader accomplishing her tasks but on her helping others accomplish theirs.

For value-add associates, the focus is no longer on their unquestioning obedience. It is on studying, understanding, and improving the process, not obeying the rules. Line employees are asked to become masters of cause and scientists of their own process.

False Decision-Point: Which One to Choose?

The bottom-up paradigm is the polar opposite of the top-down model, inverted as it is with all previous assumptions, preferences, principles, and values upside down. In this inversion, the previous power structure seems erased. But that is not so. Any attempt to remove the previous power base (the top-down approach) would almost certainly destroy the entire organization, not just the executive level.

Yet, in the early 1980s, such attempts were made, however wrongly, when we first began to learn about empowerment and its value. Back then, companies suddenly understood the immense power that is released when harnessing the minds and hearts—and not just the hands and feet—of the workforce. They rushed headlong into that; and, in their haste, some companies mistakenly dismantled their executive or middle management structure.

In wholly replacing the top-down paradigm with that of the bottom-up, those companies erroneously turned over the running of their companies to quality circles and other empowerment configurations. They were surprised when the enterprise failed—but you and I, with the benefit of hindsight, are not. We see now that they threw the baby out with the bathwater.

Two Pyramids: Two Functions

In the top-down paradigm, executives are responsible for vision, mission, values, strategy, systems, and structure. Their position at the top of the pyramid provides the long view that allows the corporation to align with its long-term objectives. The CEO sets the framework in place, answering the "what," "why," and "who":

1. What are we about? What are our products and services? What is our common purpose? What are our strategic objectives?

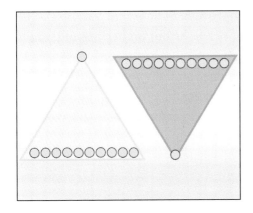

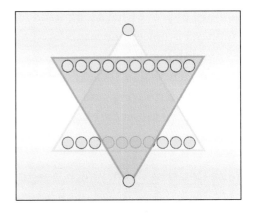

FIGURE 3.3:
DIFFERENT FUNCTION—
DIFFERENT GROUPS

FIGURE 3.4:
THE RESOLUTION
OF OPPOSITES

2. Why is any of the above important? Why bother?

3. Who is responsible for these "whats" and "whys"?

The so-called "head of the snake" is responsible for defining the *corporate intent.* By contrast, the bottom-up pyramid focuses on the "how"—how the purpose is deployed; how the objectives are met; how products and services are made and delivered; and how operations can fulfill its part of the corporate intent. In terms of the value-add level, the empowerment approach asks employees to become scientists of their own process on a local level so they can find ways to improve and upgrade that process, systematically and continuously.

These are two very different, side-by-side functions, executed by two distinct groups (Figure 3.3). In the face of such dramatic opposites, some companies struggle to decide which of the two pyramids to embrace and which to erase. These are the wrong questions.

We cannot throw either approach out. Instead, we must resolve or blend these two seeming opposites into a single paradigm. The company needs both of them. Figure 3.4 depicts this: one triangle on top of the other, situated so you can see most of both.

But there is a third element that expresses itself when we take steps to resolve seeming opposites: the circle or sphere, as shown in Figure 3.5.

If this image looks familiar to you, it is because you have seen it before, most

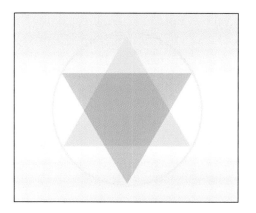

FIGURE 3.5:
ANCIENT SYMBOL
OF UNITY

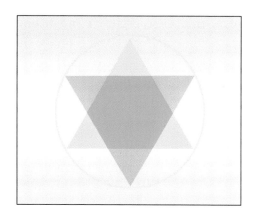

FIGURE 3.6:
THE GEOGRAPHY OF
COMMON GROUND

probably in the religious iconography of the civilized world since time imme-morial—not just in Judaism (as in the Star of David) but throughout the art and thought of ancient Mesopotamia, Persia, India, Egypt, and China, as well as mod-ern Christianity (among others).

The image is the universal symbol of unity. In its original ancient depiction, the two triangles are inscribed within a circle. The technically correct language for this recurrent image (which is actually 3-D and not flat) from the field of Sacred Geometry is: "a star tetrahedron inscribed in a sphere."

Dwell a moment on the notion that the image in Figure 3.5 is that ancient and universal symbol for unity. Could it be used as such today? Think about it.

Choose any set of opposites: black Americans and white Americans; male and female; Muslims and Jews; Pro-Choice and Pro-Life; Democrats and Republicans; managers and hourly employees; us and them. How do these sets of extremes co-exist? How can they? How do they find resolution? How can they become uni-fied?

There is only one way: They must look for common ground. The work of uni-fication is through the often arduous and always rewarding work of finding com-mon ground. Creating a unity of these is not just hard work. It is transformative. When they do combine, notice what happens to the polar opposites (Figure 3.6). Only a portion of Figure 3.6 is perfectly blended: The green section in the center. This green area is the geography of common ground. Around it remain sections of different-ness, exclusive and distinct. Pure yellow. Pure blue. Unaffected one by the other. I often gaze at this image and think of it as a terrific depiction of a strong marriage—much is shared and has to be shared, and much is separate, distinct, and independent. And the marriage is strong because of both.

Committed to finding common ground? You are in for some hard work—and tremendous reward.

Let me illustrate with a story.

Pro-Life and Pro-Choice Come to an Agreement

It would be hard to find more polar opposites than the pro-life and pro-choice movements in the U.S. Each has an iron-clad set of values and premises that supports its own correctness and brooks no argument.

So it was quite a surprise when the two groups in a small Midwestern city began talking to each other back in the mid-1980s. One said to the other, "Listen, we are each so convinced of our own rightness and the other's wrongness that one of these days we might start killing each other. Why don't we sit down and try to understand each other so we don't further polarize (even though we know we can never ever agree)."

The two groups decided to meet once a week and take turns in explaining their own perspective. They agreed on this simple set of ground rules: 1) One group would present and present thoroughly its point-of-view; 2) The other would listen; 3) The listening group had to re-state the presenting group's position until the presenting group declared that the listening group had understood.

Both groups agreed to the following definition of the term "understood": When the listening group could repeat back the position and perspective of the presenting group to the presenting group's satisfaction, it would be taken that the listening group had understood. At that point, the groups would switch roles.

With that, a coin was tossed at the first meeting to determine which group would begin. Pro-life won—and so that group began to explain its beliefs, values, and premises; and, at every step of the way, pro-choice was obliged to repeat back its understanding of what was said until pro-life said, "Yes, now you understand."

The pro-life part of the process took nearly six months. When it was complete, the roles were reversed. Pro-choice spoke; and pro-life listened and sought to comprehend and appreciate until it could repeat back the pro-choice party line to the satisfaction of the pro-choice group. That took another six months.

At the end of a year, the two groups—polar opposites—understood the other group's position, even though they still did not agree with it, not one bit.

In the wisdom of the moment, the two groups then decided that they did not want to throw the opportunity away. They decided to search for common ground— some area of endeavor they could undertake together. After yet more discussion, they realized that they both had an abiding interest in the welfare of children. They began to meet once a month to work together on children's projects.

Though the two groups kept their differences and held to them fiercely, they had found common ground (the green center) and arrived at enough agreement for them to move forward together on an issue of mutual interest.

Finding those areas of overlap requires that we pursue consensus: *The active search for disagreement until enough agreement is met for us to move forward together.* We learn a new way.

The Business Connection

That is exactly what is transpiring in companies throughout this country and around the world. Executives and senior managers are learning a new way. Hourly employees are learning a new way. Neither is easy. Both groups are indispensable to the running of the company. Each is powerful.

When we talk about transforming the work culture, we are talking about this process, which is, at its foundation, a re-balancing of power. The roles and the power bases remain distinct. Executives and senior managers still have their own set of duties, responsibilities, and functions. Hourly employees still have theirs. There is no effort to blend these. Instead, both sides commit to identifying and embracing a common purpose together: Finding common ground. For the purposes of our discussion, that might sound like this: achieving operational excellence across all company functions in order to cultivate the profit, prosperity, and long life of the company, shareholders, workforce, and the community-at-large. When found, this common purpose allows both sides to deploy their strengths for a common good. They seek to pool these strengths, not become homogenized.

Caught in the Middle

Before we take a closer look at the mechanics of this change, we need to look at another player in the shifting of this balance: middle managers and supervisors (union leaders included).

These employees are the translation point of the change, carrying messages between the apex and the base, and operationalizing the new paradigm of power/empowerment (Figure 3.7).

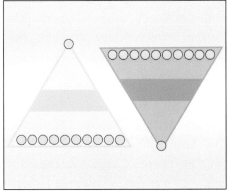

FIGURE 3.7:
MANAGERS: CAUGHT IN THE MIDDLE

This is no easy task. The goals of the general and the foot soldier are clearly defined—but lieutenants and sergeants have to make them happen. Theirs is a role of support, coaching, and influence. In a traditional organization, middle managers and supervisors are the problem-solvers of the enterprise. Most of the time, the problems are not theirs but inherited from generals and foot soldiers, with both groups expecting solutions.

Supervisors and managers are caught in the middle in the traditional organization. They are caught in the middle in the new organization. And they are caught in the middle in the transition between the two. As you will learn in this book's third section, a specific set of visual workplace technologies is designed to help them in this task and beyond. But the inversion must first be initiated.

The How of Empowerment: A Hidden Geometry

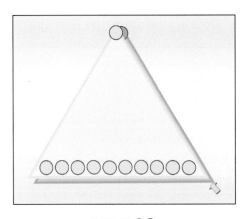

FIGURE 3.8:
THE TOP-DOWN PYRAMID
(EMPOWERMENT IS HIDDEN WITHIN IT)

The top-down pyramid is the starting point for the process of converting the work culture (Figure 3.8). That is because companies that need to convert are, by definition, functioning from the top-down model. They could never have gone into business without that or stayed in business for long. Command-and-control is the make-decisions/get-things-done line of attack. It requires task and action.

Yet, when we study this form closely, we see that the top-down pyramid con-

> *Discipline is remembering what you love.* —*Albert Einstein*

tains another one. Just inside the command-and-control pyramid is the pyramid of empowerment—dormant, waiting, and powerful only in its potential. The bottom-up paradigm is embedded in the top-down approach, its hidden prisoner.

This hidden geometry is both a seed and a promise. When we begin to see the shortcomings of the obedience paradigm, we understand that the way to address these shortcomings is by inverting (not subverting) its power. We turn to the workforce and in a sense say, "We still need obedience. But this time we want you to obey a deeper knowing than just the rules. We want you to find and then listen to your inner drive for excellence. Yours is the new power mandate: Become a scientist of the process. Get to know it for yourself. Get informed. Get educated. And then get active in making it better."

This variation on the theme of obedience is closely akin to the refreshing definition of discipline that Albert Einstein provides us. *Discipline*, Dr. Einstein tells us, *is remembering what you love.* Here we have culture as an outcome in a single phrase. In Einstein's rendering, *discipline* is synonymous with ownership, engagement, and alignment. We pursue excellence because it speaks to us on the level of our own knowing, our own desire to exercise the power within.

Could it be that the premier physicist of our era and *TIME* magazine's Man of the Century is proclaiming the power of love in the workplace? That is exactly the case.

When we love doing something, we do not need to be reminded, prodded, micro-managed or threatened. We simply do it. If we are blocked from doing it temporarily, we find a way around the obstruction and do it anyway. We love it. We want to get back to it. It feeds us.

The challenge in converting a traditional work culture to an improvement work culture is finding the way to ignite that sense of ownership, engagement, and alignment. After that, the care, momentum, and sustainment take care of themselves. They emerge naturally and powerfully from that base. The love does all the work.

This is in no way to suggest that improvement becomes continuous just because people enjoy doing it. With so many priorities competing for time and resources in most companies, wanting to do something and actually getting it done can be two different stories. As you will read, there are numerous visual principles and practices that can help us harness the drive for excellence so it can be put to work for the betterment of the corporation—and for ourselves as employees and individuals.

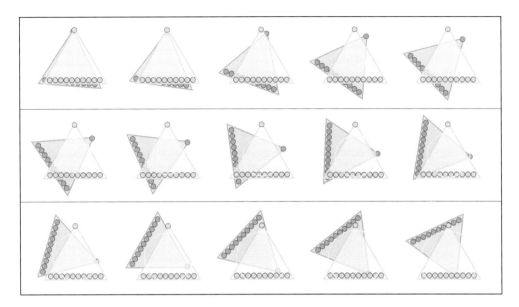

FIGURE 3.9: THE SEPARATION + INVERSION OF THE BOTTOM-UP PYRAMID

Liberating the Hidden Pyramid: A Closer Look

Transitioning into an organization that authentically reflects genuine unity is a long journey that is accomplished in three courageous steps.

The first step is taken when company management recognizes that its top-down approach works against the company's success and *decides* to break the inertia of the past; to share the power currently imprisoned in the command-and-control paradigm; and to empower the workforce so value-add associates have equal footing.

Step two is breaking the inertia—management taking the first fledging steps to activate the change.

Step three operationalizes that change into a systematic process—a conversion. This requires a long series of almost imperceptible shifts as the inertia that holds empowerment a prisoner dissolves and is slowly replaced by parity (Figure 3.9). The blue pyramid representing the imprisoned power of associates begins to gradually invert.

In workplace visuality, this literally begins when line employees are put in charge of their corners of the world and claim those corners through the *visual where* (see Chapter 5 for more).

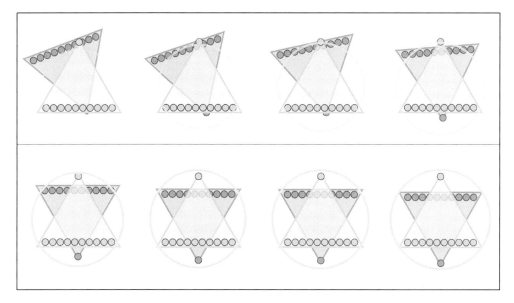

FIGURE 3.10: THE TWO MODELS APPROACH AND BLEND

In doing so, the iron-hold of the command-and-control pyramid (yellow) is loosened and the fluid power of the bottom-up pyramid (blue) is released, free at last to invert. Slowly the yellow pyramid re-orients and travels into its new position as a power partner in the company. As it turns, bit-by-bit, the unity sphere that will encircle the entire final form begins to exert itself—first as a tiny dot, then an expanding ring, next an ever-widening circle, and finally an encompassing sphere.

The blending persists in Figure 3.10 as the force within the bottom/up pyramid continues to seek its rightful positioning in the power structure. Giving up nothing of its distinctiveness, the yellow/empowerment pyramid moves into balance and overlap with its top/down partner. This elegant process of accommodation can take many months or even years. In the end, the two paradigms are nested, one on the other—perfectly balanced, yet individually distinct and accountable. Progress is incremental yet inevitable, powered as it is from within.

The end result is unity, with the simultaneous definition of both areas of commonality and areas of enduring differences. That is the nature of power.

Participation Myths

Remember, though I am illustrating this progression through a series of simple shapes and explaining it smoothly, the actual process drives change into the heart of the organization, where a host of formal and informal values reside. This conversion is rarely simple, smooth or quick. Instead, it is usually messy, confusing, and time-intensive. But one way or the other, in our experience, the separation between the two powers, the inversion, and then the final integration, are required for companies committed to excellence.

For some, however, empowerment is such a potent dynamic that they prefer to move towards it in small doses. Typically companies that decide to take it slow do so because they fear that anarchy will result, instead of unity. But they are wrong. Anarchy is nowhere to be found in this progression.

The only true danger is backsliding—backsliding into the old authoritarian paradigm; and that can only happen if the process is begun but not completed. This usually happens when the company declares that it wants an empowered workforce and a balanced work culture and then decides to proceed piecemeal—a little of this, a little of that but no substantive change. When that happens, one runs the risk of diluting the very momentum the company must gain if the shift is to be made. As a result, the conversion is never achieved.

To be sure, organizations that stay the course will experience moments of discomfort as managers witness what momentarily looks like a loss of control. This seeming loss is of the very control they know that they will have to—and in fact want to—release if they are to enter the new paradigm at all.

There can be no better moment to exercise the artistry of change—but this is also the moment when the company knows the least about what to do or how to do it. Colossal mistakes can and often do get made. Prescriptively, I will tell you that to succeed in this transformation you must designate an implementation team to oversee it—a group of skillful, experienced, emotionally sturdy individuals who will remain alert to predictable pitfalls.

There are many methods for successfully converting the work culture. No single method is sufficient to induce, produce, and then sustain the entire change. Yet, in my experience, an effective implementation of the technologies of the visual workplace comes the closest to creating this outcome.

In workplace visuality, we call that outcome: creating a workforce of visual thinkers. This is a new world-class competency, capable of shifting the enterprise into balance and unity, and catapulting it into splendid profit margins. It is the most effective way we have found for both liberating the individual will that is currently embedded in the obedience paradigm and getting the bottom-up pyramid to disengage and begin its inversion.

Employee involvement does not surface easily or naturally on its own, especially in a company accustomed to the rule of command-and-control. Often the real legacy of an organization rooted in the top-down/obedience approach is arrogance and abuse of power on the leadership side—and ballistic anger or numbness on the value-add side. Both breed a deep sense of helplessness and entrenched passivity.

In such organizations, managers often complain that the workforce does not want empowerment, remembering the many times they have offered hourly employees opportunities to participate and were refused. When the time came, line employees either sneered or said nothing; they simply sat there even when, protests management, a great deal of what was meaningful to them was at stake.

Yes, some line employees may give it a half-hearted try—or two. But then in the face of the usual "no extra time provided for improvement," associates wisely write off employee involvement as another empty promise. Not long after that, managers may also write off employee involvement—because employees do not appear interested in responding, even when given a "special invitation."

In the face of this seeming belligerence and/or indifference, managers mistakenly conclude that the workforce does not want participation, or does not appreciate participation, or does not want to be bothered. "These people don't care! They're just plain lazy," managers wrongly conclude.

What they overlook is the truth: The workforce does not know how to participate. It is a mystery to them, an unknown. They don't know what this new kind of employee involvement means since, in their view, they have always been involved in what, up to now, management has said is important—producing, doing work, adding value, showing up. The only participation they know is the work itself. That's how they have been asked to participate, year-after-year, job-after-job: "Just do your work." And they do.

And now management is asking them to do more. Or is it something else? No one knows for sure. How can such an undertaking possibly succeed?

Because most managers have experienced what I just described more than once in their careers, they tend to skip right over the "special invitation" part and go directly to one of their two favorite forms of improvement participation:

1) Doing the improvement themselves; or 2) Handpicking the best of the lot from the ranks and assigning these "high-achievers" a role in an event-based improvement activity such as a Kaizen Blitz, Special SWAT Team or the like.

I do not mean to suggest that handpicking members for your improvement teams is not a useful option, especially for event-based improvement efforts. It may be exactly right for your purposes. It is, however, not an effective way to align and unify the enterprise—or cultivate an empowered workforce.

None of these scenarios (managers doing it themselves; writing off the possibility of empowerment because "people are lazy anyway;" or handpicking the implementers) will advance the inversion of the hidden pyramid. You need a radical new vision and the courage to deploy it. That vision must be rooted in the values of the change you say you want. Only then will you know how to respond when the unusual or unforeseen occurs.

The fact is, companies in transition from a traditional to a new enterprise often do not know how to create a true participation-based organization. They do not know how to structure-in the opportunity for people to regularly and reliably contribute their ideas locally—on behalf of the corporate intent. Yet, just because the company has not yet learned how to do this does not mean that the possibility does not exist—or that employees will always either not have any ideas to contribute or simply refuse to contribute them.

Thinking so is a problem in itself. In all cases, such a mindset brings us to the wrong conclusions and closes the door on solutions that are genuinely available.

Nonetheless, one must realize that mistakes made at the earliest phase of this journey are the most difficult to correct, no less so when implementing workplace visuality as anything else. The Chinese proverb "the first step of the journey is the destination" applies here.

The Biggest Mistake

As you will learn in the reading of this book, there are no less than ten doorways into workplace visuality. Each doorway leads to a distinct category of visual function (visual order, visual standards, visual metrics, visual displays, and so on). Each doorway is opened by a different organizational group or mix of groups—each responsible for embedding a specific visual outcome into the corporate landscape. Line employees, managers, engineers, maintenance personnel, quality technicians, supervisors, executives, and support staff each make a special visual contribution.

But I will choose the first doorway to illustrate several of the main points in this chapter. Doorway 1 targets implementing the *visual where*. This is the doorway reserved for employees on the value-add level, whatever the setting—factory, hospital, insurance office, home delivery vehicle or retail store. This task is theirs.

The formula is simple: a border, address, and an ID label for everything that casts a shadow. No exception. This lays down the pattern of work that *is* the visual where—the ability of a workplace item to find its way back home, based solely on the visual location information built into it.

As explored in detail in Chapter 5, an effective implementation of the *visual where* routinely produces a 15% to 30% increase in productivity on the cell or departmental level, with parallel reductions in flow distance and lead time, as well as dramatic improvements in quality and on-time delivery. It also serves as the single trigger for the mighty work culture conversion we have just discussed—the release and gradual inversion of the empowerment pyramid.

But such outcomes require that managers not take shortcuts—though they will be tempted.

The first mistake that management can make is exactly here, at the launch of visual order. Because this pitfall comes at the very outset of the visual conversion, it can easily become the company's biggest implementation mistake. What is that mistake? Management appropriates the simple chore of installing the *visual where* for itself, assigns it only to a few hand-picked associates or delegates it to some group other than line employees.

Yes, the most fundamental error managers can make at the earliest stage of a rich and productive transformation is to commandeer the simple task of implementing the *visual where* for themselves. Such managers mean no harm. They reason only that, because the task is so simple and obvious, they can do it themselves (or contract it out) and save operators for more interesting improvement tasks. "Lines, labels, addresses! That's easy."

But they are mistaken. The very simplicity of installing the *visual where* is a key reason it can move the company through the inversion experience.

The Visual Where: Low-Hanging Fruit

Installing the *visual where* is like picking so much low-hanging fruit. When managers decide to pick that fruit themselves, they unintentionally rob the organization of a prime opportunity to *empower the value-add level workforce.*

It is exactly because installing the *visual where* is so elementary—and yet so useful to day-to-day performance—that operators should be the ones to implement it. Operators decide. Operators design. Operators explore. Operators experiment. Operators invent. You can only engender an empowered workforce if you provide the workforce with powerful tasks to undertake. This is at the heart of the I-driven approach.

In implementing visual order, we ask the group in the enterprise charged with adding value to help to improve their own work area and their own work flow by getting the workplace to speak the answer to the *where* question again and again. The dialogue is between employees and their work. Having associates install the *visual where* is a vital to getting them to connect to the physicality of the change.

This is genuine empowerment, providing the company with a new core competency that prepares it for the other transformative changes that must happen if the company is to achieve excellence.

In this first phase of the journey, employees find and follow their own internal improvement vision—every employee. Each person is asked to be in charge of his or her own locus of control and to use the need-to-know as a stimulus to populate their local real estate with visual devices and mini-systems that answer that need.

You can think of I-driven as self-motivated ("I can"). It can also easily embrace inventiveness ("I will") and inspiration ("I want."). You get the picture.

There is no way to over-emphasize the importance of the I-driven dynamic in creating and sustaining workplace visuality. Indeed, I-driven will continue as a theme again and again in the chapters of this book; and maybe after all that, I will have succeeded in making the beginnings of a case for its importance.

When we aim to establish a new way of thinking in the enterprise—visual thinking—we deliberately look for ways to make each person independent and singular in his or her actions, in his or her own improvement ideas. Let me repeat: To many, this seems counter-intuitive, the antithesis of creating a unified, team-based work culture. It is, in fact, a strong step in precisely the right direction. (See the case study that starts on the next page.)

This I-driven process, which is primarily designed to engage and empower the value-add employee, is the subject of the next chapter.

THE VISUAL TRUCK: A MINI-CASE STUDY

SEARS HOME REPAIR TRUCKS

ANGIE ALVARADO

FRANK LOPUSZYNSKI

DISTRICT 8368

- 337 Trucks
- 301 Technicians
- 421 Total Associates
- Total Area: Nevada and half of California
- Average of seven home visits per technician per day
- 376,574 Home visits one year before pilot
- 404,023 Home visits one year into the pilot

THE PURPOSE: MAKE MILLIONS

When Sears Home Services (Illinois) launched operator-led visuality in Product Repair Services, the goal was to shave five minutes off of each home visit that 8,400 repair technicians made daily, nation-wide. The multiple of those five minutes would mean millions in additional revenues.

The focus was the repair truck which contained everything technicians need to make repairs: parts, tools, manuals, a computer linked to Sears home base, and so on. Technicians were entirely in charge of their work—what they did and how they did it. No one watched. The truck was not only their lifeline, to many it felt like their company.

Under the leadership of Frank Lopuszynski, corporate Director of Operations, District 8368/Sacramento became the visual truck pilot. Angie Alvarado, District GM, became the pilot's management champion. She started at Sears 18 years before in phone sales.

THE SACRAMENTO CENTER

ANGIE ALVARDO: IN HER OWN WORDS

BEFORE: "Productivity—more work with less payroll—is a major goal in all companies. It was the same in District 8368. Our main productivity measure targeted technician repair times: how much time a technician spent in a customer's home, repairing appliances. Decreasing repair times was always the goal. We talked about it daily, and our goals and recognition programs all circled around it. Before visuality, we struggled to improve repair time without sacrificing repair quality. We had no process, no on-going method.

🔺 **Before:** Trucks got pretty darn cluttered. Legend has it that one tech, in need of a screw, decided it would be quicker to take it off the truck body itself than to try to find it under all that jumble.

Then my boss asked if I had ever heard of the visual workplace and 5S, because he needed a volunteer for a project. I had a 5S book on my shelf, so I signed on, even though I was a little insulted. After all, I had the cleanest and most organized facility in the Western Region.

Three months later, Dr. G (Gwendolyn Galsworth) walked in with her crew of visual worker bees. We toured the facility together. I introduced her to some technicians and proudly announced our success, metric after metric. Dr. G listened, took time to ask questions, and praised us on our successes.

Dr. G and I spent the next year together. I learned that, while 5S gets things clean and organized, the *visual workplace* engages your employees in sharing information—and making it readily accessible to themselves and others—through visual devices. Plus, employees get the improvement time they need to do this and (yes) improve productivity.

Productivity—that brings us back to the repair time question. Well, the answer was there all along; and it was not in better supervision or better software. The answer was in the workspace, the value field— the repair truck itself. The technician spends most of his day in the truck—driving to the customer's home, going back to the truck to locate a tool, and then one more time (we hope only one more time) to find a needed part.

So, was the answer to clean and organize the truck, as in 'Let's have another Kaizen event and clean all the trucks'? No. Some of our techs had very clean and organized trucks (like our facility). Yet their repair times and productivity were no higher than anyone else's.

The issue was *visuality*. All those neat, clean, and organized parts, for example, in near-identical little brown boxes, with near-identical small labels and

◄ **After:** Everything is accessible, clear, safe, and visually-ordered. This tech even decided to carpet the floor of her truck!

◄ This cab speaks!

THE VISUAL TRUCK

◄ The tech on this truck lists parts on these pink cards, crossing them out as consumed.

Each appliance manual on this truck is visually ordered. ➤

even smaller part numbers. That was the problem. Technicians could not tell the difference between anything. That was the struggle and the time-eater. They had been fighting with their own workspace.

Then they got trained. Visuality made sense to them. We didn't push it. They decided to get visual. Smart move. One technician, for example, realized he could address the racks that held the small boxes. So he did. Others followed. So simple. So practical.

We did not dictate a standardized workspace. We avoided that. Instead, we asked each technician to decide what worked best for him/her. We wanted them to come up with new ways. Some technicians addressed racks with pictures of the parts; others made binders with diagrams of the truck interior. Many used color coding. Everything got visual.

My team and I set a course to embrace this new and exciting concept. The technicians came into the facility with their trucks once a month to show off

Visually ordered, color-coded bins with bold addresses help a lot. ➤

their new visual ideas to management and each other. We kept lots of supplies on hand in the Visual Corner so techs could run with any improvement idea they had—bins, baskets, tape, pre-cut pegboard panels, Velcro, hooks, and more. We developed recognition programs around this monthly event, set criteria and recognized "best visual trucks."

Employee morale soared. And yes, productivity improved, too—15% across the board.

Trust was another unexpected result. Before visuality, we locked up pens and other supplies—because we were certain that people would steal them. As a result, all managers had to have a ton of keys—or know somebody who did.

We don't do that anymore. Supplies are in their addressed locations, open to whoever needs them. Supplies don't disappear. Employees don't hoard. We don't spend money on endless replenishments. People know where things are; they use what they need.

Repair time? Well, that measurement never improved. But customer satisfaction, quality repair scores, and revenue soared. The technicians spent less time in their trucks looking for parts and tools, and more time (saved time) with customers—listening, getting better information about the needed repair, and offering to fix other appliances.

Revenues went up by $1.5 million in a year. Customer satisfaction (which at Sears is rated exclusively on Perfect 10 scores) went up 300 basis points the same year. Reschedules and cancels went down by 28,000 customers—that meant we gained 28,000 customers that we would not have had because we had no capacity.

The year we launched workplace visuality, our district was 47 in a field of 67. Two years later, we were number one—in the nation!

The exam-awards process that Dr. G developed for us (discussed in Chapter 9) knitted our entire team together—in the trucks, outside in the yard, and inside the building at home base. Everyone learned and applied visual workplace principles and practices."

A GROUP OF TECHNICIANS DURING THE VISUAL PILOT TRANSFORMATION

When your entire "department" is a truck, space is at a premium. The Sears techs eagerly applied S4/Select Locations principles (smart placement) to their trucks—principles such as: store things/not air, point-of-use, use the existing architecture, put it on wheels, use the natural flow line, and so on. Take a look.

◆ The precut pegboard panels from the Visual Corner gave techs lots of ideas on how to visually use the dead space on the back doors.

These visually-ordered parts bins were mounted on a wooden frame and do more than you think. See the latch? Open it and the frame swings forward to the point-of-use—while also allowing the tech to access the shelves behind it. Close it and the items on those shelves stay safely in place. ◆

Techs also made great use of the dead space tucked up in the corner where doors open. ◆

O brave new world, that has such people in it.
William Shakespeare
The Tempest

CHAPTER | **4**

The I-Driven Culture

In far too many organizations, the social fabric of the workplace—the company work culture—is out of balance. Without a substantive change in that culture, no implementation, however excellent in intent, will be sustainable. That change must begin at the level of each employee's sense of self and of his/her place within the enterprise.

Will I Be the Hero of My Own Life?

Charles Dickens opens his classic novel, *David Copperfield*, with David pondering his young life. In the quiet of his heart, he asks: "Will I be the hero of my own life?" Over the next 400 pages, David proceeds to discover the answer to that question in the trials and adventures of becoming a man in 19th century England.

David's question is our question. Though quietly forgotten as we grow older, when each of us was young, this was the question in our hearts: "Will I be the hero of my own life?" It may have been worded differently. Maybe it sounded more like: "What will I be when I grow up?" Deep in the mystery of our childhood—and then of our adolescent heart—was a profound belief that whatever it turned out to be, "I will be excellent at it. I will excel. I will make something of my life. I will be its hero!" (My thanks to Swami Chetanananda for this challenging insight in his book, *Will I Be the Hero of My Own Life*, Rudra Press.)

This was the sentiment at the heart of a conversation I had nearly a decade ago with an employee of an aerospace manufacturer in Texas. Ted, as I will call him, had started at the firm 27 years before, fresh out of high school. His Dad worked there before him.

Ted told me that, as a kid, he would stand in his backyard and see the fighter planes cut white streamers across the sky. He remembered being thrilled, "to my bones" were his words, knowing someday he would join his Dad in making those magnificent flying machines, so slick and fast and perfect. He recalled saying to himself, "I'm gonna makes fighter planes when I grow up! That's what I'm gonna do! Just like Dad!"

Fresh out of high school, Ted was hired by that great aerospace company. "I went in to be a hero, Gwendolyn," he said. "I wanted to do something great! That was 27 years ago." Ted paused; then he asked, "What happened?"

I looked at him and saw a fine person. But I knew Ted wanted me to look deeper. He wanted me to see the hero that was still inside, waiting to get out.

I was silent.

Part of the new job description for every CEO, president, plant manager, VP, manager, and supervisor is to help employees find and manifest the hero within. Those leaders who take this on immediately widen the definition of their own contribution, their own work.

Think about it. What would happen if you took this on, whether you are a floor supervisor, in charge of finance, a production manager or the CEO of a multi-national? What would happen if you committed to helping each person who reports to you become the hero of their own work? What part of your current job would stay the same? What part would change? What part of *you* would change?

Work Culture: Identity's Mirror

How does a manager help people realize the transformative, transcendent dimension of themselves? (Remember, we include middle managers, supervisors, executives, site managers, and union leaders in the term "manager".)

In my experience, this is, pure and simple, a matter of identity. The power to transform a traditional top-down culture into one that is empowered rests on the issue of who you believe you are—and who you believe the other person is. The deepest cultural change begins at this level: our beliefs about identity.

Shifting people's identity beliefs does not happen overnight and is most easily accomplished by making the process as tangible as possible, at every step. That is, management must discover ways to translate new beliefs about who people really are into a concrete system of principles, methods, and tools.

For one thing, people need time, permission, and a protocol of behavior that reliably and predictably leads them to shift into a higher dimension of their own being. You cannot help people realize the hero within merely by communicating, supporting, and encouraging. Communicate what? Support what? Encourage what? You must offer them a structure that can contain and advance the change.

That change must start on the value-add level, where so many of the distortions about people collect—misbegotten beliefs that are part and parcel of the company's current work culture. It is here that implementing visuality in the workplace can be such a potent force for transforming the entire enterprise—and with that, the work culture that every enterprise must express.

The Need to Know: The I–Driven Approach

Remember the two driving questions discussed in Chapter 2: What do I need to know? What do I need to share? The "I" in both questions is the key to visual thinking—to finding and eliminating motion and the information deficits that trigger it through solutions that are visual.

The Need-To-Know (NTK) and Need-To-Share (NTS) are also key to creating a work culture focused on improvement. In both, the energy and power of the "I" are the driving forces. Once the "I" is systematically engaged, heroes are not far behind.

NTK and NTS happen in sequence. NTK is engaged first. "What do I need to know?" is asked and answered—visually answered—iteratively, cycle after cycle, time after time. (Please note: These two driving questions are equally as important and as powerful for supervisors, managers, CEOs, your maintenance and field staff, marketing/sales, finance, purchasing—in short, for all organizational functions, as you will see for yourself when we get to the later chapters of this book and examine the Ten-Doorways Model. In this chapter, however, we focus squarely on applying them on the value-add level—by your operators and line employees.)

At the outset and for some time, the single NTK focus on the operator-level is on the where question. Where are my pliers? Where are the parts? Where are the materials? Where are the reports? Where is my supervisor?

The result? The immediate work area becomes populated with dozens of visual devices that answer that individual's questions about "where?" That's how the *visual where* gets deeply installed for everything that casts a shadow—through borders, addresses, and, as applies, ID labels.

Over time, the logic of the *visual where* spreads across the entire company. That impact can be so far-reaching when line employees put visual order in place, that it often feels to them as though they have completed 90% of the journey to a visual workplace. In fact, only about 20% of the distance has been covered—only one of the ten doorways but one of the most powerful.

This physical conversion of the work environment only describes the outcome on the tangible, concrete level of the physical work. A second outcome surfaces that is intangible and subtle—the cultural conversion on the socio-leadership dimension of the enterprise.

This socio-leadership dimension impacts every layer of the workforce. For the purposes of this immediate discussion, we will look at its impact and meaning on the associate/operator/value-add level. That impact and meaning is this: *I am in control of my corner of the world.*

This is a mighty occurrence. When an operator states, "I am in control of my corner of the world" and feels that control, you can confidently predict that person is on his/her way to becoming a steady improvement contributor, a genuine citizen of the organization, and an authentic member of a high-performing team—even if that team is not yet formed. In the visual workplace, achieving visual control over one's corner of the world is the first step in mastering the rest of the physical landscape of work.

In my experience, the simple physical act of installing the *visual where* through an I–driven process provides us with an invaluable sense of the physical control we crave and need in the world of work. Personal confidence is a natural by-product.

For many, this sense of control is often their first experience of any degree of mastery in the world of work. From that standpoint alone, it is a revolutionary personal breakthrough. Slowly, control becomes confidence—confidence in one's own ability to address the world of work. As this sense of control and confidence spreads from individual to individual, and then from department to department, a trust in the company itself begins to emerge.

Over time (and not all that much time; several months can do the trick), these shifts in personal identity lay the groundwork for self-leadership, resourcefulness, and high levels of engagement and connection that characteristically produce high-functioning/high-performance teams.

Unless you have lived through it, it may be hard to believe the simple act of installing the *visual where* can engender leaders where before there were none. Yet I, my clients, colleagues, and trainers have witnessed this repeatedly. The journey into visuality has to change us because it changes the way in which information is delivered—and therefore the social fabric of work.

Simply put, the liberation of information *is* the liberation of the human will. When the human will is liberated, it is free to align with any purpose that makes sense to it. Excellence attracts that will. The *liberated will* normally chooses to align with the *corporate will* if excellence is at the heart of that enterprise.

Let's delve more deeply into the presenting symptoms that make cultural transformations so tricky as well as so needed.

The Phases of the Identity Evolution: From Struggling-I to Unified-I

As the implementation of workplace visuality deepens and spreads, we can see a parallel journey or evolution of the "I" (the individual) in its worldly perspective from struggling to strong to unified—from small to medium to great. The three phases of this journey are summarized as:

- **Phase 1:** The company recognizes that Struggling-I's exist and are having a detrimental impact on enterprise excellence. The company initiates a visual rollout as a remedy. The Struggling-I's begin to translate their needs-to-know into visual devices (beginning with the *visual where*). In so doing, they gain a new degree of control over their work and their performance.

- **Phase 2:** Struggling-I's have now become Strong-I's, pro-actively continuing to implement high-impact/low-cost visual solutions in and around their work area. They continue to gather strength and exhibit strong pride in their own improvement contributions and independence in their thinking.

- **Phase 3:** Strong-I's shift their focus to the need-to-share, developing visual answers to questions that others have. Because others can now more easily access vital workplace information, they are able to do their own work better and more safely. Strong-I's have become unified in their thinking and actions—informal *servant-leaders* (if you are familiar with that term, it is as life-enhancing as it sounds) in their work areas. The new "I" evolves into a Team-I or Unified-I.

Let's walk through this process, phase by phase. Recall our story about Ted. Ted was like most young people when they show up for work for the first time. He felt the hero within wanting to get out; he could not help but bring it along everywhere he went. Years go by and Ted's connection with that hero fades. We say: People change. Indeed, most people in the workforce for more than a few years are not who they were when they began. Most are beaten and bruised by the experience we call work.

At VTI we say these folks are struggling; they are *struggling-I's*. We know something of such employees. We know that their individual sense of self has often suffered many attacks, eroding their self-esteem and ability to trust. We know that, as a result, they can act in a variety of noticeable ways. Some are cynical; some non-cooperative. Others are downright nasty and belligerent; they are angry. Still others appear indifferent, unresponsive, passive or non-committal; they are numb.

If you ask the angry ones what's wrong, they will often say that the system is "dumb"—or management doesn't know what it is doing and is ruining the company. Stupid things happen, they say, and they are powerless to stop them.

On the other end of the Struggling-I spectrum are people who seem indifferent. They are likely to claim that they just don't care; they will ask to be left alone. Stupid things happen, they say, and they are powerless to stop them. People from either group tend to see their work lives as out of their control and see themselves as the hapless victims of a badly-run system.

Many times, they are right. The company is badly run; dumb things do happen all the time—and everyone does seem powerless to change that. Too much goes

---

INSET 4.1: JOURNEY OF THE "I"

Phase 1: The company recognizes that Struggling-I's exist and are having a detrimental impact on the pursuit of excellence, and determines to remedy that.

- The Struggling-I sees himself as a victim of the system, blaming others for an array of woes and troubles. Feeling powerless to change things, such individuals respond by either going numb or ballistic.
- Struggling-I's reflect a co-dependent, passive/reactive mindset.

Phase 2: The Struggling-I's begin to translate their needs-to-know into visual devices and, in so doing, gain a degree of control over their workday.

- As this process ripens, the Struggling-I—the individual—has gained strength and grown independent and proud of his role in the company.
- This "I" now reflects an independent mindset and is an individual contributor (not yet team-minded).

Phase 3: The independent "I" now recognizes his need-to-share and begins to develop visual answers to questions that others have so that they can do their own work better.

- This "I" is an individual who is strong, focused, and willing to serve the greater interests of the company.
- This "I" is team-minded, with an interdependent mindset that recognizes that no part of the organization can succeed in isolation. This "I" embraces unity as the pathway to customer-retention and greater profit margins.

---

wrong too often. Big things or little things, working seems more like walking on shifting sand than marching firmly and purposefully forward. The entire system is careening out of control, and just about everyone, including the plant manager, feels like the company is on the brink of chaos. A psychotherapist might want to call the system *dysfunctional* and the people who work there *co-dependent*—and that is certainly one perspective on this condition.

In strongly-aligned companies, Struggling-I's are rarely a problem because they are rarely hired. They are eliminated as candidates during the interview process—belligerent applicants for having an attitude problem, passive ones for being too shy. But in companies in the process of making (or about to make) the transition from a so-called traditional enterprise to one seeking excellence, the Struggling-I is typically part of the work landscape, part of what is chronically wrong with the work culture, and a big (but not insurmountable) barrier to progress, prosperity, and wealth.

Moving Too Quickly to Teams

Some executives attempt to correct the organizational condition of Struggling-I's by declaring teams into existence. This is always done with the best of intentions. The reasoning goes like this:

- Everyone has strengths.
- Everyone has weaknesses.
- If we organize people into teams, they will cover for each other's weaknesses with their strengths.
- Supervisors will be freed up to attend to larger matters.
- In the mix, we'll level the playing field and unify the workforce.
- Morale will lift; people will pay better attention to their work; they'll solve problems; we'll cut costs and improve our profit margins.
- We'll all win!
- Let's do it!

A lofty goal; but let's look at what can happen instead and often does.

The F-28 Department is asked to get into a team, appoint a team leader, and so on. Hank, Suzie, Mary, Ted, and Sam meet in a spare training room. Once the door is shut, whoever talks first, loudest, and/or fastest becomes the team leader and takes over the group.

The result? Another form of the dominance hierarchy is imposed upon the company. (See the Dilbert perspective in Figure 4.1.)

You may find this scenario distorted or over-simplified. In some companies, it may be. But in others, it describes the dynamics of team-making with precision. Teams are announced, not created. People are left to fend for themselves within the so-called *team* framework.

Even when companies proceed to teams with care, supported with training and coaching, the resultant teams may not address the underlying cultural imbalance. In so many organizations, that imbalance produces a widespread sense of instability, low control, and disempowerment as workplace constants—the symptoms of a workforce overpopulated with Struggling-I's.

FIGURE 4.1: YET ANOTHER FORM OF THE DOMINANCE HIERARCHY

How does one address this sad state? Yes, you certainly should hire for attitude and character. That is always preferred. But what do you do with folks who joined the company 10, 15, 25 years before continuous improvement became the rallying cry and enterprise excellence, the goal? They know the methods; they know the secrets; they know how to create value in the organization.

You can threaten and, if need be, fire them for not aligning with the new best thing. Yet in many companies, this is not possible because of union rules and/or because the expertise those ornery employees possess is indispensable. They currently hold the knowledge and know-how wealth of the enterprise—and they and you know it.

In such cases, company leadership often thinks it is stuck with damaged goods. Yet, there are options other than firing such people as well as perspectives other than feeling stuck. Seek instead a process that focuses on realigning the distorted will, strengthening the Struggling-I—and doing so in full cooperation with its owner, the individual. This is the visual workplace's journey of I.

The Visual Remedy: Letting the "I" Drive

Companies need a way to address positively the Struggling-I's that populate the workforce, on both an associate and a management level. In companies just starting their journey to excellence, it is common for many (if not the majority) of employees to see themselves as victims of the system and powerless to change it.

Such value-add line employees are not yet ready for teams, not yet ready to pursue improvement as a group. When the work culture needs a major overhaul, look for ways that allow people to ease into an improvement frame of mind. Evolution, not revolution, works in this case—even though the results, when they come, are often revolutionary. No Kaizen Blitzes for the moment, please. No requirement for the workforce to march together, single-purposed, to a greater tomorrow.

The divisiveness that is a by-product of a fragmented work culture does not convert into unity overnight. It can't be scheduled out of existence or bullied into oneness. The "I" is the starting point—the "I" in you, the "I" in me, and the "I" in the other. This is the work culture on its atomic level where it cannot be further divided. That is the level of wholeness.

The "I" exists on the level of will. That will is the location in each of us of our last outpost, that last quantum of which we are always and ever in charge. You and I are alike in that regard, as in no other. Outside factors and forces can get close, very close, to the *me* on the inside. Other people may presume upon or even appropriate parts of me—my hands, my feet, my brain, even my heart. But *not* my will. At some point, their demand stops and mine exerts itself, implacable and clear.

That point is the point of my will—the boundary line, a secret place of my own. This is where plans are hatched that create escape routes for the rest of me—my hands, feet, brain, and heart. The will is the place where I am in charge. It is a place of decision, intention, and knowing. It is a place of power.

Without the will's agreement, personal progress is fraught with difficulty. With it, great things are possible. Without the alignment of the personal will with the corporate will, no company can reach the full promise of excellence. With it, the organization is unified, aligned, and ready to tackle day-to-day and long-range challenges, armed with its full potential.

The will is the powerhouse of the "I." Each person has one. And it is this that we seek to resuscitate and rehabilitate when we decide to align the work culture with excellence. When, in workplace visuality, for example, we ask individuals to install the simple formula of the *visual where* (border + address + ID label), we empower them to make a mighty change in their immediate work environment, one that will benefit them both tangibly and intangibly—and the company as well.

Not everyone agrees to this at first. Early on, I–driven gives back people's right to decide if they will get on board—or not. We allow people—we ask them—to show us their stripes, in a manner of speaking. We permit them to do or not do, based on their own inner decision. Many refuse. Others watch.

And a few don't just get on board; they leap. Responding to their own internal vision, they cut a swath of improvement through the work landscape that can be dazzling. They create. They are unstoppable. The results often go far beyond the simple protocol of visual order and explode into unique visual solutions of unsurpassed usefulness and invention. (See Photo Album 6 for a set of splendid examples of visual inventiveness.)

In allowing people to participate as they are inspired to—or not—we get to see who people really are, without constant surveillance and prodding by supervisors or managers. Remember, the whole journey is about identity. Each person must march to his own drummer and not to the participation requirements of the company—not yet.

Why, you may ask, would a company allow its employees to decide if they will get on board or not? To many a manager, this sounds like *laissez-faire* or even anarchy. What business purpose can such seeming permissiveness serve?

The answer is plain. Companies that capture and engage the hearts and minds—as well as the hands and feet—of their employees reap the harvest of a spirited, engaged, and aligned workforce. The future of your profit margins depends on that.

As this chapter started out by saying: It is on the associate/value-add level that so many of the mis-assumptions about identity and work culture collect and amass. We begin to shift that culture when we ask the Struggling-I's to take and maintain control over their corners of the world by implementing the *visual where*: Install a border, address, and, as applies, an ID label for everything that casts a shadow. The change protocol is simple. It is knowable and largely do-able within the workday. Bit by bit, tool by tool, part by part, shelf by shelf, Struggling-I's gain some control, some power, over their work areas, even as they grow in personal stature.

Yet, take note: When, in this process, we invite employees to follow their own lead, their own preferences, we do so exclusively in reference to improvement activity. There is no such invitation made in reference to production performance. We cannot and do not tolerate any slackening of workload, quality or delivery requirements. Those demands are as uncompromising as ever. They do not waver.

What becomes elective for the employee at the start of the rollout is the decision to participate in the visual rollout or not. Yes, let each person make that decision. Any opportunity that lets individuals show who they are and what they want when the pressure is off is extremely valuable. Seize it. Give them the rare option to participate in improvement or not, based on their own personal preferences and own inner calling. Allow them the right to find and re-claim their own will.

Photo Album 6

Visual Inventiveness at United Electric

Creating Visual Thinkers at United Electric Controls (UEC)

United Electric Controls (Watertown, MA) is an ISO-certified company that battles daily in the highly competitive switch and controls market where precision, quality, and low-cost are givens. Today, UEC is a cellular manufacturing jewel, with a motivated, articulate, and inventive workforce—and with supervisors who are, first and foremost, superb coaches. Launching operator-led visuality was one of UEC's first improvement commitments.

**BILL ANTUNES
ACE VISUAL THINKER**

LEE SACCO LEFT HIS OFFICE
TO USE BILL'S DISPLAY

LEE SACCO MOVED HIS DESK
NEXT TO BILL'S DISPLAY

Reducing Stockouts through Visual Displays

Bill Antunes, a veteran UEC assembler who invented dozens of splendid visual solutions, developed this one:

1. When Bill or anyone else noticed a part is low, they marked it on right in blue "Low Stock"—or, if out, then in red on left "Hot Shortage."

2. The buyer (here Lee Sacco) noted this on his rounds, contacted the supplier, and marked the promised delivery date on the display.

3. The associate then circled the date, both to say thanks and to complete the communication loop.

Bill's display replaced a 3-part memo system the company had used for years. His solution led to buyers going to the areas they supported—instead of associates sending memos to them. Later, Lee Sacco and all other UEC buyers moved their desks onto the production floor.

Paperwork Improvement through Visual Order

From the moment John Pacheco, veteran machinist at UEC, was first trained in workplace visuality, he never stopped inventing visual solutions. This brilliant mini-system is just one of his many contributions. Like all of them, it captures many visual workplace principles.

Before ⬆

John realized that he did not need an eight-foot table for his paperwork so he got rid of it.

After (1) ▶

Removing a shelf from a nearby rack, John replaced it with a wooden shelf on sliders—getting double-duty out of a pre-existing value field and allowing him to pull the paperwork function to him when needed and store it out of the way the rest of the time.

After (2) ▶

Fresh paint plus borders and home addresses completed the system, still in use and in mint-condition 20 years later.

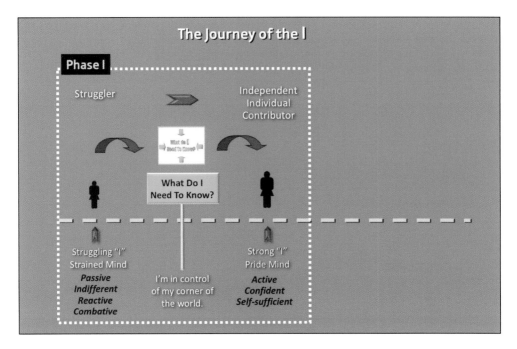

FIGURE 4.2: PHASE I—THE SHIFT FROM STRUGGLING-I TO STRONG-I

This is not as radical as it sounds. People already exercise that right—but not overtly. You may get them to show up, but they won't bring much else with them. They won't bring their full resources to bear. Yes, they show up; they comply. But they will not initiate; and they will not *own*. They will be passive. Or they will pretend to be involved; but the results will be pale by comparison with what is possible.

Companies are often grateful for pale results in the face of the alternative—nothing. Yet so much more is possible when the will is more fully engaged. When people *have* to, they do; they obey. When people *want* to, they create; they feel purpose, pride, and satisfaction, even joy.

When people can find *themselves* in the change, they own it deeply. When they I-dentify with change, not only are the results theirs, but the change is theirs, too.

Figure 4.2 shows Phase 1 of the journey of the "I"—the progression from a Struggling-I to a Strong-I. The shift happens when a person is asked to apply the need-to-know and succeeds in gaining control over his or her corner of the world.

Another way to say this is: The person finds a sense of safety, sanity, and stability at work.

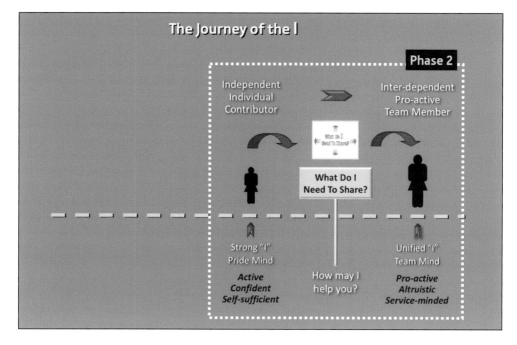

FIGURE 4.3: PHASE 2—THE SHIFT FROM STRONG-I TO UNIFIED-I

Once that control is established, something very beautiful and natural happens. The person turns to others and says, "How may I help you? What do I need to share? What do I know that you need to know—in order for you to do your work?" This is the shift that occurs in Phase 2 (Figure 4.3). In this second stage of the journey, people build on the security gained in getting control of their corner of the world and find that they can afford to think of others. And they do.

The resulting visual solutions answer the questions that others have in the work area. They address other people's motion—the motion of internal and external suppliers, internal and external customers, co-workers, and/or managers.

At this stage of workplace visuality, individuals have already aligned their personal will with the interests of the corporation and serve in the role of informal leaders. This is when the corporation reaps huge cultural and bottom-line benefits from its patience and forbearance during Phase 1, when the "I" elected to get on board—or not.

Look at Figure 4.4 to consider both phases of the journey when a series of simple, subtle, and powerful changes focus on and help cultivate one of the most

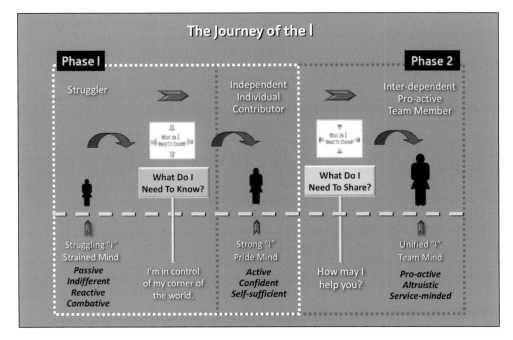

FIGURE 4.4 THE JOURNEY OF THE "I" (BOTH PHASES)

elusive aspects of enterprise excellence: the individual will, the "I".

Yes, there is a wide range of ways in which people express their involvement. The following discussion offers additional insight on this theme.

Rowers, Watchers, Grumblers: Another Perspective on the "I"

It doesn't take too many improvement initiatives to discover that people tend to respond to change in one of three ways: They embrace it; they resist it; or they don't have an opinion one way or the other—they are neutral. I call this threesome: the Rowers, the Grumblers, and the Watchers (based on a story that my sensei, Dr. Ryuji Fukuda, shared with me in the 1980s). Let's look at each role.

Rowers are the early contributors. Self-starters and independent by nature, they move ahead, heedless of barriers. They see the vision and its possibilities burning brightly before them, leap into the boat and start rowing. They already know that they want what the destination promises. While they may not yet act as a unifying force in the company, they are pro-active and confident.

Watchers hang back and let the Rowers blaze the trail. Then, if nothing bad happens to the front-runners, they may join in, however tentatively—or just continue to watch. Watchers make no deliberate effort to obstruct change. Yet they also do not easily lend it their enthusiasm. They may climb onto the boat and sit beside the Rowers; but they don't pick up an oar—not yet. For Watchers to engage, they have to be convinced that they are safe and that the change is strongly and tangibly supported by management. They don't like taking chances. They are not resisters; they suffer, instead, from the cultural impediment called *inertia*. Given reliable conditions, Watchers often become Rowers, but not quickly.

Grumblers, on the other hand, are masters at being grumpy in ways that everyone will notice. They whine, complain, moan, groan, refuse, sulk, reject, and/or deny any improvement effort. In all of this, they often like to grandstand, making sure, one suspects, that we notice their displeasure. They watch keenly for our response to their resistance. They also know that their "bad boy" behavior may well persuade an upstanding Rower to waste his time trying to help the Grumblers see things differently, change their ways, and "save them from themselves."

Grumblers are very good at grabbing our attention—and they expect us to give it. When we do, we make a fatal mistake. Instead of accepting our concern as an invitation to parley, Grumblers use it to take us for a ride, their ride. And when they have had their way with us—meaning, we double-commit to reforming them—they walk away and send the unmistakable message that they are indeed incorrigible and happy to stay that way. Grumblers are completely in charge of their own will; and, if they can, they will gladly take over ours.

(To be clear: Whatever their wily ways, Grumblers are not permitted to obstruct or sabotage an improvement activity. That is not only not cute, it can be cause for dismissal. With this in mind, take special steps to ensure: 1. that you declare the ground rules, and 2. that those rules are understood.)

When push comes to shove, the only progressive response to Grumblers is to concentrate on keeping the Rowers rowing. Watchers will continue to watch. When and if they see the boat is steady and has sprung no leaks, they will likely put a crooked smile on their face and pick up an oar or two.

Grumblers will continue to act grouchy and resistive. Yet, it is just as likely that any one of them will do an about-face and become a formidable pace-setting Rower. If you ask why the sudden change of heart, the erstwhile Grumbler is likely to declare, "I changed my mind"—and then simply walk away.

Photo Album 7

Kanban and Visual Inventiveness

I-Driven Visual Inventiveness at Plymouth Tube

With eight metalworking mills and some 900 employees, Plymouth Tube Company (Warrenville, IL) is a manufacturer of high-precision tubes and extruded shapes. Committed to implementing workplace visuality, lean, and other improvement strategies, Plymouth started its journey to manufacturing excellence in 1999. It continues it to this day.

ROBIN GRIGGS

Stock outages and parts-hoarding had become a problem at Plymouth Tube in West Monroe, LA when Robin Griggs, supplies purchaser, developed the kanban replenishment system you see in this album.

Robin came up with several innovations to make the system work locally. First, because parts bins in this rack were so small, Robin installed a time card holder on each side of the rack for kanban cards. Follow the numbered captions for more.

1. Welding parts are stored in cubbies in this rack.

2. Each bin is marked with the part number plus min/max levels.

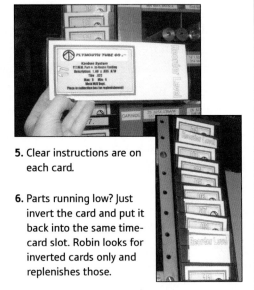

3. Cards are numbered to correspond to each small bin.

4. The card slot is numbered, too.

5. Clear instructions are on each card.

6. Parts running low? Just invert the card and put it back into the same time-card slot. Robin looks for inverted cards only and replenishes those.

In this regard, Grumblers are exactly right. Since they are in charge of their own will, they get to decide how they want to use it. As Grumblers, they are as exasperating as Rowers are inspiring.

There are many lessons here, but the primary one is—and always will be—to keep the Rowers rowing and know that Watchers and Grumblers will join in when and as they are ready.

People are Worth the Pause

Experience has taught me that people are worth the pause—a period of time when they are truly allowed, even encouraged, to be themselves, with no fear of penalty. Show them the new way; then allow everyone a bit of time to find the path—or not.

In doing this, another compelling dimension of I-driven change comes into view: People become authentic. Active/passive, cooperative/resistive, enthusiastic/grumpy, aggressive/indifferent—we can only be our authentic selves when we are met and accepted for what we are right now. When that happens, the chances for change increase. Most people don't mind change. They do mind when we try to change them.

The workplace is not a therapist couch. It is also not populated with perfect beings. Cultures in transition have many lessons to learn and huge treasures to unearth. Those treasures are hidden in the congestion and complexity of the flow of material and information in and through the facility. Treasures can also be found in the complex and sometimes congested hearts and minds of the people who have given 10, 20, 30 years of their lives to your company.

When information deficits were a way of life in your company, these people stuck it out. They took the hits. They persevered. They got bruised in the process. So it is fitting and right for us to provide them with the training, structure, time, and support they need to make the same transition within themselves that the physical workplace is undergoing on its journey to operational excellence. Your employees want that excellence too. Such victories are hard won, and they are mighty in their harvest.

We end this chapter as we began: People want to be heroes. We want the hero that we came to know in our heart when we were very young to go to work with us. We want the hero to show up there. Yet, if the company has made no room for heroes, has no structured way by which that hero can be encouraged and brought forth, it shrinks in us—even as we shrink at work.

I have found no better framework than the technologies of the visual workplace to bring this extraordinary outcome into fruition, across the company and within all organizational functions. The change begins on the associate level because, as stated repeatedly, the value-add level acts as a magnet and a mirror for all the misconceptions and imbalances in the work culture. That is one of its gifts to management.

If change is to happen at all, it must start from the ground up. In starting there, we have the chance to reconstitute the foundation of the enterprise and the fundamental definition of identity—yours, his, hers, ours, theirs, and mine.

FIGURE 1: THE IMPLEMENTATION PATHWAY

Section | Three

TECHNOLOGIES OF THE VISUAL WORKPLACE

Workplace visuality is about thinking first—and only then about visual devices. In this third section of the book, we examine two frameworks that help us understand visuality as a destination and show us ways to get there: the *Visual Workplace Implementation Pathway* and the *Ten-Doorway Model*. In our work at Visual Thinking Inc., we use both constructs to diagnose the current level of visual competency in an organization—and then as road maps for planning how to strengthen and expand that current level.

The Pathway (Figure 1) is a ladder of visual workplace technologies (methods) needed to comprehensively convert an organization into a highly-effective visual enterprise. Though many of these methods may be familiar to you, what may be new is thinking about them as a single line of logic and an integrated framework with a common purpose: to implement informational transparency within and across the enterprise. Read

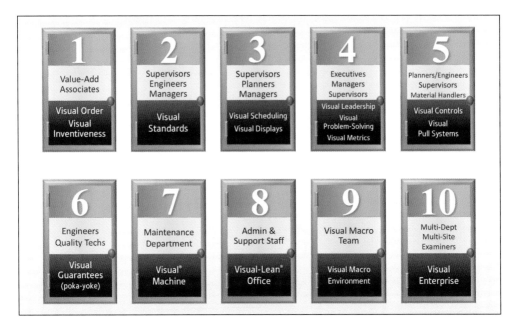

FIGURE 2: THE TEN DOORWAYS INTO A VISUAL WORKPLACE

this progression from the bottom up, with each rung its own distinct visual method. These can be implemented *in any order* and still yield the same result: a fully-functioning visual workplace, a workplace that speaks.

The purpose of the second construct, the *Ten-Doorway Model* (Figure 2), is similar but importantly different: to create a workforce of visual thinkers, enterprise-wide. Each doorway is linked: a) to a specific category of visual function; and b) to the employee group responsible for putting that function in place. For example, managers and supervisors own Doorway 3 and develop visual scheduling/visual displays; as a result, they begin to gain control over their own work—scheduling, manning, material consumption, patient release, and so on. Information deficits are still the invisible enemy, motion remains the lever, and I-driven is always the pull mechanism. But the actual improvement focus is anchored in a given doorway. A visual assessment of your site will reveal which doorway (or doorways) to open first (see Chapter 11 for more). My guideline remains: Open *any* six (in *any* order) and you are at—or very close to—world-class visuality in your industry.

In the next five chapters, these two frameworks anchor an orderly discussion of the categories of visual function—and the groups responsible for implementing them.

CHAPTER | **5**

Visual Order
Visuality's Foundation

The first level of the Implementation Pathway to a visual workplace is visual order—Doorway 1. This is the doorway that is wholly owned by line associates, those employees who work on the value-add level.

Apply the process called 5S+1 and produce the outcome called *visual order* (Figure 5.1), also known as the *visual where*.

Do not confuse visual order with industrial housekeeping or workplace organization. And do not equate 5S+1 (the method that produces visual order) with other 5Ss, 6Ss or 4Ds. They are very different.

The differences are both in content (knowledge) and the implementation approach used to apply that content (know-how). I do not mean to suggest that my system is superior to all others. It does, however, have a number of core elements (principles) that make it distinctive—and, in my experience, distinctively effective. In addition, since this book's first edition, I have developed these further, creating a new training and implementation system called "Work That Makes Sense: Operator-Led Visuality" (WTMS), with a book and online training system of the same name.

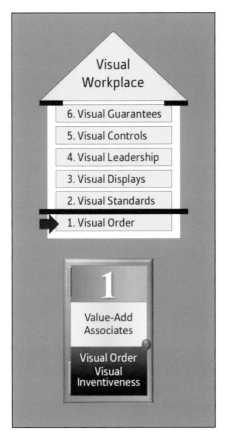

The WTMS method targets high levels of operator-created visual solutions—as soon as the workplace has been de-cluttered, cleaned, and made safe through 5S. Everything that follows below the description of S3/Secure Safety is the domain of WTMS. (For more, see the Resource Section of this book.)

Based on the results of dozens of successful implementations, 5S+1—and WTMS—produce impressive and entirely sustainable bottom-line benefits whatever the work venue: manufacturing, office, agency, hospital or open-pit mine. A 15% to 30% productivity increase, for example, is common, even in companies that have already embraced lean.

The Japanese Legacy

The five words that represent 5S in Japan can be translated into English in any number of ways. I learned this the hard way when, in 1983, I joined Productivity Inc., the then-premier source in the West for books and materials on Japanese manufacturing techniques. Within months, I was promoted to head of training and consulting and asked to find English equivalents to the five Japanese 5S terms. Knowing less than a little, I offered the following:

- *Seiri:* Sort
- *Seiton:* Shine
- *Seiso:* Set in Order
- *Seiketsu:* Standardize
- *Shitsuke:* Sustain

If these English words seem familiar, it may be because they appeared in many Productivity books and quickly spread into popular improvement jargon.

I and my staff spent the next decade trying to use that translation to produce in western companies the 5S success the Japanese had achieved in their home country. We failed, however, and failed again. The emotional push-back from US line employees, for example, was unrelenting. Managers did not like 5S much

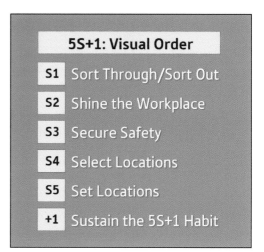

FIGURE 5.2: 5S+1/VISUAL ORDER

better. Except for a huge removal of clank and clutter, the impact of 5S on actual performance was pale, with the resulting landscape of lines and labels not only *not useful* but somehow offensive.

Something was wrong—something that could not be corralled and cured through 5S audits. I suspected it was the translation itself. But the die had been cast when my fledgling translation showed up in so many books. Those English equivalents stuck.

Only when I left Productivity in the early 1990s and started my own company, Visual Thinking Inc. (formerly Quality Methods International), did I have the chance to test my suspicion. When I re-translated the Japanese Ss into more closely linked action-oriented steps (Figure 5.2), 5S sprung to life and *5S+1/Visual Order* was born. In it, I focused on highly-visual outcomes, propelled by the engine I call *I-driven*. That was when our clients began to experience dramatic shifts in their levels of employee engagement and impressive productivity gains, both made sustainable through visuality.

I do not tell you this to share a nugget of my personal history nor to denigrate the 5S success many companies have achieved. I tell you to alert you to the fact that 5S must make sense in the language and emotional framework of *your* workforce. Otherwise, 5S can remain largely unimplementable, despite the time, effort, and auditing you and your colleagues invest in trying to make it a success.

Naming the Outcome: The Goal is Visuality

The Japanese use 5S to establish and maintain a clear, clean, safe, and orderly workplace. That has worked well in Japan and in Japanese transplants—but not so well in many western companies. Even when an initial advantage is gained, it can end there, be unsustainable or require excessive effort to keep it in place. Why?

For one thing, in nearly 35 years of implementation, I have never been very successful in rallying people around the notion of *neat/clean/orderly* as a victory—at least not enough to base an implementation on it. As for getting adults to clean up after themselves, I am not their mother and they know it. When I talked about the importance of cleanliness and order as an outcome, some people (usually women) got very animated—while others (often men) tuned me out. The group became polarized even before we got started. That's when I decided *neat/clean/orderly* was a battle I no longer wanted to fight; everyone would lose.

Instead, I began to talk with people about *implementing visuality*—creating visual answers to their recurrent questions and implementing the finding function through the *visual where*. The cleanup part, I explained, was done in order to prepare the physical work environment to hold that visual information. Never again did I attempt to make *clean* an independent outcome.

As a result, I decided to combine *visual order* with the 5S name to help people stay focused on the outcome, instead of the method. Done effectively, the process establishes a foundation for the entire visual progression, while putting into place the cultural groundwork for truly empowered employees on the value-add level.

Decades later, the 5S+1 process (and its latest and most powerful incarnation, *Work That Makes Sense*) continues to focus on workplace visuality as the outcome, not cleanliness or neatness. In visual order, the emphasis is on creating more effective visual outcomes (specifically a high-functioning *visual where*), not on promoting the method that produces it. Naming the outcome you want—not the method used—is crucial for gaining buy-in and getting people engaged and inventive.

I see a parallel each time I spot that perfect little size-10 black dress at the back of my closet, the dress I wore to a fancy Rolls-Royce dinner in the UK a few years back. There it hangs, sandwiched between the 12s and 14s I currently wear. I know I will need to eat a lot of cottage cheese and fruit to get back into that little black dress. But if I think too much about all that cottage cheese and fruit—and not enough about how fantastic I looked in that dress—I will never get into it again. I will get disheartened; and I will bail. So I keep my focus on the outcome, not the method. That keeps me going.

To me, asking people to do yet another round of 5S is like asking them to eat yet more cottage cheese and fruit. Where's the joy in that? Why should they bother? Why indeed? What would happen if you asked them, instead, to care about an outcome that fires the imagination: visual factory, visual dock, visual hospital or visual machining center—or a workplace that speaks?

Some companies complain that their 5S process is dying on the vine. "We can't seem to keep people interested," they say. Could it be that what they are asking people to do is not all that interesting? Could it be they are trying to motivate people by naming the method instead of the outcome?

When a company fails to link 5S with visuality, 5S will almost certainly get implemented in terms of its dry and repetitive minutia and not as a doorway to splendid and highly-effective forms of visual information-sharing. The process will get pushed, instead of pulled.

Visuality jumps over these pitfalls and challenges operators to implement the visual where and, in parallel, create high, even dazzling, levels of visual inventions. This happens without audits. Operators do it because they want to—and they want to because they have learned how. You have taught them!

So for starters, name an outcome that is better than clean and straight. Invite us "to create dazzling visual solutions to our chronic information deficits and become scientists of motion." Now that's something we can run with and run to. As Aleta Sherman, a colleague in Colorado, once remarked, *"Visual order is like 5S on steroids!"* She got it right.

Next we will walk through 5S+1/Visual Order, step by step. As we do, look for points of comparison between it and other 5S methods—those telling differences in emphasis, content, process, languaging, and outcome. And on the last page in this chapter, we give an overview of another mighty Doorway 1 outcome: establishing an improvement infrastructure—or strengthening an existing one.

Visual Order (Level 1—Doorway 1)

The purpose of 5S+1 is to prepare the physical environment to hold visual information; and then to install visual location information—the *visual where*—by

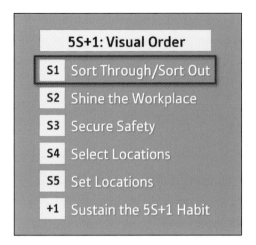

FIGURE 5.3:
SORT THROUGH/SORT OUT

applying a border, address, and, if possible, an identification tag ("ID label") for everything that casts a shadow. This simple formula gives every workplace item the ability to find its way back to home, based solely on the visual location information built on it and into it.

S1: Sort Through/Sort Out

The first step in visual order tells us to get rid of the "junk"—anything people say they don't want or don't need to support their work (Figure 5.3). These get removed from the value field and put into the local red-tag corner. Management determines the final disposition.

Sorting through and sorting out unwanted "stuff" is the indispensable first step in preparing the workplace for visual information; and it can be a lot of fun. It can also be done routinely, say once a month (or a quarter) after the initial sorting, as part of your sustainment infrastructure. Sorting works equally well for office environments where people tend to prefer naming what they want to keep rather than what they want to toss. The result is the same: "junk removal."

S1/Sort is a simple and powerful first step in preparing the work environment for visual information—with one major proviso. Because 5S+1 is propelled by I-driven change, the decision of what stays and what goes in one's own personal workspace is strictly up to the "I," up to the individual who works there.

Adjustments to the I-driven principle happen when the item is in a common space or shared, including across shifts. Then red-tagging is used but not as a voting device. It is used to surface people's preferences.

Remember our earlier discussion on the power of the "I" and the mistake companies can make in moving too quickly to teams? In 5S+1, we do not use red-tagging as an excuse to jam a team in place so there are enough people to decide in favor of getting rid of this or that offensive item. When red-tagging is used as voting, we turn our collective backs on the primacy of the "I" and diminish our ability to build an empowered workforce and bring the organization into balance.

This is a subtle point of tremendous significance. Voting automatically polarizes those who vote—the yeahs versus the nays. Polarization is implicit in voting. When used before individuals have regained their self-clarity and self-esteem—or made their way back from the vagaries and abuses of the obedience hierarchy (top-down approach)—voting may cause those individuals to crumple, or go ballistic.

Why chance it? What do you gain by forcing the issue to a vote? More importantly, what do you lose? If red-tagging is used as a proxy for voting, then the majority will rule; and, whatever the fate of the item, everyone will know that nothing in the enterprise related to empowerment has fundamentally changed.

I make this point crystal clear when assisting a company in a visual conversion. To executives and associates alike, my position on this is unwavering. I say it like this:

"I lied to you before when I said that the first 'S' is for Sort Through/Sort Out. It is not. The first 'S' is for Spirit."

If you balk at the word *spirit*, you could say the "first S is for Respect" since respect for the individual is implicit in the use of the term "spirit." Then again, others may think you are illiterate. What to do...?

When I say the first "S" is for Spirit, I refer to the spirit of the workplace and the spirit inside each of us, equally. When a company uses red-tagging as a vote, it turns S1 and the journey to workplace visuality into a battleground. The tribal majority will certainly win that battle; the offending item will be removed from the area. But the war will be lost—the war against waste, the war against motion that all those hundreds and thousands of "I"s are intended to wage. The victory of a fully empowered and unified enterprise will elude us again.

This is a great loss. It is tied to not understanding the mechanics of implementing visual order—or the power of the very first S, "sort." If incorrectly implemented, "sort" can wreak havoc on the entire future of the initiative which, at this early stage, requires that every step be carefully placed, most especially the first step. Once again, the Chinese proverb hits the nail exactly on the head: "The first step of the journey *is* the destination."

Never forget that red-tagging brings everyone face-to-face with one of the most challenging aspects of improving the physical workplace: a personal sense of owning the things that occupy it and sometimes the location itself, even though—technically speaking—those things are all company assets. People live at work. For eight to ten hours a day, this is home to your employees—and to you, too. When you undertake to physically change the material workplace, you smack up against

> *Discipline is remembering what you love.* —*Albert Einstein*

one of the strongest human instincts: the territorial imperative. It sounds like this: "Take your mitts off that thing! It's mine!"

Here at this first step of a very long journey to workplace visuality and an aligned and spirited enterprise, the company has a great deal to gain—and nothing to lose—in letting the values of the I-driven approach govern the seemingly mundane decision: Do we throw out that item or let it stay?

The moment crackles with possibility. People watch. People wait. What will you do? What will the enterprise embrace? The old way: "Do as I say"? Or the new way: "The first S is for spirit?" Decide in favor of the "I," and you break the inertia of the past. The hidden pyramid is pried free of its authoritarian counterpart and can begin the inversion process. Decide against the "I" and the habit of using power as a weapon strengthens. A great deal is at stake.

An effective implementation of visual order serves multiple purposes, across many dimensions of work life. For operations and the physical work environment, it produces order you can see, order that functions. On a micro-cultural level, visual order provides an opening for individual employees—starting on the operator/line level—to reconstruct, rehabilitate, and restore a brilliant sense of self and one's own personal power to do, change, improve, and contribute.

On a macro-cultural level, visual order is capable of converting a traditional work culture to one that builds enterprise excellence. It installs an improvement infrastructure and puts an end to myths that say there is no time to improve.

These are mighty outcomes and they are real. Their impact is as powerfully positive on the bottom line as on the work culture. Why throw them away for the sake of a red-tag item? Remember that *the first S is for spirit*. For an S1 story of inspired leadership and another of misbegotten understanding, see Inset 5.1.

S2: Shine The Workplace and Everything in It

In visual order, when people start to clean in S2, they do so in order to prepare the surfaces to hold visual information—first borders, addresses, and ID labels, and later more advanced visual devices and systems.

They are not asked to clean to make me, their boss or God happy. They are not asked to clean to demonstrate that they are capable of discipline, at least discipline in the usual sense, with all its heavy cultural overlays. People are asked to clean in order to prepare the physical workplace so that it is capable of holding visual information. That's it—and that's all. Information won't stick on dust, grease or grime.

Managers regularly obsess about cleanliness and order, but rarely do line personnel or anyone who actually has to do the cleaning, day after day. This is *not* to say that squeaky clean is not a mission-critical condition in many companies; or that cleaning cannot be fun (of course it can); or that many employees find genuine satisfaction in cleaning and in keeping things white-glove clean.

It is to say: In S2, we ask people to clean it once and clean it good, and look for ways to never ever have to clean the darn thing again. The improvement focus of S2 is squarely on cleaning prevention—because if you prevent dirt, you prevent motion. In S2, individuals and teams first look for the causes of dirt; then they look for ways to prevent it. The S2 metric I prefer is not the level of clean in a given area but the number of dirt-prevention devices that are in place. Here is the I-driven dynamic again—this time as the "I" in I-nvent. The results are excellent.

S3: Secure Safety

S3 is all about increasing your work safety quotient. As the saying goes, *Safety is cheap. Accidents are expensive.* Area operators are asked to notice risk and to correct what they can themselves. Anything else gets reported to the company's Safety Team or Committee—and shame on any company that does not have one.

Here again, with a premium on visual inventiveness, people in the area develop remarkable safety solutions to risks that sometimes only they recognize.

See Photo Album 8 for simple and innovative visual solutions linked to S2 and S3 from the Trailmobile/Canada implementation.

S4: Select Locations

S4/Select Locations is about *smart placement*—deciding where workplace items should be located in order to accelerate the flow of material, information, and people in and through the work area. S4 is the area's chance to verify or improve the area's layout before locations are locked in place in S5/Set Locations—through

INSET 5.1: MANAGEMENT CHAMPIONS—KEEPERS OF THE FLAME

There is a moment in every implementation when the future of the initiative hangs in the balance. It is an exact moment, a moment when the values of the new way run smack up against those of the old. When that moment comes, sponsors of rollout must act swiftly and decisively in favor of the change they are seeking. Here are two vignettes—one inspires, the other shocks.

S1 and the Potted Palm

PHOTO 5.1:
DOROTHY AND THE PALM

The first Visual Workplace training session at Parker Denison in Marysville, Ohio was not easy. The thirty union associates in the room had heard it all before and were not buying any of it.

After the session closed, I walked around the floor and made contact again with the participants. Dorothy Walls and Sheila Bowersmith, two accomplished machine operators, were friendly, showing me a scrawny potted palm in a plastic pot they were nursing back to life. (I made a mental note to bring in a nice ceramic pot I no longer used and offer it as a better home for the palm and its four scraggly shoots.)

A month later, on-site for session two, I stopped by before the session to see Dorothy, Sheila, and the palm. "Where's the palm?" I asked, "I have this new pot for it." I held out the ceramic pot.

"Oh they killed it," Dorothy said. "What?" I squeaked. "What on earth do you mean?" "Oh, we put a sign on it," said Shelia, "when we were doing S1. It said, 'Keep your paws off our potted palm!'" We thought it was funny but someone must have taken offense. The next day it was dead—someone sprayed it with weed killer." They sighed, smiling weakly.

I looked at both of them and said, "Excuse me. I'll be back." I went straight to the office of Ken Theiss, the GM. "May I come in? Something has happened," I said. "What's up?" said Theiss. "There's been a murder in your factory," I said. "What!" said Ken. "Yes," said I, "Someone killed Dorothy's and Shelia's potted palm." I held my breath, knowing that whatever Ken said next would either advance the visual conversion or set it back, way back. The values of the change were at stake. What would he say?

Ken said exactly the right thing! He said: "I knew that plant... (long pause). Tell me what happened." I told him. Without another word, Ken stood up, walked straight out to Dorothy's and Sheila's work area, and declared in a very loud and very clear voice that this kind of behavior would not be tolerated in his company. Within moments the word spread.

Things were different after that. Oh, the pace of change was still slower than I preferred; and there were plenty of bumps. But a new level of respect was at its foundation: respect for the change that wanted to happen and for the people undertaking it. And Ken Theiss bought Dorothy and Sheila a new palm, planted in the ceramic pot I had offered.

S1 and Daddy's Little Girls

In a different union plant, one that will remain unnamed, management launched an industrial housekeeping process (not 5S+1). The consultants that led the change put special emphasis on discipline, audits, and adhering to standards. An early standard forbade personal items at work. Not surprisingly the workforce pushed back. Management decided to take a stand. During the graveyard shift, the production manager walked the floor with big black plastic bag and threw out every personal item in it. Nothing was spared.

Five years later, I led an implementation of visual order in that same factory and met with terrific resistance. Within a month, one of the machinists filed a grievance against me. Though the union committee quickly dropped it, I remained puzzled as to my offense.

Some three years later, when the implementation had taken hold and nearly everyone was rowing and involved in the visual conversion, the machinist who had filed the grievance (whom I happened to think was a terrific guy) took me aside and began to apologize to me for filing that grievance. I told him that was not necessary, "I know I can be a bit of a handful, from time to time." "No, that's not it," he said. "Let me explain." I listened.

He told me about the previous attempt to "5S" the plant. Then he turned personal. "I have three little girls, triplets. Ever since they were tiny and had learned to draw, my girls have put little love notes in my lunch box every day. I'd find them when I ate lunch and tape them on my tool box and bench until they nearly covered both. One night about six years ago, a production manager I'd known for years went around the floor to get rid of personal items. When he got to my tool box, he tore off all those little notes and threw them away. All of them—without my permission—in the name of 5S. When I came in the next day and found them all gone, I got very angry. But I needed my job. I have three kids."

"When you showed up talking about 5S, I thought it was the same thing all over again, and I took it out on you. But it's not the same thing—it's not about rules and audits. I'm sorry."

I was speechless, moved by his apology for which there was no need and appalled by the story. The values-disconnect the company exhibited in the name of progress, in the name of 5S, was extreme. But I knew of many 5S methods that pushed this kind of missionary zeal. "Just Do It!" was a familiar battle cry—easy to spout but risky to implement and hard to sustain. All too often, managers think that discipline is the secret driving principle of the change they want. But their test is this: How would they respond if the same "discipline" was imposed on their personal items? Don't get me wrong: I believe in discipline—but as Einstein defined it (see again page 65 in Chapter 3).

S1 is the first step of the first phase of a very long journey. If there is a place where a visual initiative can go off the tracks with little hope of recovery, it is exactly at S1. Remember managers and executives: The first "S" is for Spirit—and you are the keeper of that flame.

Photo Album 8

S2 + S3 Solutions at Trailmobile/Canada

Using Visuality to Turn a Factory Around

Under the leadership of Tom Wiseman, Trailmobile launched a visual rollout in its newly-acquired facility in Toronto. At that time, the monthly accident rate was at an astonishing 46.2%; operational efficiency, 86%; and pre-delivery warranty costs, $40,000.

Within eight months of the launch, monthly employee absenteeism was down from 80% to 10%—and a previously disconnected and troubled workforce began to move as one.

◀ Roof Team
Salam Azar, Tyler France, Paul Russel, and Ed Alvez.

Roof Mezzanine ▶

The trailer roof gets installed up a level on the mezzanine. Several times a shift, large barrels of trash and scrap are carried down the steep stairs for disposal—risky even for the two men this required.

◀ ▲ S2 Motion-Busters

Look at the simple but brilliant pair of S2 solutions the Roof Team invented, once visual order and motion were understood: two chutes cut into the mezzanine floor, one for scrap, one for trash. Broad yellow borders—plus a lid on the trash chute and metal barrier around the scrap chute (painted red for safety)—complete this excellent S2 system. Motion prevention at its best!

Expect Trackable and Impressive Bottom Line Benefits

The visual implementation continued, area by area. 100 visual thinkers later: 50% of the total production floor was liberated and re-deployed; operational efficiency was at 117%; pre-delivery warranty costs were down by over 95%; and accident frequency was down by nearly 75%. Then, when gas prices rose and the market dried up, the plant had to cut back to one shift (50% fewer employees). Yet that diminished workforce sustained the 117% efficiency and increased it by 7%.

I don't believe I have ever participated in a visual conversion of such speed, precision, alignment or joy. I remember it with tremendous gratitude.

Before

After

"This visual workplace process has unlocked the potential of our employees. The potential was always there. We just couldn't see it.

Now associates are the driving force behind not just change but our journey to excellence. And new employees can light a candle from an existing flame where before there was nothing.

April Love
Director of Continuous Improvement
Trailmobile/Canada

⬆ Visual Safety Solution

Several times a day, sheets of steel are delivered to the stamping machine (above right). But, in backing up to the machine, drivers would often bump against the yellow stays (left) that support the fabrication of the trailer floor, endangering the riveters. When the stays were painted a more visible color—red—the problem disappeared.

The S2 and S3 solutions shown on these pages here represent the tiniest window on the remarkable visual inventiveness of the Trailmobile/Canada workforce.

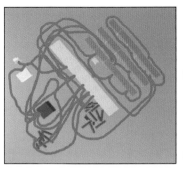

◀ LEFT
FIGURE 5.4:
WHAT-IS MAP
(BEFORE
SMART PLACEMENT)

RIGHT ▶
FIGURE 5.5:
COULD-BE MAP
(AFTER
SMART PLACEMENT)

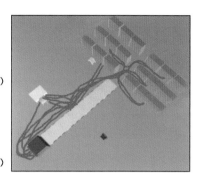

borders, addresses, and, as applies, ID labels. The governing formula in S4 for this is: *Function plus location equals flow.*

S4/Select Locations is another departure point in the 5S+1 process that differentiates it from traditional 5S methods. In it, area associates take on the work that is usually reserved for engineers and other technical staff: to re-think, re-imagine, and re-layout work content within the actual landscape of performance—the cell.

In undertaking this, line employees work in teams to construct two maps. The first, called the What-Is Map, maps the work area as it is now, with all items placed or laid out exactly as they are, right now. After that placement is mapped, the team traces the many lines of motion that this existing layout of function triggers. (See Figure 5.4 for an artist's representation of a What-Is Map.)

The Could-Be or Dream Map shows the exact same work area but with easy-to-move items, consumables, and WIP relocated to better support an accelerated flow (hard-to-move items are out of scope and left alone). This second map provides value-add employees the opportunity to re-imagine, re-shuffle, and re-arrange their work area for their own convenience—and so flow quickens, travel distance shrinks, and motion is greatly reduced or even eliminated (Figure 5.5).

With change list in hand, area associates present both maps to senior managers for appreciation and comment—but not for authorization. The changes are purposely within the control and ability of associates and are, therefore, simply undertaken. (See Chapters 4-7 in my book, *Work That Makes Sense*, for details.)

Time and again, the smart placement process produces huge and tangible breakthroughs in layout that are comparable to (and often beyond) engineer-led redesigns. Yet the non-tangible benefits are equally impressive. S4 mapping is the first time associates (who—up to now—had not been required to align with other area associates) find themselves collaborating with co-workers in order to build an accurate current-state map and imagine a greatly improved one in the Could-Be Map. The spirit of team begins to emerge.

By the time the maps are presented to managers, ownership of the physical change is high. The group then lays out the actual area to match the Dream Map and gets ready to install borders and addresses that will turn the new layout into a physical and visual footprint. They are ready for *S5/Set Locations*.

S5: Set Locations

As practiced in the West, traditional 5S is satisfied if orderliness is anchored in so-called "lines and labels"—the barest framing of designated locations. Words matter and technically speaking, a "line" is a collection of points along a continuum that has no beginning and no end. It is a geometric event, with no performance function. The term "labels" is equally neutral. For that reason and many others, I use the term "border" to name the boundary function and "address" to designate a border's close partner in traceability/retrievability.

By the time a work area is ready to implement S5/Set Locations (Figure 5.6), everyone—especially value-add associates—has a good feel for who rows, watches or grumbles (Chapter 4). This recognition is not a problem. It is simply information.

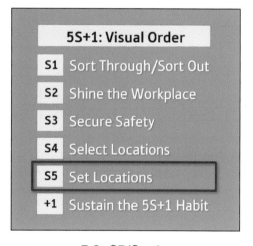

FIGURE 5.6: S5/SET LOCATIONS

When it comes time to lay down borders, those who are enthusiastic will remain so. Those who watch may laugh or smirk. And those who grumble will either say rude things or go bananas. Borders are not readily understood by people who have not yet worked in a company where visual order has been installed, comprehensively. Yet they are the single most important physical element in the pursuit of orderliness, stability, retrievability—in short, the visual where. See Photo Album 9.

The formula for the visual where is as simple as it is powerful: a) Start with

Photo Album 9

Automatic Recoil— The Visual Where in Action

Creating Visual Order that is Distinctive and Very Satisfying

In addition to remarkable cultural benefits, implementing visual order through an I-driven approach produces a flood of visual inventions, even with elements as simple as the visual where. The examples shown in this album are a mere sampling of what you can expect when you implement operator-driven visuality in your own company—work that makes sense.

Rear-Headers Address ⬆

Associates in the Rear Headers area at Trailmobile/Canada invented this superb home address announcing their department—installed directly into the production floor. Notice the person-width borders between the two workstations.

⬆ Double-Border Function at Harris

Melody Sparrow at Harris Corp. (Quincy, Illinois) made sure that this red testing stand was always in visual order—whether she was using it (dashed border) or not (solid border). Brilliant visual detail!

◀ Visual Where at Rolls-Royce

This is a corner of a Rolls-Royce factory in England. When the *experts* (RR's name for operators) decided to create the visual where for outgoing parts, they used person-width borders as a base. But they were stuck for a place to add addresses because the ceilings at this site were too high. So they built this partition and added the addresses there. Now that's ownership!

Visual Creativity in the Details of Day-to-Day Work

The solutions in this album stand witness to individuals who are gaining control over their corners of the world through visual thinking. Their visual inventions don't just solve local challenges. They serve to drive organizational improvements deeper and deeper into the landscape of work.

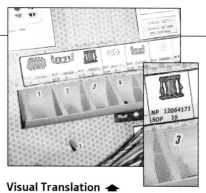

Photocopied Borders ▲

Bob Comeau, perhaps the first visual thinker ever at United Electric Controls (Boston), grew tired of outlining borders with markers, tape or paint. So he carried his tools over to the photocopy machine, laid them carefully on the glass, and hit the copy button for instant borders! Then he taped borders down and covered them with Plexiglas. Better put ID labels on those screwdrivers quick—or they will look like mine!

Visual Translation ▲

Notice the long part numbers (N/P) above each bin in this superb visual solution at the Delphi plant in Juarez, Mexico. The picture of the actual small part makes the part number recognizable at-a-glance. The "3" next to the peg tells you exactly where the part in blue bin 3 is assembled.

◀ Color-Coded Gauges

Rick Ell, a formidable visual thinker at Parker Denison, developed this color-coded gauge drawer as part of a larger system he designed for the products he machines and inspects in his area.

◀ Color-Coded to Product

This fixture for fixtures Rick designed holds so many visual and smart placement principles, they are nearly impossible to list. The short of it: This is brilliant visual thinking on a mastery level.

borders for everything that cast a shadow; b) Add an address on/near/above each border; and c) Put an ID label on each item that resides in each border. The only ID label exception is for items that are consumed: cardboard, bubble wrap, screws, brackets, sheets of steel—or M&Ms. Like this: There's a border around the bowl that holds the M&Ms, an address on that border (so you know the bowl belongs there if it is elsewhere), and an ID label on the bowl itself. But there are no ID labels on each M&M because we will consume it. Yum!

The "everything that casts a shadow" mandate applies equally to items that are easily movable (benches, carts, fans)—and to those that are not easily moved (machines, tall shelves, large tables). Yes, when we say *everything*, we mean it.

Companies need to prepare before operators can tackle automatic recoil. They need to develop a color-code system for borders; decide between plastic tape and paint; and devise a protocol by which borders can last 12 months (even in heavy forklift traffic) and be removed overnight. Supplies need to be handy too so associates can create addresses. The list goes on. The company's Lead or Macro Team typically handles these matters. We hope you have one (see Chapter 8 for more).

To re-cap: The visual where can sometimes get off to a slow start, especially if your company is new to the importance of borders. At the outset, some people may not believe you mean it—borders for everything that casts a shadow. Others may think it's just a nutty idea. Such responses are natural and not a problem. It is important to simply forge ahead and undertake the mandate. As your value-add associates begin to design and install an ever-more robust system of borders, they as well as others will start to experience their unique power: the power to establish and maintain the visual where—and something more. The story that follows explains that "something more."

The Pattern of Work

As a practitioner in the field of workplace visuality, I am often asked to assess a company's current level of visual competency. Some of these companies are well into their journey to visuality and know it—and they want to know how to go further and wider and where "next" is.

Others think they are well on their way. But, according to the criteria-based assessment instrument I use, they have barely started. Others still have barely started and know it. And yet others are thinking about thinking about getting started.

I enter a lot of companies. Over the years, I noticed that when I entered a company in the early stages of the journey, I would experience a moment of anxiety. But why? I am very good at what I do and am known to provide great value to my clients. Yet, standing there at the operational threshold, I felt nervous.

I would look out into the vast gray and brown (or white and blue) of the work environment, populated with machines, benches, and clumps of people moving about, and my inside voice would say something like this, "Oh my gosh, I haven't the foggiest idea what is going on here. No clue. All I see is nameless disarray, a muddle. Will I be able to help these fine folks? Oh my gosh! There's no visible logic, no handle. How and where do I begin?"

This mental miasma, when it came, lasted only a nanosecond; still it was undeniably there, however fleetingly. It evaporated just as quickly as I moseyed onto the floor and my cognitive flow kicked in. I became a visual system expert again. Yet, the moment of miasma always struck me as odd, both in its recurrence and in its simple message of "Yikes!" Why did it always happen? What was it about?

The reason came to me when I was teaching a visual thinking seminar in Texas, some two decades ago. I was in the midst of explaining the importance of borders through the sequence of *visual where* solutions shown in Photo Album 10.

There, in the Incoming Inspection area at Parker Denison (Marysville, Ohio), the team was repeatedly vexed when Pete and Donnie, the forklift drivers, would leave pallets in the aisles, instead of either delivering them to designated bordered locations—or, if an overflow, finding an Incoming team member to ask for help.

What to do? The team decided to paint big yellow Xs in the aisle ways to send drivers the message: "Don't drop pallets here." It didn't work. The behavior of the drivers did not change. Then the team painted the entire aisle ways solid yellow. Bingo! The behavior of the forklift drivers changed—instantly and forever. They never put pallets in the aisle ways again. But why? What happened?

Donnie and Pete had not been re-trained; nor were they scolded or threatened. As the Incoming team recounted, the drivers' behavior switched from wrong to right the moment they saw the broad yellow aisle ways for the first time. "Donnie got off his forklift and asked us what we wanted him to do with the extra pallets." They were amazed and jubilant at the same time. But I was perplexed. Why had the behavior reversed and so quickly?

At first, I wrote it off to the power of bright yellow paint. But at the Texas

Photo Album
10

The Mind is a Pattern-
Seeking Mechanism

Visual Thinking/Visual Order at Parker Denison (Marysville, OH)

I discovered long ago that visuality teaches us more and more about how to implement it *as* we implement it. Here is a client scenario that taught me a core principle of visuality and how and why it performs so powerfully in the workplace.

Before ▶

You see what remains of the company's first attempt at 5S here in Incoming Inspection —some scruffy color lines on the floor. The department was notorious for its lack of enough floor space. Forklift drivers made things more difficult (and the Incoming team irritable) by their habit of dropping pallets anywhere, including in the aisles between designated pallet locations.

◀ **After (1)**

When the Incoming team got trained in the visual where, they immediately laid down a gorgeous array of color-coded borders—orange for *incoming*, green for *outgoing* (top), and red for *hold*. Even though these helped them tell status at-a-glance, it did not change the behavior of the forklift drivers at all. They kept using the aisles for overflow pallets. What to do?

After (2) ▶

The team decided to tape big yellow Xs in each aisle to send a "don't put anything here" message. But it didn't work. The fork-lift drivers cleverly placed overflow boxes within each quadrant of the X—in the spaces left by the figure "X" itself. Some thought the drivers were joking. Either way, the team was foiled again. But they kept going.

Brain Function and The Power of the Mind

One reason the visual workplace is so effective is because our minds are hungry for information we can see. Fully 50% of our brain function is dedicated to finding and interpreting visual information. Brain function and the mind can become powerful partners in your pursuit of operational excellence if harness them for the corporate good. This is central to cultivating a workforce of visual thinkers.

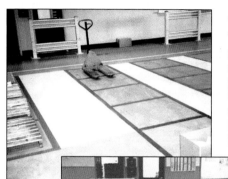

◀ After (3)

Then the team remembered examples of person-width borders from their training sessions and applied them here, in strong yellow paint. The problem behavior of the forklift drivers evaporated. Instead of leaving overflow pallets in the aisles, they asked the Incoming team what they should do instead. Huh!? Why had their behavior changed?

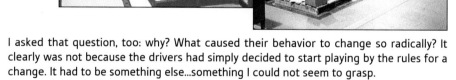

I asked that question, too: why? What caused their behavior to change so radically? It clearly was not because the drivers had simply decided to start playing by the rules for a change. It had to be something else...something I could not seem to grasp.

Then I remembered! *The mind is a pattern-seeking mechanism.* The mind will look for a pattern until it finds one. Unknowingly, the Incoming team had laid down a pattern that was more powerful than the drivers' habit. Even though they did not understand the pattern with precision, they knew something different was needed from them, a new behavior—and they asked. (See text for more.)

Of equal interest is the fact that this area maintained this level of visual functionality for five years, until Incoming Inspection was moved to another location in the facility.

seminar, people were pushing me for a better explanation. Then I remembered!

Twenty-five years earlier in New York City, I was in the process of trying (and failing) to still the noise in my head and meditate. I couldn't seem to do it. I complained to my meditation instructor; and he said: *Don't you understand, Gwendolyn, the mind is a pattern-seeking mechanism.* Huh? I didn't understand. But nearly three decades later, in Texas, I suddenly got it.

The mind is a pattern-seeking mechanism—and as such, it will seek a pattern until it finds one. If it cannot find a pattern, the mind will not stop. It continues seeking because that's what the mind does: It seeks patterns.

Many of us have experienced this in our personal relationships—the mind's insistence upon finding an organizing logic to things, a pattern. There you are at home, while your significant-other is speaking to you with a great deal of animation. It is clear that your honey is trying to make a point, urgently. And you are trying to get that point. But you can't quite make sense of the sounds and the words that are coming at you. Your mind is seeking a pattern and drawing a blank. Finally, feeling either nervous or very nervous, you say, "Honey, I really am trying. I can hear you. I know it's important. But I can't seem to understand what you mean...."

Your mind is seeking the pattern but not finding it. So it slips into a mild (or intense) level of stress. If the lack of pattern persists, the stress level rises. In extreme cases, the mind checks out (goes numb) or goes ballistic. Sound familiar?

That is exactly what I described as my experience at the start of this discussion when entering a certain kind of factory for the first time. New employees often experience it too. We look a bit dazed, distracted. In reality, our minds are very occupied, busy seeking a pattern, a place to hang our psychic hat—some way to link what is *new* and *unknown* with what is *familiar* and *known*. That is a common experience but not commonly understood.

When we lay down borders, we lay down the pattern of work. We lay down the physical logic of work—visible meaning—for all to see, especially newcomers, whether visitors or new employees. When borders are applied for *everything that casts a shadow,* we see and we understand. This is the pattern the mind seeks and needs to find. Newcomers can and will adapt to the absence of a pattern, in a week or two. But before that, they make a point of finding buddies, tribal insiders who can help them *make sense* out of their new work environment in the most physical, visual sense of the phrase. They need to I-dentify with their surroundings.

Within a month, they grow used to the absence of pattern. They have their tribe and are better able to cope. Questions asked and answered become the glue that hold the scary unknown at arm's length. But with those questions comes a ton of motion. How different the first experience of the company would be if borders (the pattern) were already in place, waiting to greet visitors and newcomers alike with its message of sanity, safety, and stability.

From that day on, I enter new factories, prepared for a nameless disarray and the absence of pattern. From time to time, I am happily disappointed.

Visuality is a system of thinking first and then a system of devices. As thinking, it utilizes brain function and harnesses it for your company's benefit—beginning with the border mandate and the pattern-seeking power of the mind. The result is well and repeatedly documented: 15% to 30% productivity gain, larger profit margins, and a spirited, engaged, and inventive workforce, willing and able to contribute its mental, emotional, and physical resources to the enterprise. This was excellently demonstrated, once again, at Parker Denison in year one of its visual conversion. For the story, see Photo Album 11: Right Angles Can Cause Motion.

Now we move to the higher dimension of Pathway Level 1 and Doorway 1: *Customer-Driven Visuality* (Figure 5.7).

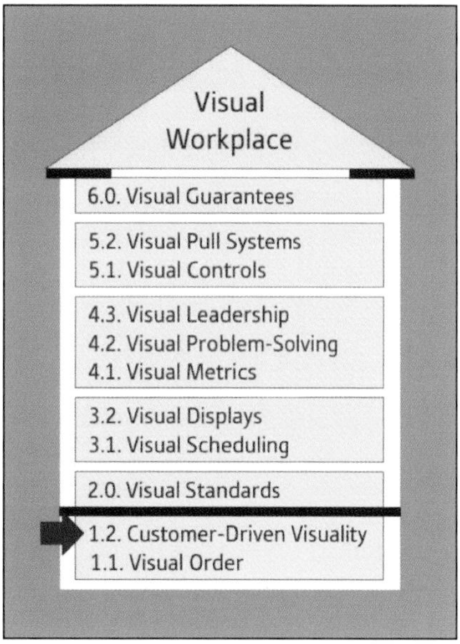

Visual Workplace

6.0. Visual Guarantees

5.2. Visual Pull Systems
5.1. Visual Controls

4.3. Visual Leadership
4.2. Visual Problem-Solving
4.1. Visual Metrics

3.2. Visual Displays
3.1. Visual Scheduling

2.0. Visual Standards

1.2. Customer-Driven Visuality
1.1. Visual Order

FIGURE 5.7:
CUSTOMER-DRIVEN VISUALITY
(LEVEL 1.2)

Customer-Driven Visuality

When associates succeed in addressing their need-to-know by thoroughly installing the visual answer to the *where* question, they gain compelling control over their corner of the world. As a result, they feel safe, in charge, and far more capable and confident of making in-process decisions than in the pre-visual workplace. Their "I" has begun to shine.

One of the remarkable by-products of this strengthened "I" is a shift from what-do-I-need-to-know to what-do-I-need-to-share. This is the beginning of the unified I, simply expressed in the question: "How may I help you?" Employees become service-minded, widening their impact scope to include others.

Photo Album 11

Customer-Driven Visual Solutions

How May I Help You? What Do I Need to Share?

After we have visually satisfied our own need-to-know, we quite naturally turn to other people and ask how we may help. This produces an entire new crop of visual devices and mini-systems, this time focused on sharing information visually in order to help others become more successful in their own work. It makes sense, then, that the customer-driven devices you see in this album were the result of collaborative efforts between Strong-Is.

Piet Mooren

Jean Heijink

⬆ Example 1: Customer-Driven Material Handling ▶

Piet Mooren, a veteran welder at Royal Nooteboom Trailers (RNT/Holland), invented the very first customer-driven visual device in the company, shown here. Piet wanted to share what material he needed next with Jean Heijink, the forklift driver, without Jean having to get off his forklift or even talk to Piet. So Piet made a magnetic plate on which he wrote the part number in question—in this case "2131." Low-cost/high-impact, this customer-driven visual device worked perfectly!

◀ Example 2: Customer-Driven Visual Metric

Value-add associates at Skyworks Solutions (Boston) created this visual measure as part of their need-to-share.

Measurement is normally management's domain, but that did not stop this team. They advertised their on-time delivery personal best (100%), along with their latest performance level (93%) to highlight the importance of meeting customer requirements.

Want to strengthen this metric? Add when the chart was last updated, along with a section for causes when 100% is not met. Enable the metric to drive improvement even harder.

Revitalizing Your Traditional 5S Rollout

After "lines & labels" are applied, traditional 5S often fizzles out because people never learn what "further" means and how to get there. 5S audits are rarely a lasting solution. When we learn to use motion as the lever, however, we discover that every work environment offers a nearly endless supply of information deficits—and, therefore, a huge potential for visual devices and mini-systems. Revitalize your 5S initiative by training people in the science of motion, info deficits, and the need-to-know/share. Make sure to show them lots of visual solutions from industries outside of their own. Remember: Visuality is a system of thinking *first*.

At-a-distance

Example 3: The Customer-Driven Store

When associates in charge of the company store at Harris Corp. (Montreal) were trained in customer-driven visuality, they sprang into action, visually answering the one question their customers (fellow associates) constantly asked: *Do you have* _____(fill in the blank)? They mounted the most frequently-requested items in display cases at the store counter and gave each item a number. From then on, co-workers simply asked for what they needed by number, completely eliminating the back-and-forth that used to plague even the simplest request.

Close up

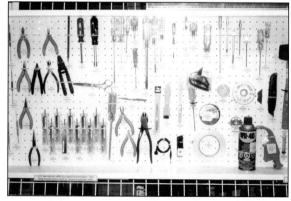

Rowers are already on board with this. What a treat to see Watchers join the service-minded—with Grumblers, often before them. This call-to-service can be a beautiful contagion that spreads from area to area and across the company. When we learn to think visually and master our immediate work, something inside us relaxes, and we can grow as people and contributors. We want to extend our mastery and help others, whether they are co-workers, internal suppliers and customers—or external ones. I call this visual workplace level: *Customer-Driven Visuality*. See Photo Album 12 (this chapter's last page) for three first-rate examples of the unified I, simply expressed in the question: "How may I help you?" Employees become service-minded, widening their impact scope to include others.

Whoever you are—co-worker, manager, supplier or guest—when you enter an area where customer-driven visuality is in place, you immediately feel safer, smarter, and more connected—more connected to yourself, to others, and to the goals of the enterprise. You become aligned with a greater intent, the corporate will to excellence. You and the enterprise have moved yet another step towards unity.

In visuality, a customer-driven orientation inevitably leads you beyond the where question to the other five core questions: What? When? Who? How Many? and How? But be careful, achieving a highly-functioning visual workplace is not simply a matter of creating devices that visually answer those six questions. That will get you somewhere but not to full visual functionality—or anywhere near it.

Visuality is a system of thinking first. Visual devices derive from that—not the other way around. When visual thinkers reach for it, customer-driven visuality will drive them to create more robust, and therefore more advanced, visual outcomes. These are the other levels of the implementation pathway and the other doors in the Ten-Doorway Model.

In theory, these advanced visual outcomes are created by employees other than line associates. But never mind. When such outcomes emerge as the result of visual thinking, they rightly get created by whoever is inspired to create them. They are, after all, simply the extension of that thinking and the use of motion as the lever.

If your version of 5S seems stalled, try this: Train your workforce in operator-led visuality—first, in the principles and practices of visual order and then in customer-driven visuality—and see a whole new crop of visual solutions blossom from employees who are spirited, engaged, and contributing. And while associates are engaged in this important work, management has mission-critical work to undertake behind the scenes. So much depends on that. A summary follows.

Your Improvement Infrastructure

Doorway 1 offers more than the visual where as an outcome, crucial though that is. It is also when you create the infrastructure for your company's improvement process. Done well, that architecture becomes a core element in your company's operational excellence platform. The following is a brief summary of the main points.

1. **Your Vision Place.** Before you launch, choose another company or community location as your inspirational touchstone—an external vision place until you have created your own. Think of MacDonald's, the airport, a library, multiplex cinema, office supply store or, my favorite, Disney World.

2. **Systematic Methodology.** Vision without a step-by-step implementation roadmap is only a hope. Select a robust and orderly improvement method that has produced proven, measurable results. Then follow it.

3. **Excellent Training Materials.** How will you transfer visual principles, knowledge, know-how, and excitement to others? You need an excellent training package, one with scores (if not hundreds) of splendid visual solutions and explanations—not just from your industry but from many industries.

4. **On-Site Leadership.** Company conversions do not happen overnight, not if the gains are to endure. To succeed, you need a small team of high-functioning, emotionally-sturdy individuals who are willing and able to be held accountable for the progress of the rollout, in terms of improvement in both work culture and the bottom-line.

5. **Focus through the Laminated Map.** Rolling out improvement too fast or too wide is a sure way to fail. Use this handy tool: Outline departments on a laminated map of your company; then decide where to begin. Develop the ability to say *yes* to the few and *wait* to the many as early success insurance.

6. **An Established Improvement Time Policy.** In the battle between production time and improvement time, production will always win. Without a written improvement time policy, there is a danger that needed improvement will never happen. The lack of such a policy is one of the greatest corporate roadblocks to your improvement success.

With these six elements in place early on, the likelihood of your Doorway 1 success rises exponentially. For a more detailed treatment, please see my book, *Work That Makes Sense.*

Photo Album 12

Right Angles Can Cause Motion

Visual Performance at Parker Denison

Parker Denison (PD) is a union shop (Marysville, OH) that produces high-precision hydraulic pumps. When PD committed to visual order, employees began to invent a compelling array of visual solutions that dazzled current and potential customers. This was a level of employee engagement the company had been seeking for decades. Here's one of many stories that demonstrates this.

⬆ Before

Though the yellow grid looks pretty, its rigid right angles caused a lot of motion!

Borders are the heart of the visual where. A revolutionary border innovation at PD was invented by forklift driver, Bill Podolski, and his colleagues. WIP pick-up/drop-off took them twice as long because borders were laid at right angles to the aisles. So they combined angled/slanty borders with person-width borders and a new visual best practice was born.

⬆ After

Bill's work on a forklift was made easy by slanty borders. ⬇

⬆ After

The green slanty borders on left are for fast-moving WIP. The yellow person-width border in the center provides access. Slow-moving WIP is locked in the blue grid on right.

People don't come to Toyota to work.
They come to think.

Taiichi Ohno
Co-architect
Toyota Production System

C H A P T E R | **6**

Visual Standards and Visual Scheduling/Visual Displays

In the process of installing the visual where, your value-add associates become visual thinkers and easily cross over into more advanced forms of workplace visuality beyond the visual where: visual standards, displays, metrics, controls, and poka-yoke devices (visual guarantees). Strictly speaking, those device types are owned by other doorways—but, for visual thinkers, nothing is out of bounds. With their focus squarely on motion and the information deficits that cause it, associate-level thinkers cut a broad swath across all levels of visual solutions.

Not only is there no problem in this, there is a great deal to celebrate. We are by birth visual beings—and we learn to be visual thinkers. Once that thinking becomes rooted in our thought processes, we simply solve. Nothing is off limits, including the devised boundaries I have placed around each doorway.

Still, within the doorway model, other organizational groups take the official lead on the visual conversion process beyond visual order.

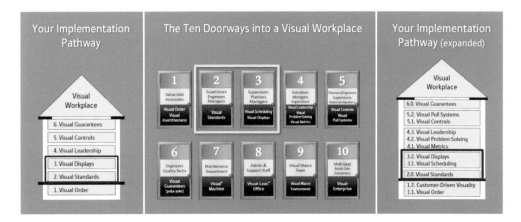

FIGURE 6.1:

DOORWAYS + LEVELS: VISUAL STANDARDS & VISUAL SCHEDULING + DISPLAYS

It goes without saying (doesn't it?) that executives, managers, supervisors, engineers as well as other support personnel apply visual order in their own value fields too—offices, desks, shelves, cabinets, and credenzas. Installing the visual where for their own work environment is not just evidence of walking the talk, it is a major attack on motion that can positively impact the entire organization.

Each doorway represents a specific organizational function. Employees in that group are responsible for creating visual devices that support, stabilize, and strengthen the performance associated with that doorway—its category of visual function. As the need arises, they also develop devices tied to other doorways. Everyone contributes visual devices in the company's war on informational waste: incomplete, incorrect, irrelevant or missing information. That's how the war is won.

In this chapter, we present the next two doorways and the next two pathway levels (Figure 6.1): Visual Standards and Visual Scheduling Boards/Visual Displays.

Visual Standards (Level 2—Doorway 2)

The second of the ten doorways into the visual workplace is opened by supervisors and engineers, and targets Visual Standards (Figure 6.2).

However much line employees may contribute to making operational standards visual (and this can be considerable), visual standards are the principal domain of engineers, managers, and supervisors. They are held principally accountable for the precise performance of work—engineers in constructing appropriate standards; and managers and supervisors in communicating them and overseeing their execution.

Standards define what is supposed to happen in the process of work—that which is planned, expected, and normal. Conversely, when standards are weak or simply fail, abnormalities result in the form of errors, mistakes, defects, rework, scrap, unplanned downtime, and associated late deliveries. Engineers, managers, and supervisors are expected, as part of their job, to identify and remedy problems and develop improved standards. That makes them very much the owners of Doorway 2.

As part of that, they are always looking for ways to make technical and procedural standards more accessible, immediate, and compelling. Converting written specs and SOPs into a visual format is a useful option. Here's the when, what, why, and how of visual standards.

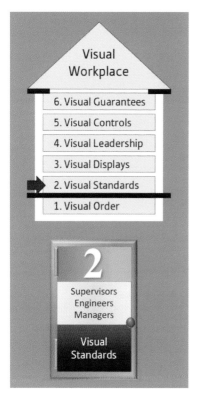

FIGURE 6.2:

VISUAL STANDARDS

Implementing visual standards is best undertaken after visual order is launched and a semblance of location stability and predictability begins to emerge in the work environment. There is no sense publishing and promoting visual standards where the barest fundamentals of everyday work are still out of reach. As soon as visual order grabs and begins to create a sense of safety and stability in the area, it's time to open Doorway 2: Visual Standards.

The purpose of visual standards is to capture technical and procedural standards (as defined in Chapter 2) in an easy-to-understand visual format—and have them handy. Done well, they can be an important performance support, and so a core part of your quality assurance system.

Visual standards are least effective when pre-manufactured by management or your engineering staff. Why? Because they will lack both behavioral and environmental elements and, therefore, they will be incomplete, inaccurate, irrelevant—and therefore misleading. A more

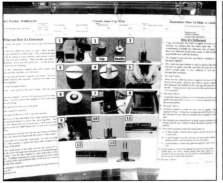

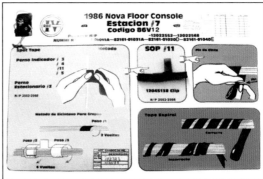

PHOTO 6.1:

VISUAL SOP/LASER CUP WELD

A multi-step SOP that includes what, why, and how, made more effective because it is very visual. (Parker Denison, Marysville, Ohio)

PHOTO 6.2:

SINGLE-POINT SOP: TAPING STANDARD

This visual standard shows the telling detail—the correct and incorrect way to tape a wiring harness. (Delphi Automotive, Juarez, Mexico)

effective way to create visual standards is through the active collaboration of engineers and supervisors with the operators who execute the work content. Engineers provide the basic framework; operators fill in the telling human-based detail; and supervisors facilitate to ensure the job gets done and properly.

This is arduous work that takes time, focus, and determination. There are lots of services and even more software that can help (one of my favorites is ExpertOJT). But the decision to undertake this work comes first—and that decision is yours.

Before we move on to finer points about visual standards, let's acknowledge that there is a good amount of confusion about the terms standards, standardization, and standard work. For my take on this, see Inset 6.1: Standard Confusion.

Two Types of Visual SOPS and Other Pointers

There are two types of visual procedural standards. The first is visual SOPs: SOPs that capture every step of an operation in telling visual detail, step by step by step (Photo 6.1). Thoroughness counts as much as correct sequencing. But it isn't enough to simply map the steps, even with the right collaborators. Each visual SOP must also be tested and proofed. This is mission-critical because testing these SOPs leads to improvements—however minute—that are inevitable when minds join.

Inset 6.1: Standard Confusion

Most discussions about standards, standard work, and standardization end in confusion. No surprise since the words look and sound similar. Unless we make careful distinctions between the three terms, there will be trouble on three levels.

The first level of trouble is that managers love the entire concept of standards and thirst for standardization. To them, it means control, uniformity, stability—and, most appealing, predictability. They want it—but they don't always understand what the "it" is.

The second level of trouble is that the three terms are importantly different. If we mix them together, we lose the important strength of each and so gain no strength at all.

The third level of trouble is that one of the three above terms is a problem, a genuine problem, for operational excellence. Let's begin with definitions.

1. STANDARDS are the bedrock of all work, paving the way to repeatable, predictable outcomes. They spell out the details of the work and the work content—the how and the what: *What* specifications/attributes need to be achieved and *how* we achieve them.

2. STANDARD WORK (SW) is not the same as a standard. SW segments work content into its elements or steps, in the orderly and correct sequence. Begin with the big chunks; refine them into minute details, and then apply time. SW is the core component of pull—a time-based flow. It is the only known way to pace operations to your customer's need: takt.

3. STANDARDIZATION is the process of developing and implementing regularity or sameness among and between things, concepts, methods, etc.—in order to make what is different (however slightly) uniform and known and therefore easily repeatable.

The above definitions plainly show us that the three terms are not the same. But they are often used interchangeably—with alarming results. In the name of the good, some companies seek to standardize everything in the mistaken notion that doing so gives them the ability to do the right thing again and again without error, providing a surefire way to acquire and retain the gold ring called *sustainability*. This is simply not true.

The Problem. The rush to "standardize everything" is especially a problem when a company wants high-functioning visuality. Every visual implementation needs a set of standards to guide that rollout. But look at what they are: arrows on all shelves, upper/lower case addresses, audits created by area teams, etc. Nowhere is it important to require that categories of visual devices be uniform, let alone identical. If you try that, the visual conversion will grind to a halt.

Visual Best Practices. Visual thinkers develop visual devices by identifying ever-deepening layers of information deficits. The focus is on thinking, combined with high levels of inventiveness. The enemy is not just defeated but eliminated. Sameness or cookie-cutter visuality is incapable of building a workplace that speaks. Focus on visual best practices instead.

In addition to improved safety and quality outcomes, building a library of visual SOPs paves the way to standard work, the required forerunner of pull and the highly-prized accelerated flow.

The second type of visual SOPs has a narrow, single-point focus. I call these single-point SOPs (Photo 6.2). They target the tricky bits found in work content—not the operation, step-by-step. The bull's eye is the telling detail. As an early step, supervisors and quality engineers isolate the segments of a procedure that they know, from experience, to be difficult, complex or ambiguous. While these call for more permanent solutions—poka-yoke devices/visual guarantees or even product or process re-design—single-point SOPs offer a near-term fix, conveying a plain visual message: Watch out for this. It's tricky bit. Pay close attention.

Single-point SOPs become especially useful when you enlist the aid of value-add associates in identifying the bits. Get ready to reap a harvest. Don't worry if, over a short period of time, the quantity of these grow. This is simply proof that many of your quality problems are tied to human execution—and we humans would like to do better. So keep collecting.

Just as you build a central library of visual SOPs, build a library branch for single-point SOPS. Store each type in separate buckets, bins or plastic sleeves. Sub-sort each group, for example, by product or model and keep them handy in the work areas. Ask each associate to select one-a-week (or one-a-day) to focus on; people know their trouble spots. This resource is of key importance for newcomers or when there is a quality slip. Visual SOPs will get old and tiresome for veteran employees if you make it required just because, like spinach, it's supposed to be good for you.

Make visual standards and visual SOPs a dynamic part of your quality system. For example, schedule a quality campaign once a quarter (or even monthly), when everyone in the department re-verifies the details on your visual standards, pointing out needed changes.

In this way, visual standards become yet another way to weave I-driven/self-leadership into the everyday life of your department and keep things fresh.

Here are some further pointers.

1. Simplify and reformat the standard (both procedural and technical) into a highly-visual and user-friendly layout.

2. Include drawings and photos to illustrate key product points, along with

photos of people executing the tasks. Remember: A picture is worth a 1000 words and a ton of insight; use them.

3. Print your work out on card stock and then laminate those cards. You want this material stiff enough to not fold or flop around.

4. Develop ways for posting relevant laminated cards at or very near the point-of-use to keep them in people's line of sight. Use magnets, pressure clips and...

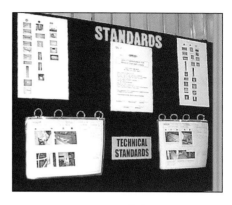

PHOTO 6.3:

ROOF FABRICATION STANDARDS

Notice the two 3-ring binders, each with a set of visual standards. (Trailmobile/Canada, Toronto)

- Clothes lines directly over work benches (and clothes pins, of course).
- Plastic storage sleeves that affix to the backs of doors, sides of machines and the like.
- The spine of a 3-ring binder (without the covers), mounted at point-of-use (Photo 6.3).

An operative word here is "relevant." As already mentioned and to repeat with emphasis: It is imperative that you find reasons and ways for the visual standards in your department to change frequently so they remain a useful and dynamic part of your improvement approach. Keep the focus sharp. As with anything seen too much, visual standards can recede into the background like wallpaper if they are not shuffled often. This is an effectiveness consideration, not cosmetic.

Visual Standards: Lower Your Expectations

Please be warned. Making your standards visual can help your company in its war against mistakes, human error, and human indifference. But in a limited way, only. If you are like most people, you want to believe that putting crystal clear information in front of us means that we will pay more attention and adhere more perfectly because that information is in our face. This is simply not true. And please don't blame us for that. Just because we don't always use those visual standards you so carefully construct- ed doesn't mean we don't care or are not interested in improving our performance.

The reason we may not use them is more closely tied to how information is formatted than to our attitude—more closely tied to brain function than a lack of interest. The culprit is the flat, two-dimensional format of a visual standard. That piece of laminated card stock may tell us what we are supposed to do; but it also relies on our willingness to do it, our consent. In this regard, visual standards have no power at all. A flat piece of paper cannot make me—or anybody—do anything, even if the paper is colorful, laminated, and issued by the Pope himself.

Experienced visual thinkers know this; and they know how to remedy it. That is because, in their training, they learned about the power levels of visual devices (Chapter 1). A visual standard fails when the required behavior does not engage. The motion continues. Seeing that, the visual thinker knows a more powerful device is needed, perhaps several devices—a visual mini-system.

Ever notice a speed limit sign on the side of the road that tells drivers to go slow because children are playing? But they don't. Even though drivers have been told that they might hurt a child, they don't decelerate. Visual thinkers unite! Quick: Reduce driver options. Don't just tell them the right thing to so: Make them do it!

Translate the speed limit sign into a more powerful visual device, one, for example, that uses structure to carry the message—a visual control: a speed bump? The speed bump enforces the message by forcing a behavior change. The driver's will is sidestepped and, with it, choice. The driver does the right thing. Visual controls trump visual standards.

Managers, engineers, and supervisors: You own Doorway 2 and are responsible for publishing accurate, complete, and timely standards and making them visual. Others may help, but you are accountable. Just don't get too excited about the ability of visual standards to help ensure safety, quality, cost, speed, or your profit margins. And do not blame your associates—or yourselves—when those devilishly handsome devices fail to create performance excellence. They are trying their best. But their best is, by definition, never good enough.

Luckily, there are nine other categories of visual function that can help—nine other doorways.

Visual Displays & Visual Scheduling (Level 3—Doorway 3)

Supervisors, managers, and schedulers own Doorway Three. Open it and you discover Visual Displays and Visual Scheduling Boards (Figure 6.3).

Visual Displays

Visual displays are the higher aspect or dimension of visual standards, capturing as they do the same range of visual answers to the core questions (where, what, when, who, how many, and how) as the previous doorway, but this time in a highly interactive format.

For companies making the transition from traditional to new manufacturing, visual displays are the glue that holds the company together while it reduces batch sizes and implements pull. In this, displays are indispensable.

Among their remarkable characteristics, visual displays are capable of holding vast amounts of inter-related information in real time, for all to see, enabling us to understand the status of a given situation in a single glance, make sound decisions, and confidently take timely, appropriate, and aligned action—either as an individual or as a team.

Displays versus the Computer

Those not well-acquainted with the superb functionality of visual displays may question why displays are needed at all. Some will point to the computer as the tool of choice because it is capable of sharing tons more information than a display, faster, and in ever-spiraling layers of complexity. And to this we say: Yes, we know; that is just the problem.

The hotel display in Photo 6.4 makes this point nicely. Some will think this display's information is so plain that it cries out for a computer-based solution. Think a moment longer and we see that the touch-interface provides us with instant flexibility. Plus, brain function research tells us that a change we change with our hands gets embedded as kinetic memory. This, in turn, connects us with the *implications of that change* far more powerfully than a computer interface can. In short, the sense-nexus of touch and sight in this display transforms visual information-sharing into meaning.

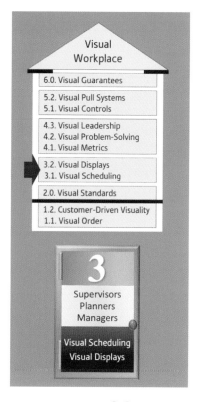

FIGURE 6.3:
VISUAL SCHEDULING &
VISUAL DISPLAYS (LEVEL 3)

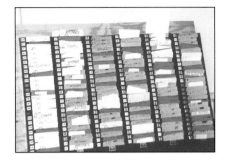

PHOTO 6.4: HOTEL DISPLAY
This homemade yet powerful hotel display allows everyone—and anyone—to know which rooms are ready for occupancy (green) and which are not (red). Before the display, all that information was in the computer. The front desk clerk spent much of his time hunting down the right information which was often not accurate. Hurried questions followed—a lot of motion! (Quincy, Illinois)

The kind of information required to make sound decisions has context, focus, and weight; the result is meaning. Anyone who has ever worked with computer-based information has experienced the frequent and surprising fragmentation of information that computers can create in a nanosecond. When meaning devolves into data and data into minutiae, it is often hard to get a picture big enough to take appropriate action. The resulting analysis/paralysis can choke the decision-making process.

With visual displays, the display owners co-locate the answers to their need-to-know questions on a single, interactive format—the board. The information range on that board can be narrow or extensive. In both cases, a place is needed where related data can pool and influence each other so that a bigger picture—a snapshot of reality—is revealed.

Visual displays are not redundant in a world governed by computers. Instead, displays are the means by which we can, in real time, display data from multiple sources (including but not limited to the computer) and predict their discrete and multi-variant impact on operations and flow. In this regard, especially for companies in transition, displays are powerful and unsurpassed in their usefulness.

The Supervisor's Pain

With rare exception, visual displays start from a supervisor's own personal need-to-know—and then, after a time, the need-to-share. Line supervisors struggle to keep track of literally dozens of data points that constantly change. These, in turn, trigger dozens of macro and micro decisions during the course of a single work shift: time to alert an upstream customer that the unit will arrive later than previously thought (or earlier); time to perform an unscheduled changeover in order to compensate for that; time to shift three assemblers over to the downstream operation where a bottleneck is beginning to form; gosh, the second shift cell leader is not going to make it in—stomach flu again.

Without a display that captures the latest information in real time, supervisors, planners, and managers are in a constant state of alert and alarm because one or the other operational element is, or is not, tipping in a favorable direction—and they have no idea which or when or how they should respond until it actually happens. They are out of control. I call this the supervisor's pain. The purpose of a visual display, at its highest level of performance, is to make that pain visible, put it into the two-dimensional format of a large board, address the pain, and then to reduce it. Visual displays are I-driven.

Supervisors are supposed to know everything. Yet, they cannot. They are defeated before they begin. Likewise, managers are supposed to know everything—and what they don't know, they turn to supervisors to supply. Especially in a traditional manufacturing setting, the truth is one of the most elusive elements of the work environment. Look as you might, you simply cannot find it. You may see it moving across the distant horizon, but as you move towards it, it changes or disappears.

The visual workplace is about making the truth hold still long enough for us to see it, assess it, make a sound decision, and then take timely appropriate action. Nothing does this better than visual displays. They are designed to provide snapshots of the truth across the spectrum of workplace concerns.

Although displays are exclusively focused, at first, on what the supervisor needs to know, they serve the informational needs of everyone. Look at the display that Frank Mulder, chief of Stores (Magazin), created at Royal Nooteboom Trailers (RNT). Frank had worked at RNT for 20 years when he attended his first visual displays workshop. The result was the splendid display you see in Photo 6.5, as interesting in its positive impact as it was beautiful.

Frank needed to know everything. With 15 material handlers, inspectors, and store staff, working across two shifts, Frank could easily lose track of the detail. Scheduling was not the problem—managing the exceptions was. His direct reports seem to come and go as they wished, deciding to leave early at a moment's notice, coming in late (again) because little Greta couldn't find her tutu (this actually happened), and the like. The schedule was whimsical at best. And it was also hidden in the computer.

FRANK MULDER   HENK HOP

PHOTO 6.5: VISUAL BOARD/STORE
Each of the three panels on this board represents a week. Daily tasks are listed and color-coded on the far left. Then comes a list in yellow of the 15 area employees. Frank Mulder, board owner and chief supervisor of Stores, assigns tasks to people in 3-week blocks for everyone to see and know—and Frank first. If there is a change, Frank makes it there—and everyone knows it.(Royal Nooteboom Trailers, Holland)

Frank wanted to find a way to get his crew to recognize the impact on him, other team members, and the work itself when someone came in late or "decided" to leave early. With Holland's particularly broad definition of personal independence, Dutch work rules—and the values that drive them—are not the same as they are in the USA. Enforcement was not an option.

There came a time when just keeping track of his staff and dealing with daily exceptions became so tedious and complicated that Frank was about to put in for a transfer. Frank knew he needed another way—or a way out.

When he learned in the workshop about visual displays—and learned that they began with his need-to-know—he immediately started to build one for his overriding need to know who was in today and what they were supposed to do. And he got the board to tell him (and everyone else) both things, three weeks out.

As Frank hoped, exhibiting specific team member duties in a public, centralized location, motivated team members to hold themselves accountable—coupled with the very visible changes that happened for all to see when someone asked for a personal exception (again). Tardiness and arbitrary absenteeism decreased. Frank's first visual display was a resounding success.

But also keep in mind this process point: the display in Photo 6.5 did not look like that when Frank began. He started as we all do—with a sheet of paper, a pencil, and some sticky notes. He made a first draft, tried it out, saw what worked and what didn't, listened for his own questions (his own need-to-know), and kept making refinements. He conferred with displays coordinator Henk Hop, who coached and lent insight into what a display should and could do; Henk kept moving Frank in the right direction.

What was that direction? The single-focused (and some may say, "selfish") capture of Frank's need-to-know questions. Henk Hop made sure that Frank's visual solution was I-driven. As invariably happens with displays, when Frank had developed a display based on his personal need-to-know, the resultant device provided vital information to others because the answers were posted in a central location and in a highly-visible, interactive format. The details of the displays changed as the truth changed. And people's behavior aligned. Splendid!

That's the way it goes with supervisors. When they know what's going on at-a-glance, thanks to a visual display, you know what's going on at-a-glance. This creates a tremendous sense of safety, sanity, and stability in the workplace—a condition more precious than gold. Why? Because those three conditions—safety, sanity, and stability—open up the possibility of unity. Unity redefines profit.

Visual Scheduling

Visual displays are the more advanced form of the Doorway 3 function. Visual scheduling boards are the simpler form. I purposely began our discussion with displays so you could appreciate some of the many dimensions or layers of meaning they can hold. Visual scheduling has a flatter purpose, not as much depth yet extraordinarily informative, especially if you are making the transition from traditional operations to the new enterprise. Please keep that in mind as we walk through this section.

Visual scheduling captures simple information-sharing, often focused on a single data dimension: parts ordering, order tracking, production scheduling, re-work tracking, stock outs, maintenance scheduling, ECN release, and the like. Its main property is its simplicity. Look at the scheduling board in Photo 6.6. It lists in order of need: serial number, start date, due date, status, and leaves a space for comments—clear and direct.

Visual scheduling boards are an elementary first step. But make no mistake: They still capture supervisor pain, the supervisor's need to know even as others can see and use it as well.

Think about it. The absence of scheduling information—plain as it is—has wide negative consequences: making the wrong thing, making it out of order, missing

ADAM CELL - AN/TSQ-252					
Serial Number	Induction Date	Due Out Date	ON / OFF	SCHEDULE	COMMENTS
60051 - Mag.			OFF		PROC/FINAL
50105 - Bench	7/23	9/2	OFF		TEST/FINAL
57009	6/30	9/28	OFF		BENCH/T
57009	11/9	10/7	OFF		MEN/AFT
60014 - Freda	9/3	11/28	OFF		INT BUILD
50150 - Troops	9/15	11/4	OFF		INT BUILD
90039	9/10	12/16	OFF		NOT STARTED
90010	9/21	11/20	OFF		FINAL WELD
60001 - Saul K.	9/3		OFF		TANK WELD
57011	9/10		OFF		PAINT
57015	9/17		OFF		PAINT
50065	9/21		OFF		FINAL
50153					(NEW BUILD)

PHOTO 6.6:
VISUAL SCHEDULING BOARD
(MILITARY DEPOT, PENNSYLVANIA)

the delivery date because you, well, forgot, and so on and so forth. The result? Instability, uncertainty, hunting around, wandering around, a demoralized, often angry workforce, especially your supervisors. If this sounds the slightest bit familiar, get a visual scheduling board up at once. Slap it up.

I have been in such plants when delivering my Visual Thinking Seminar. Participants are so starved for information that, during our lunch break, they often construct a makeshift scheduling board for their department and get it going before lunch is over. Prior to the seminar, they had simply never thought of centrally-locating that information and presenting it visually, for all to see. They had never realized this format was the tool they were looking for. Once they understood, they snapped into action. Indeed, this is the way many of us react when we realize the answer to our struggle was literally right in front of our eyes: the visual workplace.

It is not enough for supervisors to have today's schedule folded in their pocket on a scrap of paper or as a computer printout. Nor is it enough for them to leave that printout with the operator, or let the traveler (the work order that accompanies a bin or pallet) convey needed information. Build a board, plain and clear and out in the open for all and anyone to see and use. When there is nowhere to go for this plain, ordinary, unremarkable information, its appearance on a public board is cause for celebration. The liberation of information is the liberation of the human will. Hurray.

Let's revisit Royal Nooteboom Trailers where Frank Mulder created his multi-layered manning display as a solution to what was eating his lunch. Frank's colleague and friend, Toon van Uden was chief supervisor of the Euro Trailer Line and had attended the same visual displays/scheduling workshop as Frank—but his response was very different. Toon built his board around a simple yes/no (ya/ne) question: "Has the material I need for this order been delivered to the line?" (Photo 6.7). That was the need-to-know question uppermost in the worry part of Toon's mind. The only change he made in the seven months before he retired was to mount the paper on a board and screw the board onto a tall rack.

I wondered why so little was enough and asked Toon. "Gwendolyn," he said (with Henk Hop translating from the Dutch), "I have worked here for 30 years and am very good at my job. The only thing I can't handle is not knowing if the material has arrived or not. If it hasn't and I know it, I know what to do. If it has and I know it, I know what to do. *Not* knowing makes me nuts!"

PHOTO 6.7: TOON AND HIS MATERIAL DELIVERY DISPLAY

There it is again. Toon wanted a sense of control—and visuality again delivered, the same way it does for value-add associates through the visual where, to name just one more of many.

Toon's encounter with the opportunity that visual displays and visual scheduling boards offer is typical and it is sound. How we answer our need-to-know questions is not static, nor is it predictable. Needs evolve. Missing answers are discovered and visually answered, with new sectors of meaning routinely added. The board captures the journey and our work become more stable, more transparent. We are more in control. A new normal is set in place that can serve as a platform for the next improvement cycle. Doorway 3 offers a pair of powerful and exquisitely useful formats for capturing the layers of information which, when absent, eat their lunch and therefore yours. See Photo Album 13 for more examples.

Visual Scheduling~In Multiples

If one visual scheduling board is helpful, what would happen if we clustered several in a room? Why not a dedicated space with walls covered by real-time data in the form of charts, tables, displays that allow us to see the current state, both broadly and in detail. The Japanese word for this is *obeya* or *big room*. Often called an Opex Room (Photo 6.8), its purpose is to organize mission-critical information in a format that is highly-visible and highly flexible in order to make it easy to understand status at-a-glance and make important decisions based solely on the information shared in that room.

PHOTO 6.8: OPEX ROOM

Visual Displays and Visual Scheduling Boards

Information in an Interactive Format for All to See and Use

Impressive in sharing complex information that changes often, visual boards are used to gain speed, transparency, and control over fast-moving processes—until process velocity exceeds the board's capacity to communicate. Whether hospital, bank, office or factory, they anchor and address a wide range of scheduling and communication challenges.

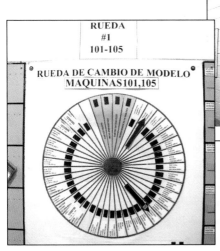

Wheel of Parts Display + Kanban ◆ ▶

A kanban board flanks each visual scheduling wheel. Part numbers dot circumference. Big arrows backed with Velcro point to the parts Machines 101 and 102 are running now. The four yellow top sections point to changeover, parts service and piloting, and preventive maintenance.
(Deltronicos, Matamoras, Mexico)

Maintenance Work Order Display ▶

This display, located in the main aisle of the plant, is Maintenance's way of letting everyone know (including its own team) what's been done (green), waiting to be done (yellow), and long overdue (red).
(Delphi-Plant 20, Anderson, Indiana)

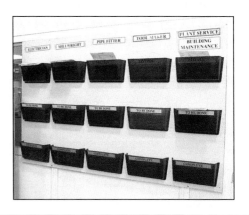

Keep Upgrading Your Board, Iteration after Iteration

All visual boards begin with the need-to-know of individuals looking for an easier way to get and give accurate, timely, and complete answers to recurrent questions. Do not expect to succeed with your first draft. Begin with sticky notes. Test it. Improve it. Then cycle through again. Rolls-Royce in Germany requires six upgrades before they consider a display in reasonable working order—and before they would invest any money in it. Until then, everything is homemade. Nothing is purchased.

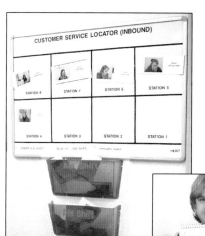

◀ "Who's on First" Board

Customer Service Supervisor Brenda Holetz designed this board to schedule and keep track of customer service reps, many of whom were Moms and worked irregular hours. Before, Brenda—and everyone else—had to check and re-check everything: who's in/which station/how long? But no more, thanks to visuality.

(Sears Product Repair Services, Sacramento, California)

BRENDA WITH
DRAFT ONE

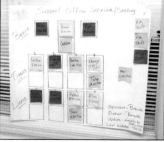

BRENDA'S SECOND DRAFT

◀ Complex Assembly Display

This meticulous visual scheduling board at Rolls-Royce tracks complex sub-assemblies. Work order magnets move across bands of color—each representing a given operation or stage.

(Rolls-Royce, Oberursel, Germany)

Similar to NASA Control in Texas, active problem-solving takes place on demand and on the spot. Daily sessions typically last less than an hour—enough time to digest and prioritize but not enough to get bogged down.

Visual Team Boards

There is one more format I want to share with you before we leave Doorway 3: *Visual Team Boards*. These boards come in as wide a variety of layouts as there are teams, with each team fashioning the format to its needs. The purpose is always the same: Provide the team with a visual focal point for idea generation, discussion, decision-making, and activity tracking. As the following example shows, the formula is straight forward.

A five-member submarine design team set up the board in Figure 6.4 and had a first meeting. Ideas abounded, captured in sticky notes, color-coded to person, and posted on the far left of the four columns. From there, each sticky note moved across the sections in real time, based on their completion status: 25%, 50%, 75%, 100%. Updated daily, the board becomes the tracking device that shares status at-a-glance. Any idea that got stalled was moved to the top for special attention. New sections—such as *NEXT*—were added as needed. Subject matter experts and decision-makers made a cameo appearance from time to time. Two months later, the design segment closed—and the team reconfigured the board for the next phase

Try this out. Launch a Visual Team Board and meet your team goals.

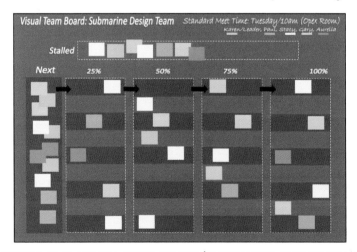

FIGURE 6.4: VISUAL TEAM BOARD/SUBMARINE DESIGN TEAM

CHAPTER | **7**

Visual Leadership: Visual Metrics, Visual Problem-Solving & Hoshin

Vance Packard told us back in 1962 that: "Leadership appears to be the art of getting others *to want* to do something you are convinced should be done." Would it surprise you to learn that the technologies of the visual workplace play a vital role in achieving exactly what Packard describes—getting people to follow you because they want the same things that you as a leader want?

In this chapter, we examine Doorway 4—the art and science of corporate leadership through a process I developed in response to nearly 20 years of working closely with GMs, CEOs, presidents, vice presidents, and site managers (Figure 7.1). They wanted to run their organizations with effectiveness, clarity, economy, and imagination. They wanted to lead. Instead, most of them merely coped. They struggled. They got through. They managed.

I watched as they did this and pondered what visuality could contribute to helping executives transform their work into positions that responded more effec-

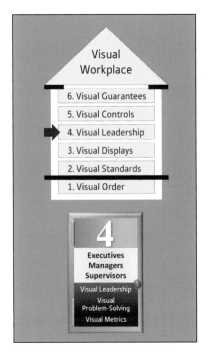

FIGURE 7.1:
LEVEL 4/DOORWAY 4
VISUAL LEADERSHIP

tively to the demands and goals of their companies—and to their own aspirations and needs, I-driven. The principles and practices of visual leadership began to take shape.

Here, for the record, is my personal view of leadership. I do not consider the ability to lead as a gift bestowed upon that rare individual with a burning charismatic persona and an exquisite business school education. My view is more commonplace. I believe that skilled leadership can be cultivated through the application and mastery of a set of highly-visual formats that help executives do the very things they must do and want to do: decide and drive. This is the heart of effective leadership.

These formats, or visual devices, form the architecture that leaders—and leaders-in-the-making—need in order to identify strategic priorities and link them to meaningful tactical projects that can be resourced, and metrics that can drive those projects. In short, they provide leaders with a reliable framework for saying say *yes* to the few and *wait* to the many.

This also means visual leadership principles and practices address the special form of motion leaders struggle with when the information they need is either inaccurate, incomplete, late, too late, not relevant, hard-to-acquire or simply missing. That special form of motion is: bad decisions or no decision at all. Yes, successful visual leaders become scientists of motion. As with others in the enterprise, they become ace visual thinkers.

Leadership, however, is also an interpretive art, with the way forward rarely a clear ribbon of highway. Here, visual formats serve the visual leader as well, promoting depth and clarity of insight, far beyond simple accountability. All of this is Doorway 4.

Doorway 4 spans three visual leadership mechanisms or tools: visual metrics (not the same as KPIs), visual problem-solving, and the suite of executive leadership practices called visual policy deployment—my formulation of hoshin.

Are you surprised that I include metrics and problem-solving as executive-level tools? Experience has taught me that both provide information vital to the stability and growth of the enterprise and, therefore, are vital to successful stewardship. The decision about which metrics model and problem-solving approach to deploy in an organization is pivotal, not casual. That's why that decision needs to happen on the highest level—in the board room—of the company.

While space does not allow me to provide the details of building and deploying the several visual constructs this chapter covers, I do describe a set of useful considerations for you to reflect upon in reference to leadership in your organization. In doing so, I trust you will find some steps you can take to strengthen the current level of leadership effectiveness in your company—and perhaps even in terms of your own personal effectiveness as a leader.

Visual Metrics (Level 4.1—Doorway 4)

The executive defines the corporate intent, shaping the way forward through that decision and many subsequent choices. While direct reports, managers, supervisors, and other players can, and often do, offer substantial inputs, Doorway 4—which has measurement systems as its foundation—is owned by the executive (Figure 7.2). The selection of the company's measurement approach is, therefore, for the executive to make, always with significant negative or positive consequences, depending on that pick.

Company measures and measurement systems have had the spotlight for decades and remain key means by which the enterprise can see and track its own performance. Early on, Japan was instrumental in driving home this point with its template of core performance measures—safety, quality, cost, and delivery (SQCD). Authors Kaplan and Norton adapted this framework in the 1990s in their Balanced

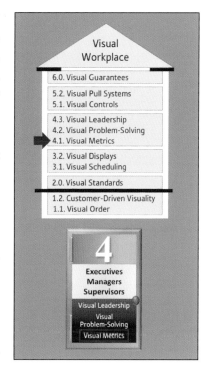

FIGURE 7.2:
VISUAL METRICS (LEVEL 4.1)

Photo Album 14

Metrics That Monitor Only

Tracking Performance is Not the Same as Improving It

The measurement devices and displays in this album are used by many companies to display the results of their key performance indicators. Usually these are computer-generated, not easily read, and published weekly. We repeat: While extraordinarily useful as a snapshot of current weekly and monthly conditions, their use as improvement drivers is limited. Though they are visual, they are not visual metrics.

◀ Plant-wide Metrics Board

This display is located on the site's main aisle so employees, customers, and other visitors can see it on their way to the production floor.

(Plymouth Tube, West Monroe, Louisiana)

Metrics Array ▶

Another proudly-presented set of performance metrics, these data show but do not drive performance indicators in this 3,000-person auto-motive supplier factory.

(Delphi Rimir, Matamoras, Mexico)

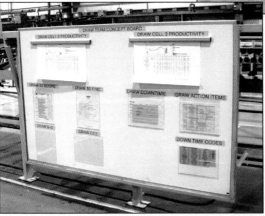

◀ Cell-Board

This cell-level measurement display provides team members with daily performance feedback, published weekly.

(Plymouth Tube, West Monroe, Louisiana)

Scorecard approach, adding the term "KPIs/key performance indicators" to the mix—measures that monitor results and promote an understanding of the link between performance and outcome.

Unquestionably, KPIs provide useful snapshots of a company's performance results. Though visible, however, KPIs are of limited use in a visual enterprise where the emphasis is not just on "seeing"—but on seeing as a *driver of improvement*. KPIs monitor only; they do not drive. As currently used, KPIs have not yet achieved the synergies or precision required of measures that can transform that which they measure. "Close," as my 93-year old Mom would say, "but no cigar." See the KPI boards in *Photo Album 14: Metrics That Monitor Only*.

In a visual workplace, I call the measurement mechanism that drives—and can transform—a *visual metric*. I coined the term in order to differentiate that which is *merely seen* from that which has a *dynamic purpose*. Which is to say that, while they share some traits with KPIs, visual metrics are also singularly different from them.

Similar to a KPI, a visual metric is a quantum or data point that provides feedback on a given performance and its outcome. But its unwavering first focus is on improving that performance and, as a result, the outcomes which that performance triggers. A visual metric never collects data unless those data are used, immediately, to drive the metric in the direction of improvement. That action is undertaken at once in order to improve those data. This is a vital distinction.

We all know companies that collect KPI data in order to analyze them. But that analysis does not necessarily trigger change, even when the problem is obvious and change is clearly needed. KPIs may be used to track problem results for days, weeks or even months. All too often, however, those data simply sit on sheets of paper, computer screens or slick LCD displays—and nothing changes. After all, the thinking seems to go, this problem has been around for a while, does not appear to be going anywhere, so what does it matter if we wait a few more weeks —or months. And when that time is up, the next move is often to collect more data. This is a particularly maddening cycle to witness if that problem is one you and your colleagues need to live and cope with in real time.

Survey after survey shows that many companies collect 20 to 30 key performance indicators weekly for every work area. A few of these are department-specific. The rest are variations on the themes of safety, quality, cost, and delivery and generate a huge amount of data to read—but far too much to parse and digest.

Do not misunderstand me. Companies will always need to collect SQCD data. The question is: to what end? To monitor performance or to improve it? They are not the same thing.

A visual metric does more than monitor performance, track results, and pinpoint problems. *It illuminates cause.* Then, anchored in cause, it drives improvement activity down the causal chain until viable solutions are identified and installed and the problem is eliminated. Visual metrics do this (and can do this) because you build them to do so. As you will see in a moment, the "drive" capability of a visual metric does not happen by accident. It is structured into place.

Visual Metric: Seven Traits

Used effectively, a visual metric relentlessly drives until breakthrough happens. The problem condition is eliminated, and the new improved condition is stabilized, embedded through visuality into the living landscape of work. It is an authentic improvement driver. Here are seven traits of a visual metric to consider:

1. **I-driven.** Visual metrics are always I-driven. They are in the voice of the user—the person or group that owns, causes, receives, and/or is in a position to help solve the problem. Not one of those I's—*but all of them*. I call this the user cluster.

2. **Concrete.** Because they are I-driven, visual metrics are expressed in concrete, relevant terms, not percentage points or abstractions. An effective visual metric speaks in the voice of the user—terms meaningful to any and all members of the user cluster.

3. **Action-Oriented/At Once.** Visual metrics are always tied to action. As soon as the data express a problem (in Japanese terms, "an abnormality"), people spring into corrective action. If there is an interval between knowledge (the data) and action, it is kept as short as possible. The principle is: Corrective action is undertaken immediately—at once.

4. **Short Collection Intervals.** Because of the "at once" requirement, a visual metric collects data at close intervals—every hour (hour after hour); or, even better, in 15-minute increments; or, better yet, exactly as the data occur.

Once-a-day collection is acceptable for starters, especially if that is a stretch goal for a company. But daily collection is not yet close enough for measurement effectiveness. Because the overarching purpose of visual metrics is to illuminate cause, and since cause has many layers and is also dynamic, we need tight collection intervals.

5. **Points of Comparison.** An effective visual metric is made more powerful when combined with points of comparison: previous versus now data; planned versus actual data; area 2086B versus our area; personal best versus AQL-required; shift 2 versus shift 3 versus shift 1, and so on. Points of comparison make it easier to understand the direction of change and the detail of what's different—cause.

6. **Illuminates Cause.** (I mentioned this trait above; now let's un-nest it.) A visual metric tracks and illuminates cause. To understand how this works, first make a sharp distinction between effect and cause—with *effect* as the result and *cause* as the trigger. Next, segment cause into groups or sections (another name for this is *cause segmentation*) so you get the data to speak. When you segment cause as it is collected, your understanding of the problem becomes increasingly refined, granular. Segmenting data means putting results into logic buckets as you collect them. Do this and exact solutions often surface in the act of measuring.

7. **Post Prominently.** Visual metrics are posted prominently for all to see and consider. This also ensures easy access for timely data postings. (Of course, if the data are confidential, take steps to protect access.)

• • • •

In summary, visual metrics track and illuminate cause, segment complex problems, and drive improvement from the I-dentify level. The focus is on daily improvement. See Photo 7.1 for an excellent example of many of the traits just described. Can you name them?

See *Photo Album 15: Visual Metrics Almost* for two measures that represent a format upgrade over the traditional KPI approach and tip in the direction of a visual metric, even though more is needed.

Visual Metrics Drive Improvement

The first two metrics in this album embody some of the characteristics of an effective visual metric, but not all. The third metric is so large and visible that one might quickly assume it is a visual metric—but, most decidedly, it is not.

◀ Cell Metric

This visual metric is in a fast-paced machine cell. Note inclusion of the goal versus actual comparison points. (Wiremold, Connecticut)

Machine Metric ▶

This metric on a high-speed molding machine shows planned versus actual machine productivity as comparison points. The colored squares represent categories of known slow downs or stoppages, with sub-surface sensors that trigger the light in the appropriate box when one of these occurs. (Wiremold, Connecticut)

◀ Management Metric Only

This device is not a visual metric. Even though it tracks productivity, it does not drive improvement. And while it is big, bright, and easy to see, it lacks the required points of comparison (among other elements). Dating back to 1986, before computers took over the role, the device was made extra large so the numbers could be seen from a wide second-floor window where managers sat. (Packard Electric, Rio Bravo IV, Juarez, Mexico)

Who Owns the Metric?

Remember who owns Doorway 4: the executive, the head honcho. Whether GM or CEO, the executive gets to determine which measurement approach would be of most use and relevance to the enterprise. Other executives may—and often do—influence that decision, sometimes heavily. Ultimately, however, the decision is for the ranking executive to make. Sanctioned in that way, the measurement system cascades down through site chiefs, managers, supervisors, and team leads.

But ask yourself: Do the data that travel back to the executive suite hold solutions—or just more unpleasant surprises?

If problems are captured as visual metrics, they are already in the voice of the local user. Therefore, they are destined to return to leadership, solved. Anything that returns unsolved is bound to be out-of-scope, owned by those who operate on organizational layers above the local level. Visual metrics will serve that layer as well, but the voice has to be changed to fit. That is the secret of it all.

Because they are I-driven, visual metrics can play a pivotal role in capturing local data equivalents from every level of the organization. Each organizational function must find its own measurement voice.

You may think you are doing a good job in linking measures company-wide through your use of a Balanced Scorecard framework or the like. Yet the true test of a measurement system is whether the measures provide the level of feedback people require to carry out improvements, aggressively on their own, within their locus of control.

It is easy enough to disconnect from a problem you are in no position to solve. Yet the reverse is also true. It is easy to clamor for a solution to a problem when you know you are not in a position to solve it. I believe the popular term used for that heightened sense of righteousness is: "missionary zeal." Inducing employees to actually own problems is one of the more difficult and illusive conditions a company can face in the early stages of its improvement journey—the elusive I-dentity dynamic.

Visual leaders can do much to ensure problem-ownership through the right choice of measurement systems. The wrong choice of measures will produce distance between the problem and those who are in a position to solve it. The right choice will trigger high levels of problem ownership and genuine excitement about getting the problem permanently solved. Making the right choice defines the visual leader.

Said another way, the visual metrics approach is specifically designed to make certain that the people who cause the problem, receive it, or can help solve it, will want—in the manner of Vance Packard—to own that problem and participate in improving it. This is a moment of genuine breakthrough for any company on the journey to operational excellence.

Visual Metrics in Action

Socorro Garza, whose commitment to excellence is both ongoing and deep, is such a visual leader. Legendary in her commitment to excellence, Ms. Garza was, when we met, the highly-successful head of quality at Deltronicos (Matamoros, Mexico)—and a woman who had recently declined the opportunity to become one of Mexico's first female plant managers because, in her words, "I still have more to learn about quality."

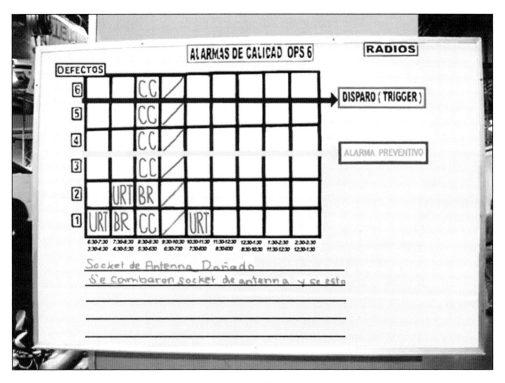

PHOTO 7.1:
SUPERB VISUAL METRIC AND IMPROVEMENT DRIVER
(DELTRONICOS, MATAMORAS, MEXICO)

The superb visual metric in Photo 7.1 is her handiwork—the result of her decision to crack the code on quality by developing a local measure that would drive improvement down the causal chain by illuminating cause. These are my words, not hers. Nonetheless, that is exactly what she did.

At the time, Ms. Garza worked at a site with some 2,000 employees who produced 35,000 high-end car radio systems per month. She developed the metrics board under discussion for a 35-person, one-piece flow, assembly line in the center of the factory. Setting to the side her hat as quality director, she showed up every day as acting supervisor because she wanted to personally test the innovative metrics format she had devised. Here's a closer look at its mechanics.

1. The format is in hourly increments across two shifts. (See the horizontal axis at the bottom of the chart: shift 1 starts at 6:30 am; shift 2 at 3:30 pm.)

2. The yellow and red horizontal lines in the center pre-set the action trigger-points, respectively, at three defects and then five.

3. Three defects of any type in a single hour will breach the yellow line and trigger an action ("alarma preventivo"). When that happens, Socorro alerts the line that something is afoot: Pay special attention.

4. If defects reach a count of five in a single hour, the red line is breached, and the line is stopped for immediate corrective action. (This is precisely what happened at 10:30 am on the day I was onsite.)

5. A permanent record is made when a photo of the board is taken at the end of each shift. Then the board is cleaned and the next shift supervisor re-starts the process.

So that's a live profile of a visual metric in action: what it is, how it works—and why it works so well. Marvelous visual thinking.

Yes, the area on the lower right is where people can post comments about the defect occurrence, a beginning attempt to get at cause. But that is small potatoes compared to the robust visual problem-solving process we are about to examine in the next level of Doorway 4. Ms. Garza's metric board, with its laser focus on quality, would have been only a heartbeat away from finding solutions to the causes had she continued down the causal pathway through the methodologies of Doorway 4.

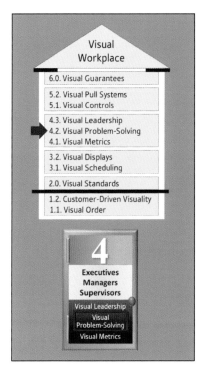

FIGURE 7.3:
VISUAL PROBLEM-SOLVING
(LEVEL 4.2)

PHOTO 7.2:
The after-market director at Australia's premier bus manufacturer, Volgren, leads a ScoreBoard project with one of the several teams focused on reducing after-delivery/warranty costs.

Visual Problem-Solving (Level 4.2—Doorway 4)

Measures that drive improvement—visual metrics—lead us directly to the next level in the pathway to a full-functioning visual workplace and the second dimension of Doorway 4: *Visual Problem-Solving* (Figure 7.3).

I am well-acquainted with—and have a great deal of respect for—many problem-solving approaches that are current in today's marketplace: DMAIC, 8-D, A3, 7 Quality Tools, 5-Whys, and others. All of them have a visual aspect, some more evident than others. But none, in my view, share enough of the principles of visuality to rank as a genuinely visual improvement driver. None incorporate enough visual principles to qualify as a robust process for solving chronic, costly, complex problems, visually. Here, I refer to principles such as: I-driven, embedded action, and dynamic information-sharing that aligns and unifies many voices (many users).

The ScoreBoarding (SB) Methodology is such a process of visual problem-solving, structuring in robust measurement with interactive cause-identification and systematic solution-making, all from an I-driven base. The SB architecture promotes parity amongst participants and unsurpassed connectivity, allowing participants to dig deep into the causal chain and engage in cycle after cycle of thinking together. It is a splendid mechanism. (See Photo 7.2 for an example of ScoreBoard in action.)

ScoreBoarding: Conceptually

Studying the Toyota Production System was a passion of my early career. For me, it was more like research because the internal mechanisms that drove TPS were not easy to find. The Japanese shared a lot; but they were not given to sharing everything. As with many aspects of TPS, a great deal was hidden—in plain sight, perhaps, but hidden nonetheless. Certainly, it was that way with how TPS treated and solved problems.

I spent nearly ten years delving into the Japanese Way in the 1980s, under the watchful eyes of my two master senseis: Dr. Shigeo Shingo, co-architect with Taiichi Ohno of TPS, and Dr. Ryuji Fukuda, former head of quality at Sumitomo, Japan's electronics giant. (Fukuda was also the first Japanese practitioner to introduce the X-Type Matrix to the West, among many other of his firsts.)

In the years since, my interest in and scrutiny of TPS, in particular, has not lessened. Now some 35 years later, I hold the fixed and firm conclusion that TPS is about one thing above all else: causality—the journey down and back up the causal chain…bad cause, good cause. What took me so long?

Dr. Fukuda put me on the scent one day as we chatted in an exquisite Tokyo hotel, sipping Japanese exquisite tea from exquisite Japanese cups. The topic was standards. Good student that I was, I asked him, "Sensei, what is your definition of a standard?" He replied that he preferred the term reliable method, which he defined as follows:

A reliable method is made up of only those elements which, when not followed, result in a predictable defect or waste.

I nearly dropped my teacup. Stunned by the elegance of this inverted definition, I immediately understood that it contained a conceptual revolution. His definition changed everything, opening for me an entirely new perspective on what problems are and how they get solved—permanently. In a flash, I saw that metrics could be designed to illuminate cause, much in the way that Socorro Garza would do in the remarkable metrics array discussed earlier in this chapter.

Fukuda's definition also made me realize that a reliable method (an SOP) was simply a sequence of good causes. That good causes produce good effects (un-problems)—and bad causes produce bad effects (problems). There it was again: causality.

This understanding is so simple that there is danger one might dismiss it as simplistic or even simple-minded. It is not. It is, instead, the exquisite doorway to excellence. Better causes mean better standards; better standards mean better results. I also realized that a problem is either a weak standard, a set of weak standards—or no standard at all. Now that's a problem!

When a company expects employees (operators and managers, alike) to produce exact outcomes in the absence of timely, accurate, complete, and easy-to-access standards, we are back to the "make-stuff-up" syndrome, symptomatic of an information-scarce work environment.

This exquisite effect/cause logic became the foundation of the CEDAC process (cause-and-effect-diagram-with-the-addition-of-cards), Fukuda's adaptation of the Isikawa diagram during his days at Sumitomo. But CEDAC had a great deal more flexibility and capability.

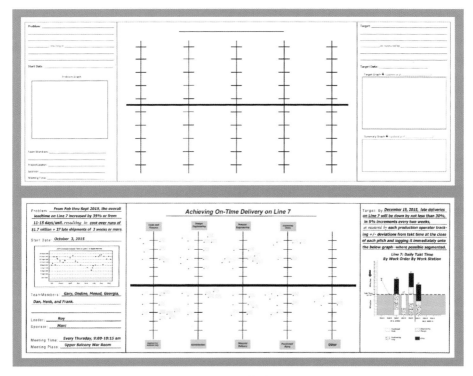

FIGURE 7.4:

The blank diagram (top) comes alive when cross-functional teams meet in front of and respond to its framework. In action (below), the ScoreBoard Diagram remains the tool of choice for solving chronic, costly, complex problems.

In the early 1980s, Fukuda asked me to turn that process into a methodology that western companies would understand and use. And I did. With Fukuda's permission, my adaptation of CEDAC became known as the ScoreBoard methodology, the one we are discussing now. It has remained the format of choice when my clients have to deal with chronic, costly, complex problems—the kind that don't fit on a fish bone and that lose their synergy when we try to segment them into the A3 architecture.

ScoreBoarding in Action

As I walk through the core elements of this superb method, consider how it supports and amplifies I-driven visuality. Think about ways you could integrate some of its strengths into your current problem-solving approach. See Figure 7.4.

1. Capture an array of good and bad causes on sticky notes and post on a large, highly-visible, interactive diagram (3 foot by 5 foot is the usual size).

2. Back the diagram in cardboard that is scored in the center so it folds easily so you can carry the diagram around, despite its size.

3. Anchor the problem-solving in a visual metric, one that illuminates cause so you can drive the investigation down the causal chain.

4. Collect this metric in real time, in the shortest possible interval—not less than once a day, preferably hourly. Always include at least one point of comparison.

5. Segment the metric by cause or some other meaningful category, such as time or location.

6. Make sure that everyone and anyone can access and contribute to the diagram, easily. (If the project is confidential, mask to block access.)

7. Make a concerted commitment to involve all users—those individuals who cause, receive, or can help solve the problem condition. Avoid substituting a representative elite for the many.

8. Collect causes and generate improvement ideas non-selectively, with a bias for diversity.

9. Organize the format around discrete—even unique—cause categories, in lieu of highly generalized or ones, like machine, material, man, method, etc.

Photo Album
16

Visual Problem-Solving

Solving Problems Permanently

Visual problem-solving shares weak standards openly so that all can participate in identifying causes and developing solutions. Consider laying out the problem in a large and an open format, posted directly in the area where the problem exists. This can go a long way to ensuring wide ownership of, and interest, in detailed causes and solutions that last.

◆ Visual Problem-Solving at RNT

This Visual ScoreBoard was posted directly on the production floor at Royal Nooteboom Trailers. Employees added sticky notes whenever they noticed a cause or thought of a solution ➥

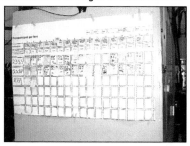

➥ Finding the Value in Inspection

Inspection can be said to be 100% non-value-adding (NVA); yet, it is a vital verification process for government contracts. When the inspection team at Pratt & Whitney (P&W) attacked NVA in the area, they meticulously tracked each work order, coupled with aggressive cause and solutions finding. (Pratt & Whitney, Connecticut)

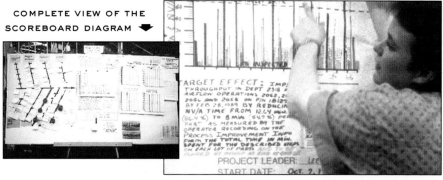

COMPLETE VIEW OF THE
SCOREBOARD DIAGRAM ➥

➦ Here Paula Robins points to the tight-interval visual metric that drove this process.

10. Solicit improvement ideas that are either anchored in the previously generated causes or intuited. It doesn't matter. All such ideas are guided through a refining process that will strengthen the valid and set aside the unsubstantiated.

11. Operationalize the understanding that success depends on a high and on-going level of interactivity and engagement.

In ScoreBoarding, you are tackling chronic, complex problems, so expect the need for a good amount of time to resolve them into sustainable solutions that have been systematically proofed and verified. Throughout this time, your segmented metric continues to provide feedback on your progress and on the legitimacy of proposed solutions. (See examples in Photo Album 16: Visual Problem-Solving.)

In the course of a project, the ScoreBoard method generates a raft of new standards—new reliable methods—that have substituted good cause for all those bad causes that generated the problem condition to begin with. The final step is to turn as many of those good causes (solutions) into visual devices so they become part of the process itself, embedded and governing our behavior seamlessly and sustainably, without speaking a word.

· · · ·

Returning to our opening discussion, the visual leadership process identifies the ranking executive as the person who mandates the development of a robust system of metrics, linked with systematic problem-solving. Executives need these systems in place if they are to make the jump from management to authentic leadership. As leader, the executive is responsible for two macro conditions in the enterprise: stability and growth. Though visual metrics and robust visual problem-solving are key to this, they are not sufficient by themselves. A third leadership dimension is needed: Hoshin/Visual Policy Deployment, the next pathway level and the completion of Doorway 4.

Visual Deployment of Policy: Hoshin (Level 4.3—Doorway 4)

Compelling, natural leaders are rare in any field, business and industry included. Combine that with the fact that nearly every workplace is flooded with priorities that constantly compete for resources and attention and we are left to wonder how a company acquires the champions it needs and wants. Good question. And my

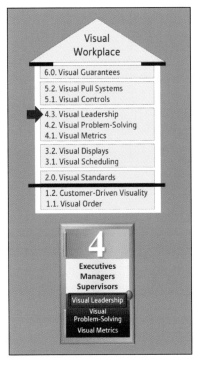

FIGURE 7.5:
VISUAL POLICY DEPLOYMENT
(LEVEL 4.3)

good answer (which you heard me proclaim earlier in this chapter) is: by teaching executives the principles and practices of visual leadership.

In this section, we examine the third level of Doorway 4 and two of the several core visual formats that executives learn to use in order to say *yes* to the few and *wait* to the many (Figure 7.5). The ability of executives to do this, in turn, gives them the clarity and confidence to decide on and drive their vision for enterprise stability and growth. They lead.

The two formats are: the Operations System Improvement Template (OSIT) and the X-Type Matrix. While there are several other leadership tools of great importance to the visual executive, these two are the first in the skill-building sequence. Let me add, again, that my purpose in presenting them is not to provide details on their construction and deployment—or how to troubleshoot them if they get stalled. There are simply not enough pages in this book. I focus, instead, on describing the visual architecture of each format—their boundedness—and how the power of those limits helps executives learn the fine art and science of how to decide, a vital step in becoming an accomplished visual leader.

The House

The Toyota Production System (TPS) model is a most widely-recognized formulation of a production system, captured in a 2D format (Figure 7.6). Companies are drawn to the iconic shape of the TPS temple or house. Its architecture exudes strength, decisiveness, integration, and stability. It has power—the power of structure, the power of limits.

Look at those columns or pillars: straight, strong, calculated, and capable of bearing the weight of the goal—the roof. That goal is clearly stated: "Highest Quality, Lowest Cost, Shortest Lead Time." The two columns represent the two

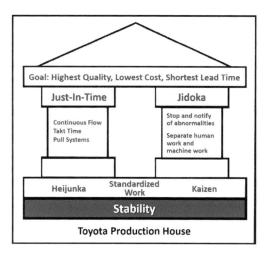

FIGURE 7.6:

The iconic TPS House shares clues but not the formula for how to use it to transform a company's operational approach.

INSET 7.1: TPS as LAUNDRY LIST

GOAL: HIGHEST QUALITY, LOWEST COST, SHORTEST LEAD TIME

    JUST-IN-TIME

    CONTINUOUS FLOW

    TAKT TIME

    PULL SYSTEM

    JIDOKA

    STOP AND NOTIFY OF ABNORMALITIES

    SEPARATE MAN'S WORK & MACHINE'S WORK

    HEIJUNKA

    STANDARDIZED WORK

    KAIZEN

    STABILITY

The elements of the TPS House are barely understandable without visual formatting and the logic of the house architecture. They become merely a list of words, without relationship, sequence, valence or synergy.

---

methodologies that operationalize that goal:

1. Just-in-Time, the capstone of pillar one, with its elements populating the column itself: Continuous flow, Takt time, and Pull System; and

2. Jidoka—pillar two's capstone and JIT's partner—with its two organizing practices (translated, I think, from the Japanese, by the Japanese): "Stop and notify of abnormalities" and "Separate man's work & machine's work."

Other allied tools are spread below—Heijunka, Standardized Work, and Kaizen—with a clear statement of outcome at the foundation: *stability*, because that is the result of the synergy of the elements above that blue band.

Visuality is part and parcel of the Toyota way. Like the House of TPS, a great deal is hidden in plain sight. Look at all those terms, populating the structure of the house. Remove the architecture and we are left with nothing more than a laundry list of words, without relationship, hierarchy, valence or synergy (Inset 7.1). Return the architecture and we instantly understand that the terms are interrelated elements. They work together as part of a system, a larger synergy inherent in the design. This is the architecture of Toyota's corporate intent on the operational level.

We look, we see, we understand. We understand this because of the way our brain functions. Do you remember our discussion in Chapter 5 of the mind and its compulsion to seek and find patterns, simply as part of its function? In that chapter, we saw brain function serving the goals of Doorway 1: the visual where and operator-led visuality. We see it working here in support of visual leadership, Doorway 4.

The principles and practices of visuality support the leadership function and can, if you use it, create an entirely new level of executive leaders—forward-moving, visionary, pragmatic, highly-effective, and successful. The TPS House is the company's corporate intent, made powerful because of the limits in that structure. As employees, including executives, cast their eyes upon these limits, they say: "Ahhh, I get it: That is who we are and that is what we are doing together. We are not doing *everything*. We are doing *this!*" In the best of all possible worlds—your world, their next words will be: "I get it. I want it. Let's go!"

Limitation by Design

Models of this kind are physical formulations of intent, demonstrating the power of sharing ideas as structure. That is why the visual leader needs them. They point the way to a future that is not yet here but is also not that far away. It is a future we will create together—using a template as the first part of that journey.

The big mistake, however, is to assume that having such a template automatically turns the individual components of your operational vision into a system. The TPS House, for example, simply shows you an array of operational elements in relationship to each other. It does not show you a way to achieve them. That template lacks a driving mechanism. It is therefore not dynamic. It is a snapshot of the future but without a pathway that shows us how to reach it, together. This is usual for material that Toyota releases to the general public—us. The TPS House shows us what but does not show us how—when "how" is mission-critical.

Few of the world's top-ranking companies ever share the telling detail of how. In the language of Sci-Fi, that's the secret blueprint of the DeathStar. Darth Vader knows the one thing we are looking for; and he is keeping it to himself. When we don't realize there is a secret, we don't ask to know it.

The "how" dimension of the TPS House is unseen. It is hidden away. Like the mainspring in an heirloom Swiss watch, it cannot be seen on the outside but it makes the TPS model work. That main spring operationalizes our laundry list of terms and turns it into speed, perfect quality, cultural growth, and profit margin.

When the VP sent you that high-gloss poster of the corporation's vision/mission/values house, she forgot to tell you how to turn that into a dynamic system of improvement. Instead, you tack the poster to the boardroom wall, and watch it turn yellow along the edges. You forgot to operationalize the house. You forgot to ask how.

Have you noticed what I notice about us westerners? We tend to buy the packaging and not worry about what the packaging contains. Pretty lights, said the little spotted deer. We forget to ask what's inside. We got seduced by a pretty poster that might have helped us if we had only asked it to. Oh no!

My effort, over the past decade and a half, to un-nest the secrets of the TPS

FIGURE 7.7:
THE OPERATIONS SYSTEM
IMPROVEMENT TEMPLATE (OSIT)

House has resulted in a new formulation that incorporates what is needed, in my view, to harness the power of that model. Because I believe that a company's production system must focus squarely on improvement, I incorporated that goal into its name: *Operations System Improvement Template* (OSIT). See Figure 7.7.

OSIT incorporates the power of visuality and adds elements that allow us to make the transition from *the what* to *the how*, as part of the same process. Knowing what you know now and relying on the visual format itself to teach, I believe you can learn a good deal simply by studying the visual architecture of the OSIT model.

The X-Type Matrix

The X-Type Matrix shares the core visual characteristics of the OSIT template. It has visible structure, and therefore limits; it shows relationship; it forces sequencing that drives thinking and connectivity. The structure of this architecture is powerful. The structure is its command (Figure 7.8).

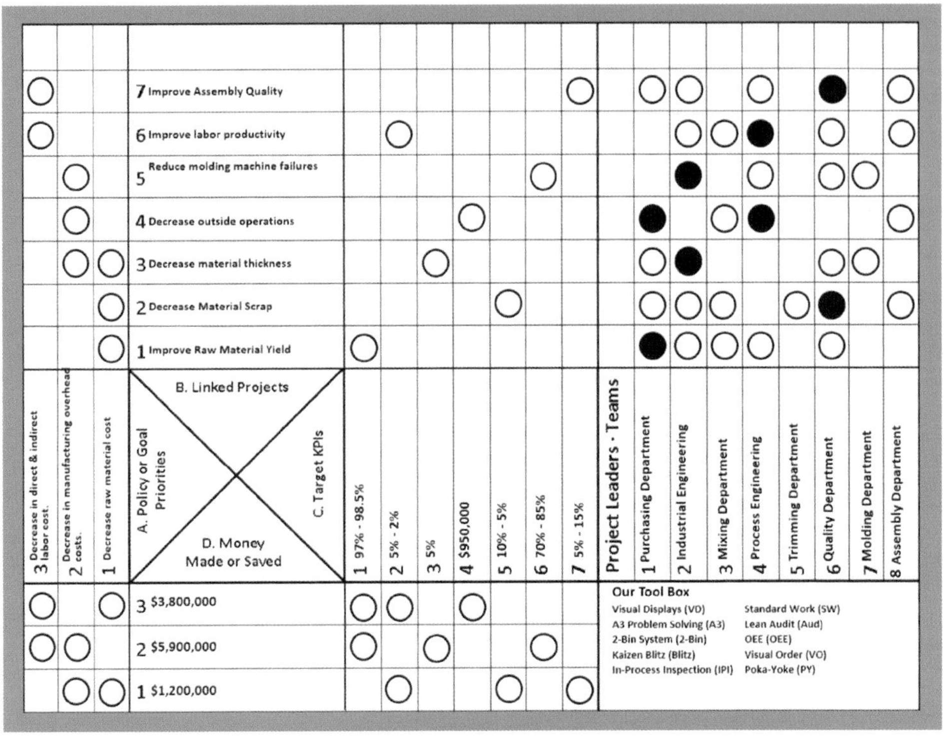
7 Improve Assembly Quality
6 Improve labor productivity
5 Reduce molding machine failures
4 Decrease outside operations
3 Decrease material thickness
2 Decrease Material Scrap
1 Improve Raw Material Yield
B. Linked Projects
A. Policy or Goal Priorities
C. Target KPIs
D. Money Made or Saved
3 Decrease in direct & indirect labor cost.
2 Decrease in manufacturing overhead costs.
1 Decrease raw material cost
1 97% - 98.5%
2 5% - 2%
3 5%
4 $950,000
5 10% - 5%
6 70% - 85%
7 5% - 15%
Project Leaders · Teams
1 Purchasing Department
2 Industrial Engineering
3 Mixing Department
4 Process Engineering
5 Trimming Department
6 Quality Department
7 Molding Department
8 Assembly Department
3 $3,800,000
2 $5,900,000
1 $1,200,000
Our Tool Box
Visual Displays (VD)
A3 Problem Solving (A3)
2-Bin System (2-Bin)
Kaizen Blitz (Blitz)
In-Process Inspection (IPI)
Standard Work (SW)
Lean Audit (Aud)
OEE (OEE)
Visual Order (VO)
Poka-Yoke (PY)

FIGURE 7.8:

The X-Type Matrix requires executives to obey the limits built into its visual format as the means for transforming why and how top-level decisions are made—and therefore how effectively the company can gain stability and grow into its strategic future.

Similar to the TPS House, the X-Type is a formulation that is often misunderstood and, therefore, underutilized. In my experience, this misunderstanding does not lead us to harm. It leads to us setting aside this formidable construct and, with it, its promise. Instead of learning how to use it, we blame the tool for the considerable time that has been wasted–that we have wasted—in trying to get it to cough up its secrets, the wrong way. We are right to be annoyed—not at the tool but at the way it was taught to us.

The X-Type is the immediate next step after OSIT. In fact, the X-Type is *how we operationalize* OSIT. This is its purpose: to translate and align your company's vision, mission, and strategy into an actionable, cross-functional plan that you can afford: your annual plan on a single page.

Look at its format, with a bold X on the middle left. Look at its lock-step grid that connects goals to action. Circle clockwise around the X, starting at the 9:00 o'clock mark. Move through the quadrants (A, B, C, D) and you pass through the key elements of your plan: goals, projects, targets, and money made or money saved.

See how each goal (A) gets linked to a specific project (B)—or several projects. Look how those projects then associate with specific improvement targets (C). Then notice the "Project Leaders + Teams" section to the far, middle right. See how each project connects to a KPI—and to the people and functions that will be held accountable for successful X-Type outcomes.

The X-Type Matrix is the supreme vehicle for aligning and driving the enterprise to its improvement future.

Look closer still and you will realize that the Matrix is mighty in reverse—for what it prevents. Hard as you may try, you cannot fit into it every favorite thing you, as executive, dream about accomplishing in the next 12 months. It will not allow you to get greedy. Even if you decide to make the font smaller and expand the format size, you will still not be able to fit *everything*. The very boundedness of the format enforces discipline, the discipline of market leaders.

Once a goal enters the X-architecture, it must connect with the projects, targeted measures, outcomes, and resources required to achieve it. Not just one of these, or three—but *all* of them. The limits are built in—and they inform, instruct, and require. They do not give up and allow. They do not concede. You have to fit into the matrix and not the other way around.

The X-Type doesn't give an inch. You learn or the tool stops helping you. You set it aside, blaming the tool—when, in fact, the tool went into a HOLD state until you learn the lesson it was designed to teach: You will fail as a leader if you do not curb your appetite and cultivate lean-ness. Oh wonderful.

More than any other of the several formats in the visual leadership array, the X-type Matrix teaches executives their most important function: how to say *yes* to the few and *wait* to the many.

As you learn the discipline and requirements of the X-Type—and as it guides you to greater skill in deciding and driving, you will become adept at making it speak to you, visually, on a finer level of detail and nuance. In the era of BFFs—best friends forever—the X-Type will become yours.

Visual Leadership: Leaders of Improvement

The visual principles, tools, practices, and concepts of Doorway 4 are aimed at helping executives become better, more effective, leaders of the corporate intent.

With the symmetry that governs the new leadership, executives take on a new identity. Mere executives no more, they become leaders of improvement. Transformation becomes their major focus. And as they transform the process, they are transformed in the process. They have learned a new way of growing themselves and the company, the distinctive feature of which is: They do it.

CHAPTER | **8**

Visual Controls, Visual Pull Systems, and Visual Guarantees

In this chapter, we address the all-powerful control and guarantee functions of the implementation pathway—and doors 5 and 6 in the Ten-Doorway Model: visual controls/visual pull systems and visual guarantees (poka-yoke systems).

Before we do, let me clarify the distinction between the pathway and the doors, the two organizing frameworks that have guided us thus far through the third section of this book. The pathway (Figure 8.1) stacks the methods of visuality in a bottom-up progression, from the grossest level (visual order) to the most refined (visual guarantees). The sequence is conceptual,

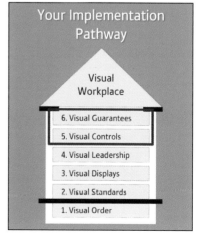

FIGURE 8.1: LEVELS 5 & 6

not prescriptive. While the vast majority of companies begin with Level 1.0/Visual Order because they need to strengthen their value-add function, the pathway does not require you to march through the six visual methodologies, ladder-like, from the bottom up, as you implement.

If, for example, a company has 5S viably in place and is hemorrhaging from product and process defects, it can take the elevator to the sixth floor, so to speak, and immediately implement visual guarantees (aka, poka-yoke systems). Another company might begin on Level 4, with visual metrics or visual problem-solving.

Your company enters the pathway at a level that is right for it, knowing that your visual journey will not be over with that single success. And that's the point. The pathway describes the array of visual functions needed for you to cultivate and then master your company's informational landscape so that the enterprise becomes sturdy, stable, and poised for growth.

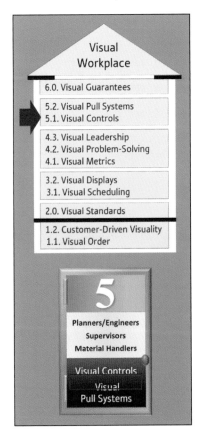

FIGURE 8.2: DOORWAY 5
VISUAL CONTROLS

The doorway model is similar to the stacked pathway, but with this important difference: Each doorway is category of visual function that is linked to a specific organizational group. That group, in turn, is responsible for putting in place the respective visual competency. Associates implement visual order; engineers and supervisors deploy visual standards; and so on.

Each group has its own visual mandate. Once implemented, a new visual practice becomes instrumental in helping that group achieve and stabilize its operational outcomes. The agents of each doorway are its champions as well as its benefactors.

Visual Controls
(Level 5.1—Doorway 5)

The purpose of *Visual Controls* is to install information deeply into the landscape of work so that people can and must do the right thing (Figure 8.2). The name I use for this is: *embedded-ness*, information that is structured into the physical work environment—planted in place as a device.

Devices on the control level don't *tell* us anything. Nor do they attempt to clarify, motivate or influence. They simply *make* us do the right thing, with increasing surety—or prevent us from doing the wrong thing. Either way, they embed adherence into the process of work itself; and therein lies their extreme usefulness.

The same control principle seen in visual control devices will later govern visual pull systems. The only category of visual function more powerful is a visual guarantee which, at its most refined, eliminates the possibility of choice entirely.

PHOTO 8.1:
QUANTITY AT-A-GLANCE

Low-cost/high-impact visual controls are widely used in operations, for example, to devise and control material delivery and consumption. This makes close allies of your technical staff, value-add associates, and material handlers. These applications are not just for factories. Materials are used in every work setting, including hospitals and offices where visual controls are key to addressing and regulating material cost and material flow. Visual controls are operational work horses.

Visual Controls in Action

The control side of a visual control is achieved through physical structure—the physical sizing of the material's footprint, captured, for example, in a bin size or visible floor footprints. In all cases, the control principle establishes limits that regulate size, number, volume, range, and other quantifiable values. In doing so, this type of device visually answers the quantity-based core questions of how many, how much, when, and how long?

Photo 8.1 is a repeat of a visual control you saw in Chapter 2 that uses borders to embed quantity. This is the power of limits. Exact information is shared visually through structure. No words are needed to guide, limit, and control behavior—an outcome for which this category of visual function is deservedly famous.

The structure explicit in a visual control constantly provides the exact information people need to continue adding value, whatever that value may be. Brain function and the mind's hunger for pattern identification are again fast allies. Increasingly, visual controls out-distance the grosser forms of visual information found in borders,

 **Photo Album 17**

Visually Controlling Answers

A Window on Seton's Total Visual Conversion

Seton is a direct-mail house, specializing in workplace identification products. Recognizing the alignment between its products and the visual paradigm, Seton asked VTI for help in implementing a visual workplace. The results were spectacular by any measure, fueled by highly-creative employees on the value-add level and supportive, aligned managers.

CARLOS DELEON

ERIC JOHNSON

◀ **Eric Johnson** and **Carlos DeLeon** in the Screen Department had to prepare enough silk screens during the day to keep the night shift supplied—anywhere from 46-52 screens. They spent a lot of time counting screens (motion) during the day. But first they had to find them. To do that, they implemented the *visual where.* ➔

THE VISUAL WHERE

◀ Though borders and addresses helped, they did not end all motion. Many times a shift, Carlos and Eric were bent over counting how many screens were ready; then they had to calculate how many more were needed. Too much motion! So they invented the visual control device to the left. That answered both questions—where and how many—in a single solution. Splendid!

Take note: The term *visual controls* is not the same thing as *visual devices*. A visual control is the type of visual device that structures in human and machine behavior.

addresses, and ID labels. The visual where may form the foundation of workplace visuality—but it is visual controls that drive precision into performance.

Because the margin of personal choice becomes so narrow, visual controls require little or no interpretation. The device itself is the message. Here the link between visuality and the adage we quoted in Chapter 1 becomes inextricably linked: visuality, and more precisely visual controls, are key to helping people *do ordinary things extraordinarily well.*

PHOTO 8.2: VISUAL SAFETY CONTROL

Associates at Seton Identification Products, a catalogue company in Connecticut, implemented visual control solutions broadly in its fabrication and distribution areas. Photo 8.2 is a visual safety control that sends a clear message: Stack bales of recycled cardboard up to the six-foot mark (emblazoned on the wall) and no further. Area associates already know that stacking above that control line is risky; this control sends a loud reminder. See Photo Album 17 for another inventive Seton visual control.

Inventing visual controls is not as intuitive a process as devising elementary forms of visuality. Training is needed so people understand what controls are, how they work, and how to amp their power. This applies equally to then design-to-task applications and visual pull systems coming up next.

Visual control mechanisms are remarkably effective. Please learn to do them right so they can build and multiply. If you see members of your workforce arrive at these high-level solutions "on their own," don't be fooled. They are the result of visual thinking—diligently minimizing motion by identifying the information deficits that trigger that motion, on ever more subtle levels.

PHOTO 8.3: DESIGN-TO-TASK TOOLS
Value-add associates at Parker Hannifin Aerospace (Irvine, CA) had organized their tools on shadow boards. Then they learned about design-to-task and adopted the blue-foam cutout system you see here. Positioned ergonomically, each box system is dedicated to a different assembly task. Plus the yellow lining under the foam makes it easy to spot missing items, at-a-glance.

Visually Controlling Tasks

Design-to-task is a crucial component of excellence in every work setting with repeated tasks, and a powerful form of visual control. Look for ways to apply this core principle to every work setting, especially assembly.

This cart is dedicated to quick changeovers in LM-Aero's Tube Shop. The top is covered in thick, stiff foam, cut out for a design-to-task array of tools and fixtures for area machines. (Lockheed-Martin, Ft. Worth, Texas) ▶

To the right is another design-to-task delivery system at LM-Aero. It regulates and protects expensive parts as well the highly-specialized tools needed to assemble them. This approach is now a Visual Best Practice across all LM-Aero sites. ▶

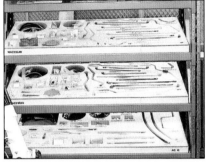

◀ Machinists at Rolls-Royce Aerospace applied exactly the same design-to-task principles to tool drawers. Visuality works like a charm! (Rolls-Royce, Oberursel, Germany)

🔺 Design-to-task is a critical visual principle at this hospital pharmacy in the Midwest where technicians prepare design-to-task kits for specific emergency conditions.

Strengthening Controls through Design-to-Task

Devices on the control level are amplified by combining them with other visual workplace principles. *Design-to-task* is one of the most splendid.

Design-to-task means physically co-locating many different items needed for a given task or operation. Tools are often the focal point (Photo 8.3).

Simply gather the tools needed for a particular operation in a specific location or container—a drawer, shelf, cart, cabinet or the like. Boldly designate a home for each item. Put the items in their homes and—presto-chango!—you can tell at-a-glance if everything you need to start and complete a task is in place, even if the task will take hours or days. Try to insert an extra item that does not belong and it simply won't fit. That's the whole idea: to design the space (smart placement) and everything in it around a given task—design-to-task.

The principle of design-to-task can be applied to every work environment with repetitive work, most especially where pre-set protocols govern the delivery of value, such as in assembly, overhaul depots, and hospitals. (See Photo Album 18 for other excellent design-to-task solutions.)

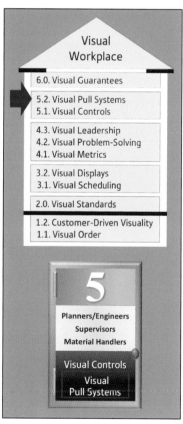

Visual Pull Systems
(Level 5.2—Doorway 5)

Let me repeat: Visual controls use structure (size, volume, and number) to share information. The result? We can perform our work more safely and with greater precision, with little or no additional thought. These devices become even more powerful when linked with visual controls in associated operations—for example, in material storage and handling, replenishment, and scheduling.

When linked, they trigger a chain of responses and produce, for example, a person/process/machine interface (demand-pull) that creates economies in all these operational functions. I call such a set of controls a *Visual Pull System* (Figure 8.3).

FIGURE 8.3:
VISUAL PULL SYSTEMS

Kanban & Heijunka

An Assortment of Visual Pull Systems

This album includes classic and innovative kanban approaches, plus an extensive heijunka system.

⬆ Material handlers keep an eye on this 4-slot kanban square and replenish before the last slot is voided—empty.

High-volume production at Wiremold (CT) is kept on track through an extensive system of heijunka boxes. ⬇

⬆ About one in 12 men has some degree of color blindness (less in women). Because of that operators at Freudenberg-NOK (Cleveland, GA) invented a pull system, using animal fronts and backs (instead of color) to match material with the correct machines. The simpler you make a visual, the better. This one is modeled on the "Garanimal" concept of kids matching, for example, the alligator shirt with alligator pants.

◀ Here is a close-up of some of the 350 individual heijunkas in the above macro-array, the one and only master schedule for this site— and the refined culmination of its pursuit of operational excellence.

⬆ Each Wiremold cell has its own heijunka, easing the way to smooth out work order fluctuations. Where does the journey to heijunka begin? A robust and complete deployment of the visual where.

Min-Max Levels

At its most elementary, visible min/max (mini-mum-maximum) levels represent the simplest of visual pull systems. Storage units marked to indicate the most amount of material allowed—as well as the restock level—make it easy for us to tell at-a-glance when material is in full supply or running out, whether raw material, parts, medicine or paper clips (Photo 8.4).

PHOTO 8.4:
MIN/MAX CONTROLS

The low-level mark triggers material handlers to replenish the supply. The visual vacuum between full level and the trigger point pulls more into place; hence the term *visual pull system*. Visuality is used to design a vacuum into the process (that red line), positioning the vacuum to suck in replenishment purely because a void occurred. Void re-occurrence and avoidance is the principle behind the pull system known as *kanban*.

Kanban

Seen most frequently in highly-repetitive operations, kanban is a more sophisticated form of visual pull. Yet, the concept of visual min/max levels applies here as well—only this time as the control element links with the demands of the critical path (the "value stream" in the language of lean). Working together, visual information sharing and lean tools create the framework for an accelerated flow that can be controlled at will—that is, at the drumbeat, pleasure, and pull of the customer (*takt*). This is a lofty visual goal and an attainable one, no matter the industry.

The term *kanban* refers to the physical card (or ticket) that visually signals the need for replenishment, delivery, removal of material, WIP or finished goods in an operation. Since these operations are always downstream, the pull dynamic is achieved—the dynamic of the void. Bins can often replace cards, as in well-known two-bin systems, and can be equally effective.

Generally speaking, kanban and other demand-leveling techniques are most extensively used in the early and middle stages of a company's lean journey as a way to formulate, manage, and control the volume of production. Yet, because of its visual efficacy, these devices rarely disappear entirely as an operational link, even when speed increases dramatically and the distance between operations shrinks. Kanban evolves with it.

Photo Album 20

Traffic-Light Pull

Visual Material Handling

The pull system in this airbag factory in Mexico demonstrates the power of keeping things simple by keeping them visual—made even more impressive because of the site's 1,500-person size workforce.

Red/yellow/green stripes appear on work stations and machines across the site's many value streams—even on the stacks of bobbins at individual sewing machines. One size fits all! This traffic-light pull system is the single way material is controlled at this factory—delivered, consumed, and replenished.

◆ Each of the more than dozen component bins seen here benefits from the same simple traffic-light pull system of replenishment.

◆ Even the bobbins are on traffic-light pull. *Painstakingly simple* means *painstakingly implemented.*

◀ Even the spools at the top of the stream have redundant visual pull devices.

In mixed-model environments, demand-flow devices often give way to high-speed *heijunka* systems, which schedule demand and smooth out or manage order fluctuations linked to variety, batch size, timing, and sequence.

Heijunka (Japanese for "make flat and level") is a specific mechanism that segments the total volume of orders into scheduling intervals. Visually speaking, heijunka is a box that physically separates these intervals into time slots that will hold actual work orders (kanbans) in sequence. Actual product labels (printed in advance) can produce a kanban shortcut. Please think about this.

For the limited purposes of this overview, understand that min/max levels, kanban, and heijunka are all visual pull systems. As such, they are vital components of workplace visuality and the critical physical links that denote a visual-lean® work environment. (See Photo Album 19 for more.)

Traffic-Light Pull

Kanban and heijunka are not the only formats for a visual pull system available to a company. Traffic-light color coding is another effective visual method to signal and control the pull of material delivery and consumption. This is an approach that is so simple, its effectiveness never fails to surprise and delight.

We go to Matamoras, Mexico to contemplate the best system I have seen to date—found in an airbag factory, dominated by cutting and sewing operations.

In the center of Photo 8.5 is a flat piece of wood, painted in a stack of red/yellow/green bands. It is part of this company's material delivery system and found at the first operation where large wheels of cloth are cut into smaller sections for patterning into airbags.

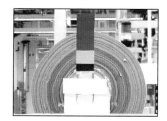

PHOTO 8.5:
TRAFFIC-LIGHT
PULL DEVICE

How does this visual device work? Consider the stacked colors for a moment and it will come clear. Yes, that's right: When the material handlers see that the roll material is getting close to the yellow mark, they know delivery of a new roll is needed soon. Indeed, it must be delivered before the fabric level hits the red. If not, the machine will run out and shut down. This stoppage will then make its way downstream, domino-style, affecting all stations in this tightly run pull-based facility.

This elegant visual pull system is made even more impressive when we learn that its core 3-color mechanism is the *only* one used for material delivery throughout the entire plant. That's right: a single device, repeated locally, governs material handling in each and every operation throughout this 1,500-person plant—with the *width of each band* as the controlling attribute. See Photo Album 20 for more on this splendid visual control system.

Pop Quiz. You may not have been a visual thinker when you first opened this book, but you are fast becoming one by now. So here's a question for you: Is the device you see in Photo 8.5 at the early stages of its adoption—or is it mature? That is, was it installed a few weeks ago for the first time—or has it already gone through many iterations. What do you think the right answer is—and why do you think it? (You'll find my response at the end of this chapter.)

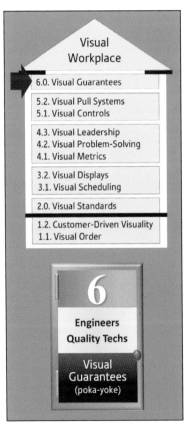

FIGURE 8.4: LEVEL 6
VISUAL GUARANTEES

Visual Guarantees
(Level 6—Doorway 6)

In workplace visuality, the most refined form of information-sharing is captured in *Visual Guarantees* (Figure 8.4). Also known as poka-yoke, mistake-proof, and fail-safe devices, visual guarantees are highly effective in accomplishing the goal of all workplace visuality: reliably and repeatedly helping us do the right thing—or avoid doing the wrong thing—in every workplace situation. In short: perfect performance.

As with all aspects of the visual workplace, visual guarantees are a part of the universal language for your operations. They work with supreme power and effectiveness in any work set-ting—from assembly to machining, from discrete to continuous settings, from hospitals and offices, and across all industries, in every work venue.

Guarantees fall into distinct categories or types, depending on the degree to which each device is able to ensure—guarantee—a perfor-mance outcome. A closer look shows that, as with all visual devices, guarantees are visual answers,

PHOTO 8.6:
GAS PUMP, CIRCA 1900

PHOTO 8.7:
A MODERN GAS PUMP

The modern gas pump began as a hose in a bucket on a pole, high enough for gravity to fill the gas tank. When cylinders replaced buckets (Photo 8.6), quantity levels etched in the glass were the first visual device. Technology marched forward, along with customer choice, maximized in today's gas pump (Photo 8.7) and supported by dozens visual devices, including visual guarantees.

only on an extremely refined level—on the level of *attribute*.

A visual guarantee translates or embeds minute operational detail into the process of work itself. Actual devices range from highly-imaginative mechanical apparatus to sensors and limit switches—all of them are ingenious and highly functional.

Think of the gas pumps at your local service station. The pump is covered with an array of visual information-sharing devices, showing the type of gas, price, octane, credit cards accepted, and where to insert it. On the level of specific action—that is, when we lift the pump from its seat and begin process of filling—those information details disappear and their meaning becomes one with the performance of function. We fill the tank. (See Photos 8.6 and 8.7.)

Further, it used to be that gas would pour over the asphalt if you put the nozzle back incorrectly. Today, the design of the nozzle makes it structurally impossible to re-seat the nozzle incorrectly. Short of not replacing it at all, there is only one way it fits in place—and that is the right way. Whether you have been driving for thirty years and are used to pumping your own gas, or just got your driver's license and are at the pump for the first time, you will put the gas handle back properly. You have no choice; and neither do I. It's visually guaranteed.

The more effective a visual guarantee, the more deeply the information (the

Photo Album 21

Visual Guarantees

Visual Guarantee Masterpiece of Luis Catatao

Visual guarantees are point-of-use solutions that impact the stream of value, directly. The one featured below completely eliminated the possibility of an error that had lead to many defects, across many operators.

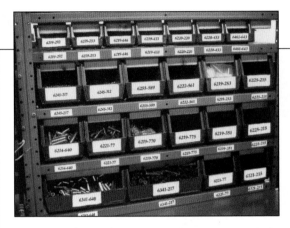

◀ The 28 bins in this rack at United Electric Controls (Watertown, MA) hold small parts for seven different switch-and-control assemblies. Because many of those small parts looked similar, operators made assembly mistakes that were only discovered in final test.

Value-add associate, Luis Catatao, was determined to find a way to put an end to those mistakes. ▶

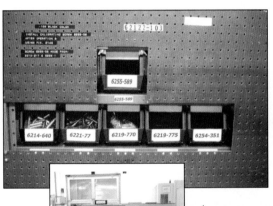

◀ Luis's solution was dazzling: a set of seven masking templates, one for each of the seven models. Each template had cut-outs for the bins with parts for a given model, *only*—making it impossible for an operator to access the wrong part.

◀ Mix-ups related to machine inserts were not uncommon at Rolls-Royce Aerospace (Oberursel, Germany). When machine associates saw Luis's invention, they knew they had a solution. They made templates for the five sets of inserts needed for their five models. Here you see a black template for one model, and a blue one in the foreground for another. (Visual inventiveness relies on us seeing lots of visual solutions from many industries.)

message) is embedded into the item or process itself—so close to the point-of-use that the guarantee and the process or item are one.

That is exactly the point of visual guarantees. They remove choice so that we can only do the right thing. Doing the wrong thing is simply not an option. In a manner of speaking, a visual guarantee sets aside the human will and replaces it with one that is mechanical or electronic—and precisely aligned with the corporate intent. (See Photo Album 21.)

Doorway 6 Owner

Your company's quality function owns the doorway to visual guarantees, often working in concert with design and process engineers—and always with value-add associates. In fact, 60%-70% of the actual solutions developed in Doorway 6 result from the close collaboration between your associates and your quality techs and engineers. Working together, they hunt down motion and the information deficits that trigger that motion and develop effective mistake-proof devices. Sound familiar? Yes, visual thinking is part and parcel of your quality assurance plan.

The systematic implementation of visual guarantees typically happens late in the visual rollout, after the cultural foundation is firmly in place and most of the doorways have been opened, to a greater or lesser extent. Once again, a robust deployment of the visual where sets the stage for more advanced visual functions. This is primarily because an effective implementation of borders and addresses minimize grosser forms of motion (and their associated information deficits)—or eliminates them entirely and clears the way for finer visual thinking.

If your company is hemorrhaging from quality problems, however, do not wait to implement visual guarantees until that visual/cultural foundation is in place. Hop the elevator to the top of the pathway and attack your quality problems with the fierceness that threats to your survival warrant.

In the absence of threatening conditions, however, this phase of the visual rollout begins with quality personnel getting trained in visual guarantees so that they can then train others. Intense learning, accompanied by plenty of trial and error, marks the first few application cycles. As skill levels build, so does the visual imagination. It is then only a matter of time before a core group becomes proficient in the method.

In most companies, the quality assurance department is eager to lead visual guarantee activity and to work with the very people (line employees) who, up to now, have worried about (or dreaded) QA's arrival in their area, like more bad news in a plague year. Instead, QA is welcomed as the hero it has become in elevating the process through visual thinking and the people who use it.

As in all robust implementations, creating visual guarantees is an iterative process with applications everywhere—in production, maintenance, material handling, supplier development, engineering, finance, and marketing, you name it. The result? Defects are minimized, or entirely eliminated, to an extent previously unimaginable; and in the process, the workforce becomes masters of cause on the attribute level.

This is what Dr. Shigeo Shingo meant when he wrote his book, *Zero Quality Control: Source Inspection and the Poka-Yoke Systems* and declared the cultivation of *poka-yoke* systems as the goal of all quality. Eliminate the quality function entirely by building quality—perfection—into the process of work.

Every enterprise that pursues sustainability resolves, at some stage, to imple-

---

Inset 8.1: Answer to the question about Photo 8.5

The device in Photo 8.5 is mature. It didn't look like this when it was first installed—it couldn't. The thickness of the color bands tells the story: wide green, narrow yellow, and almost non-existent red. Whoever relies on this device to pull the timely delivery of the next roll of fabric gained confidence, over time, that the approach *would* work because it *had* worked.

When the device was first implemented, it looked more like the photo on the right, with its wide band of red providing the forklift driver with plenty of warning (and time) to act. As a result, materials handlers were successful and operators learned to trust the approach.

Visuality allows us to "see" the needs of the user. At the outset, no operator or material handler could have trusted the tight demands of that narrow red band. Would you?

Visual principles connect operations with work culture and improve both.

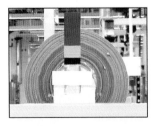

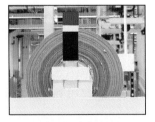

A MATURE APPLICATION   AT THE BEGINNING

ment visual guarantees as part of its strategic commitment to excellence. The return on this investment can be enormous, and the time to start is now.

• • • •

Visual guarantees are the culmination of the stacked pathway because poka-yoke devices address the *most* refined level of information-sharing: attributes. By the same token, visual guarantees is the final of the six methods central to the visual conversion of the enterprise, represented in the Ten-Doorway Model.

To this point, we focused on their applications in generalized operations: the factory, the hospital, the workplace. In Chapter 9, we extend the doorways to two specialized settings where the same array of six methods are applied, first, to the machine (Doorway 7) and, then, to offices. This chapter also describes two macro functions in workplace visuality: one for creating visual linkages between departments (Doorway 9); and the other for developing a visual performance language across multiple sites, a comprehensive language of visual best practices (Doorway 10).

Before we move to our next chapter, please remember that the methods in the Implementation Pathway or Ten-Doorway Model are not implemented in lock-step order. In fact, it would be a mistake to do so. Though both frameworks represent an orderly, theoretical logic, this logic is not a prescription.

The correct order is to: Assess first; decide; and then implement. Determine the sequence of visual conversion based on your business case: your company's targeted need for stability and growth—because that is what the technologies of the visual workplace produce. Once your assessment is clear, you are bound to pick the doorway or doorways most relevant for you. (You will find a great deal more on this in Chapter 11.)

The real problem is not whether machines think—but whether men do.

B. F. Skinner

CHAPTER | **9**

Visual Machine®, Visual-Lean® Office & the Macro Visual Environment

The previous four chapters provided the basics of the first six doorways and, similarly, of the six levels in the stacked Implementation Pathway. These six represent the core methodologies in achieving a fully-functioning visual workplace (Figure 9.1).

In the first part of this chapter, we apply those six visual methods to the machine as we make it visually-capable—then do the same for office settings. Then we consider the macro-visual environment and the final two doorways of the Ten-Doorway Model (Figure 9.2). It is worth repeating that the stacked pathway does not continue past Level 6 (visual guarantees) because that template concerns itself with visual methods and not who owns them. So the doorways take over.

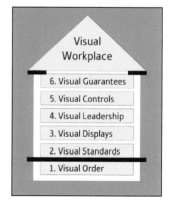

FIGURE 9.1: PATHWAY

Doorway 7: The Visual Machine®

Even though machines represent a company's most expensive asset, they are often taken for granted. The logic (or lack thereof) goes something like this: "Machines work—and when they don't work, call Maintenance. It can't be helped. Machines break down. And that's all there is to it."

Similar notions apply to the time it takes to changeover and setup equipment for a new production run. Yet, there is a great deal a company can do—everyone can do—to improve machine effectiveness, changeover times, and equipment availability. The visual improvement technology known as *The Visual Machine®* is a major component of this. The visual machine lets equipment speak.

In creating a visual machine, you apply the full array of methods discussed in the previous chapters of this section: all of the first six doorways, the entire stacked pathway (Figure 9.3). The exact starting point may vary. For example, if you are faced with long changeovers—and to many, any changeover longer than ten minutes is considered excessive, regardless of machine type—make that the focus for making your equipment visual. (See Inset 9.1)

Machinery and visuality are a perfect fit. You can only shrink changeover times by implementing most, if not all, of the six core methods. Begin with visual order on and around the machine and for all the fixtures, tools, and material locations that support your machine utilization. Work your way from there.

In our experience, there is no end to the benefit you can create by applying

FIGURE 9.2: FINAL FOUR DOORWAYS

The Implementation Pathway to a visual workplace concludes with Level 6/visual guarantees. The Doorways, however, continue through four more categories.

The next two doorways are linked to specific workplace settings: Doorway 7 to the Visual Machine® and Doorway 8 to the Visual-Lean® Office. Then we move onto the macro-visual environment.

Because this book is designed to provide concepts and awareness, I overview these four remaining doorways rather than explain the exact details for putting them in place.

visual principles to the machine environment. Positive outcomes abound. Where machine assets dominate, we suggest that companies begin and anchor their enterprise-wide visual conversion exactly there.

FIGURE 9.3: DOORWAY 7
THE VISUAL MACHINE®

Doorway 7 Owner

Maintenance owns Doorway 7. Much as we discussed with quality assurance and visual guarantees, Maintenance can (and I think *should*) take on a leadership role in the drive to make the machine *speak*.

Certainly, there are many exceptions. Yet, in far too many organizations, maintenance technicians are burdened with the knowledge that if they don't keep the machines going, the company will fail—and that they, along with many other people, could lose their jobs. They often also believe that the rest of the workforce represents the weakest link in a machine's overall effectiveness.

They know what you know: for example, that 60%-70% of all machine breakdowns are caused by mistakes in lubrication—primarily due to information deficits and, therefore, human error.

In the best of conditions, Maintenance has a daunting workload. In the worst, that workload can be demoralizing. When machine conditions are bad, everyone seems to be against the maintenance crew. At the same time, the maintenance staff may find they have to fight for everything—parts, tools, resources, time, you name it; and fight with everyone, sometimes even with operators who, to them, often seem more skilled at causing breakdowns than preventing them. Faced with this, it is not hard to see why the maintenance crew sometimes has a reputation for being grumpy.

Imagine their jubilation when management commits to implementing the visual machine. In this simple, powerful approach, information vital to running, maintaining, changing over, and repairing equipment is visually installed directly in, on, and around the machinery itself. Through dozens of low-cost/high-impact visual devices and mini-systems, maintenance and operators alike can do what

---

INSET 9.1: THE VISUAL MACHINE MEETS QCO AND TPM

Since the mid-1980s, thousands of companies around the world have found the flexibility and machine utilization they need to stay competitive by implementing Total Productive Maintenance (TPM) and Quick Changeover (QCO) methods.

The Visual Machine® uses visuality as the doorway to many of the same outstanding performance outcomes—with the added benefit that operators can get quickly and strongly involved from the very early stages.

Have you already launched TPM and QCO? I hope so. Then use the principles and tools of the visual machine as a powerful complement to them.

In one company, setup took at least four hours on a 1,000-ton stamping press. Sixty days later, after the team applied QCO and the Visual Machine, the same setup took 1.5 hours. Six months after that, it was done in three minutes. That's not a typo! It does say "three minutes!"

In another company (with 5,000 screw machines), the best changeover anyone could achieve was an hour—and then on only 1,250 of those machines (25%). The rest took much more time. Two years later, the best changeovers took 100 seconds or less—and on a startling 62% of the machines (3,100). And those are not typos either!

Astonishing? Yes. Unusual? Not anymore. Changeovers happen fast these days—at 80% to 90% of what they once were, thanks in great part to making the machine and all that supports it *visual*.

---

needs to be done in support of maximum machine availability—quickly, safely, and accurately. See Photo Album 22.

Here is a short list of basic visual devices that let the machine speak:

- Match-marks that help everyone and anyone see at-a-glance if bolts and slides are over-tightened or loosening.

- Color-coded lubrication tags, lube diagrams, and lube cart so the right lubricant is used in the right quantity and at the right location.

- See-through red/yellow/green faces on temperature, speed, and pressure gauges so we can see at-a-glance if the machine is running normally or abnormally.

- Visual safety indicators and procedures on the machine at the exact point of use to reduce or even eliminate the possibility of risk.

- Visually ordered/color-coded material and tooling placement to make it easy for everyone and anyone to locate the correct WIP and dies for machine changeover.

The Visual Machine®

An implementation of the visual machine casts a wide net that can visually transform fixture and tooling protocols, lubrication and changeover practices, the maintenance function, and, of course, the machine itself.

◆ Belts and pulleys are now in visual order on an unused upper wall.

◆ This machine is up and running, with two changeovers in queue.

◀ The visual machine tells us what's normal—and therefore what's not.

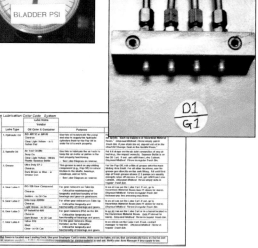

◆ Quick changeover carts are visual carts.

◆ Color-coded lubrication charts and lube discs minimize costly mistakes.

Visual devices and mini-systems make machinery self-explaining so we can be self-regulating. They build common sense and a common improvement language directly into the physical work environment. The visual machine doesn't just help us do the right thing repeatedly, reliably and fast, it helps us prevent problems.

In a world without visual devices and visual mini-systems, operators and maintainers alike are forced to rely on memory or costly trial-and-error to fill in for information deficits. The result? Long changeovers, long repair lead times, lost production, unhappy customers, and a demoralized workforce. Machine-based visual solutions put an end to all of that and refocus us on better questions, such as: What is the highest level of equipment effectiveness and availability we can achieve?

Doorway 8: The Visual-Lean® Office

The excellence revolution had been around for more than a decade before companies began to realize that the same principles and practices that made operations faster, safer, better, and more profitable were applicable to other settings. BINGO! Non-operational functions became targets for conversion. From there it was an easy step to seek operational excellence in offices everywhere—and in hospitals, banks, retail stores, airports, at-home services, schools and colleges, and government agencies.

The knowledge content of workplace visuality is so universally relevant, it pertains to all work venues. Wherever work is undertaken, visual principles and practices will make as dramatic a positive impact as they do in factories.

At VTI, the method we use for improving these settings is the *Visual-Lean*® *Office*. Similar to visual machine applications, office conversions encompass the full scope of visual workplace technologies and outcomes (Figure 9.4).

A Word about Office Implementations

While the knowledge base for achieving a visual office is identical to that in operations, the know-how base is considerably different. That is, the *what* is the same, but the *how* is very different. Said another way, the most powerful variable in converting an office to visuality is the work culture. Here are the reasons:

1. **People are accustomed to groups.** People in offices are used to getting their work done in a group context, not in isolation from others. Working in groups, if not in

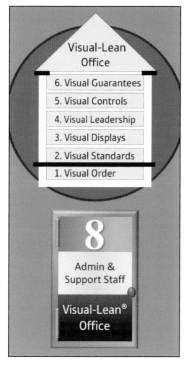

FIGURE 9.4: DOORWAY 8
VISUAL-LEAN® OFFICE

teams, is the norm in office settings. This is not to say that the groups always work well, but there is a built-in awareness that office outputs are owned by the department, not individuals.

For example, unlike a production cell, it is difficult for Accounting to separate a financial report into its discrete components, the way one can with a sub-assembly. Even though many people may contribute to the report's sections, the boundaries between those sections quickly blur and ownership becomes a joint event.

2. **People own their work.** People in offices feel a greater sense of ownership over their jobs. They understand how pieces fit and recognize what they contribute to the whole much more readily than production personnel do. By the same token, because individuals identify more closely with their work outputs, they often feel greater pride in their quality outputs and greater distress if their work is not up to standard.

It has occurred to me more than once that the scope and focus of those who work in offices are more closely aligned to those of a good manager, often understanding the big picture and the purpose of their work, with great insight and appreciation.

3. **People are more self-supervising.** People in offices are used to more self-regulation. While they may require or even seek supervision on tasks, they rarely need or seek help on skill. The educational sequence that landed one person an office job is, more often than not, similar (if not identical) to that of an office peer.

For the most part, office personnel know what their job is and how to do it. Being micromanaged is a frequent complaint; people prefer instead an approach that "tells me what to do—not how to do it."

4. **People protect their territory.** Who hasn't heard offices called "small king-doms?" That's usually said with some venom, but to me it makes sense. "Don't

Photo Album 23

The Visual-Lean® Office

Visual Inventiveness in the Office

Office visuality is vital to a company's pursuit of excellence, with office personnel eager and able to make so many inventive visual contributions.

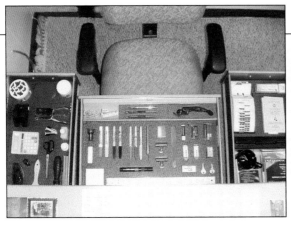

➤ The executive who sits at this desk walks the talk.

➤ Full-disclosure in this excellent customer-driven home address helps everyone.

➤ Not just a forms holder—but one that speaks.

➤ No question about when the next pony express arrives.

Office Visuality

The visual component of the Visual-Lean® Office deploys a full range of visual technologies as seen in the offices of this Sears Product Repair Center (Sacramento, CA).

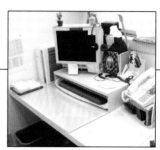

▲ Customer-service value field: before and after.

▲ Every drawer has a table of contents.

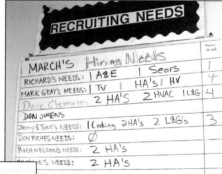

▲ Why keep hidden the information that so many need to know?

HR took a ton of motion out of weekly orientation activity with this visually-ordered supply cabinet. ▶

▲ This is the red-tag "corner."

touch my desk" is a constant reminder in our offices at VTI. I have a huge sense of ownership over my piles; and I respect that need in others.

The fact is people in offices tend to be more protective of their work domains than production personnel. They do not like anyone messing with their value fields, their desks. It might as well be their purse or briefcase that is invaded. As things would have it, the habit of sharing one's desk with another is not generally practiced in the office community (not yet anyway). By comparison, workbenches are commonly shared, but they are rarely "owned."

In consideration of these, VTI starts to implement workplace visuality in offices in a manner that is substantially different from the way we launch on the shop floor. Although the telling details are beyond the scope of this book, let me clue you in on a few more of the most significant changes in our approach in offices.

For one thing, since time is the inventory of the office, we typically launch improvements to the value stream (lean) in close sequence to (sometimes in parallel with) the steps of an office conversion to visuality. On the visual side, instead of waiting to implement the *visual where*, we use standards of visual practices, including the *visual where*, as an application pathway. Standards of office visuality drive the office initiative.

Yet, there is also much that remains unchanged from our production floor implementation. For example, we never deviate from our commitment to create I-driven visuality. Nor do we lower our expectation that office personnel will invent remarkable, never-seen-before, visual solutions.

Office personnel are as eager as anyone to self-solve their problems. In that regard, the vast majority of office personnel, including in hospitals, demonstrate a keen interest in studying and understanding visual devices from all settings, including manufacturing. Wisely, they do not insist on seeing only examples from their own kind of work environment. Anyone with a grasp of the eight building blocks will see past the narrow local details of great visual solutions from other settings and generalize to their own need. This is a hallmark of good visual thinking and commonplace among those who are properly trained in visual knowledge and know-how. (See Photo Album 23.)

• • • •

The final two Doorways (9 and 10) are not about a group of specific visual methods. Instead, they focus on linking up the organization and attaining a truly comprehensive outcome: a visually-capable enterprise.

Especially in larger facilities or across geographic locations, spreading visuality deeper, wider, and more quickly becomes a task requiring an unwavering focus as well as the means for integrating and standardizing a wide assortment of visual solutions. All this must be done without stifling the very creativity that has generated the local inventiveness at the heart of a series of Visual Best Practices.

Setting and implementing standards for workplace visuality are sizeable undertakings. The final two doorways in VTI's approach to visual information-sharing recognizes the importance of this outcome and provides innovative concepts, tools, and frameworks to address it.

Doorway 9: The Macro Visual Environment

As a visual workplace initiative gathers speed (and by the fifth or sixth month it will), management will face many micro decisions that, summed up, can have a large impact on the company's macro environment. It is important, therefore, to form a special team to attend to them. That is precisely the purpose of *Doorway 9: The Visual Macro Environment* (Figure 9.5).

FIGURE 9.5: VISUAL MACRO ENVIRONMENT

This focus is a wide one and therefore requires a special team. A main goal of a company's visual-macro team is to identify, standardize, and institute macro-visual mechanisms that will knit together diverse organizational functions into a single visual landscape. Such mechanisms can include:

- A coordinated color-coding system across multiple sites
- Coordinated in and out locations for material handling
- Building visually-integrated pull systems
- An array of visual links between all functions and across all sites
- A growing framework of Visual Best Practices at each organizational level

This team is also poised to take on special projects that can move to resolution quickly. Delays in incoming material inspection, for example, may be a trouble spot. Let the visual macro team take on the challenge and find a set of rich visual solutions to address it. Naturally, they will interface with area supervisors and value-add associates. But the key usefulness of this team is as owners of systems-level problems, with a mandate to cut through layers of inertia and resistance and get the job done effectively, through the savvy application of visual principles and practices.

In no way does this activity conflict with—or override—training and implementation on the area level. No burnt bridges, please. Visual-macro team members work in parallel with local efforts, not instead of them.

Here is a set of outputs developed by a visual-macro team of one of my UK clients, in support of a sustainable visual where (Doorway 1), specifically for addresses.

1. All barcode addresses on shelving must be backed in a contrasting color to clarify location.

2. Cancelled or out-of-date barcodes must be removed.

3. Any shelf address must have an arrow, showing to which shelf that address applies.

4. Any address containing words must use upper and lower case.

5. Every department will identify the top of its value stream and put its address there.

These five standards require that addresses (a visual device) attain a uniform level of function—in this case, readability. But be careful: None of this requires people to make their visual devices look alike, look the same, or even be the same. There are a gazillion ways to create highly-effective addresses. Let them all be used, ensuring their effectiveness through these never-miss rules. These are the kind of standards that trigger us to become scientists of our processes, not mindless copycats. I am sure you recognize the difference.

Needless to say, those who serve on this macro team must be master visual thinkers themselves—*visual senseis*, in the popular parlance. They must: 1) be able to identify minute and strategic forms of motion triggered by macro applications; and 2) be practiced in minimizing or even eliminating that motion through solutions that are visual.

Whether the workforce size is 2000 people or 20, companies of every description need a visual-macro team, not just large or multi-site organizations. The macro needs of a rollout start to surface as soon as more than one department undertakes visuality. Therefore set up this in-house team early, in full recognition that it cannot grasp the full implications of its purpose until tested. Let the visual knowledge and know-how of team members grow, over time, into visual expertise. And let them start early. They will learn a great deal through the doing, as long as they are well anchored in visual thinking concepts, principles, and examples—lots and lots examples.

The most important thing is for them to learn enough (and then know enough) to ask the right questions and recognize the right answers.

Another powerful template for this is found next, in *Doorway 10: The Visual Enterprise.*

Doorway 10: The Visual Enterprise

A large workforce and/or multiple sites create new sets of challenges when a company wants to implement a structured, sustainable approach to workplace visuality.

Doorway 10 opens to a comprehensive visual conversion process that continues to promote and reward visual inventiveness, build individual and team leadership, and achieve fine bottomline results (Figure 9.6).

The cookie-cutter approach is death to workplace visuality. Visual devices and systems need the juice of local imaginations devising splendid solutions to problems that are often invisible to those outside the department. No company can afford to give up that juice. It is crucial to sustainability and to solutions that really work.

FIGURE 9.6:
VISUAL ENTERPRISE

For the past two decades, VTI's team of visual coaches and trainers has been implementing a powerful framework of principle-based exams that build enterprise coherency and alignment through visuality. You may think I refer to an audit process when I describe the central mechanism as an exam. I do not. An audit is a closed-ended formulation that tests and rewards compliance. Our visual enterprise exams are driven by visual principles that allow visual thinkers to go deeper and wider in their pursuit of motion as the footprint of the enemy.

For example, in assessing Doorway 1/Visual Order, we do not ask if the things of the workplace are neat and orderly. Instead, we seek to assess *the extent to which* specific visual principles are in place: store things/not air, use the existing architecture, sort the universe, point-of-use, and so on and so forth. The exam questions are as dynamic as visual thinking itself, always looking for ways to help people see more clearly and more completely as they deepen their understanding of the science of motion and the power of visuality to dissolve workplace struggle.

This final doorway opens when senior management decides the site is ready for visual consolidation through the stepwise exam process. As you can already see, these exams are not designed to find fault, assess blame or root out inadequacies. Instead, they present a set of principles and practices that allows the workforce to understand what winning means in workplace visuality and how to implement it accordingly. At the conclusion of an exam cycle, each department gets a score, based on the extent to which it succeeded (not failed) in implementing these principles and practices.

Exams are administered by a set of cross-functional site examiners, preferably volunteers from every organizational level, with highly educated visual eyesight and a deep desire to see visuality spread. They are I-driven, the company's visual leaders, and ace visual thinkers in their own right.

The exam questions are captured in a detailed set of visual scorecards that describes the visual requirements for the micro and macro work environments throughout the facility and, as applies, across far-flung sites. In other words, they describe a corporate-wide set of criteria-based visual principles and practices that incorporate all pathway levels and all doorways. It is a heady experience.

Rolling out workplace visuality to a large site or multiple locations is not simply a matter of doing multiple applications of the same procedure. Scale makes its own demands. The level of specialized visual needs required in a large organizational environment runs roughly parallel to the scope and level of specialized information which that same organization routinely requires. Complex companies demand complex rollouts.

A robust implementation framework is required. It will take time to put this firmly in place as the core element of your sustainment process. Enterprise-wide visuality is capable of producing remarkable cost-savings along with work culture alignment. A company committed to excellence should seek—not shrink from—the highest possible level of visual integration and coherency.

• • • •

With this, we conclude our treatment of the technologies of the visual workplace as discrete methods and outcomes. In the next section of this book, we consider three final themes: visual management, the doorways as an assessment tool (plus a visual conversion mini-case study), and the visual-lean® alliance.

FIGURE I: THE IMPLEMENTATION PATHWAY

Section | Four

VISUAL THINKING

Now that you know about visual workplace technologies and the stunning cultural and bottom-line benefits they produce, never forget that their purpose is to build and support that single mechanism for creating and delivering value—the enterprise.

The first of this book's final two chapters surfaces and corrects several misunderstandings about the fit between visual management and the visual workplace. This is an important discussion. Without getting the difference straight, you may well over-estimate the capability of the first to advance the enterprise—and grossly under-estimate the scope and power of the second to do the same. Either way, your company loses. Chapter 10 is my attempt to change that outcome.

Chapter 11 provides a valuable conclusion to this book's discussion. First, it describes how the Ten-Doorway Model can be used as an assessment instrument that allows you to decide which doorway is most important to open first and why. A company case study of Royal Nooteboom Trailers (RNT) in Holland follows, illustrating the doorways in action over the course of a five-year visual conversion. Guided by the over-arching goal of self-sufficiency, RNT and its workforce walked through seven of the ten doorways and, as a result, gained splendid cultural and bottom-line outcomes that were sustainable. What started as a strong operator-led visual implementation transitioned to the basics of lean, and finally became a successful visual-lean® alliance in the operations of the company's five sites. RNT was transformed, as were the people who worked there, including executive leaders—all self-leaders and ready to continue the journey to excellence on their own and yet in tight alignment with others. It was a heady and entirely satisfying experience.

With that glory described, albeit in summary, this book concludes with an invitation for you to make the decision to get visual, cultivate a workforce of visual thinkers, and let the workplace speak.

Words are free.
It's how you use them that can cost you.

Mom's Law

CHAPTER | **10**

Visual Management vs. Visual Workplace

Lately, the term *visual management* is on the lips of many business leaders, management gurus, and consultants as today's "answer" to operational excellence. Avid attention on visual information-sharing of any kind is, of course, a step in the right direction and, therefore, good news. Except for this: Many of those people—perhaps including you—are treating visual management as though it is the same as a fully-functioning visual workplace when, in fact, it is not.

Definition of Visual Management

What is visual management? How is it defined? And how does it fit in with workplace visuality and the technologies of the visual workplace—the focus of this book?

Visual management (VM) is a measurement approach that monitors organizational results and then displays those results in flat/2-D formats. Some popular formats include: KPI dashboards; LCD data monitors; glass walls; vision/mission statements; hour-by-hour tracking charts, to name but a few. Whatever your list of visual management constructs, they share a single goal: to make it easy for managers to see and understand what is going on in the organization on a more abstract and summative level than the work content itself. In other words, VM makes it easy to tell merely by looking.

The flat figures of VM—a sheet of paper, a flat screen, a poster, a chart—are packed with at-a-glance evidence about the organizational direction, pace, and results. They visually share what the enterprise does and how well (or not so well) it does it.

The purpose of visual management is twofold: first, to share the company's direction and intent; and, second, to frame critical results data so their meaning is clearly understood—and adjustments can be made. While that makes visual management an important part of the visual workplace continuum, it is not a substitute for it.

In their sum, VM formats are designed to connect and align a company's many activities to deliver the right value to the customer, on time, safely, and within the constraints of that company's cost structure.

VM devices compel our interest because the information they convey is so vital to the stability and growth of the enterprise—and because these devices are visual. Science has already established that we humans are creatures of our senses. As shared in Chapter 1, 50% of the brain's resources are dedicated to finding and interpreting visual data. In this regard, the power of visual formats to convey, connect, and illuminate is unsurpassed. Humans are masters of spatial interpretation, which rivals by a hundredfold our ability to retain and understand non-visual/abstract events. Seeing is not only believing. Seeing makes it so.

Yet a number of studies show that visual management devices have had little or no trackable impact on the bottom line. For example, in the five years between 2007 and 2012, companies in Europe and the US invested a startling five billion dollars in setting up visual management systems—yet they experienced less than a 5% success rate, with success defined as measurable KPI improvement. What went wrong?

Visual Management: The Subset

Part of the problem stems from thinking that visual management and the visual workplace are the same thing. They are not. The terms *cannot* be used interchangeably.

To begin to unpack this common mistake, let's revisit the tried and tested definition of a visual workplace I use throughout this book:

The visual workplace is a self-ordering, self-explaining, self-regulating, and self-improving workplace—where what is <u>supposed</u> to happen <u>does</u> happen on time, every time, day or night, because of visual devices.

When the visual workplace is effectively implemented, it visually shares the informational details of your operational system—along the goals and results of that system. The array of visual solutions this produces can be vast and include, for example: color coding; visual standards; the visual where (border/addresses); visual scheduling and visual display boards; visual controls and visual pull systems; visual machine devices; visual guarantees/poka-yoke systems—as well as KPI dashboards; LCD monitors, Obeya rooms, and other visible tracking systems.

Yes, that's right: The visual workplace (and its interchangeable term, *workplace visuality*) encompasses visual management and much, much more. Workplace visuality is the umbrella framework; visual management is a subset—and not the other way around. A highly-effective visual workplace demonstrates the full spectrum of visual functions, including visual management. It becomes the visible language of your current operational system, whether your organization is a factory, healthcare center, government agency, office or open-pit mine.

Yes, visual management is mission-critical and should be pursued by every company interested in stability, accountability, and growth—as long as you understand that visual management is *only one* in a progression of core visual functions that comprise the visual workplace. It does not and cannot stand alone.

Far too many companies and practitioners *think* they understand what visual management is—and, by inference, the visual workplace. Yet, the ways in which they *don't* understand prevent them from utilizing visuality effectively. This is not just a mistake in thinking; it is the loss of the huge improvement opportunity you have been reading about in this book.

The Visual Workplace Continuum

Look at Figure 10.1. It shows the eight categories of visual functions found in an advanced visual work environment. (Note: The continuum is a condensed version of the Ten-Doorway Model that we examined in Section Three, only mapped onto a horizontal axis.)

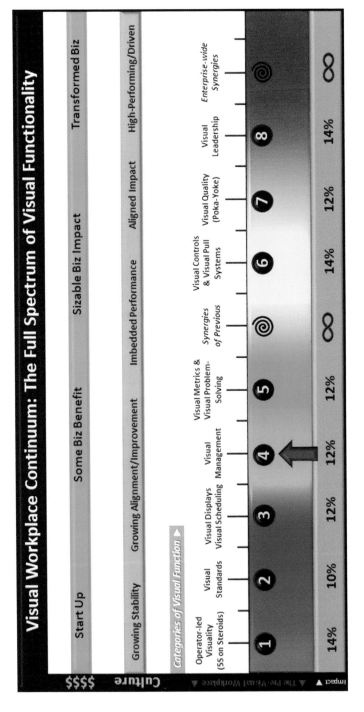

FIGURE 10.1:

THE SPECTRUM OF VISUAL FUNCTION

This progression shows eight categories of visual function in theoretical order. Remember to implement them as the needs and goals of your company require. The pink band at the bottom shows a rough estimate of the impact that each visual function has on the stability, alignment, and growth of the enterprise. Visual management is one—and only one—such function. It is most effective when implemented as part of a larger, enterprise-wide, visual workplace transformation.

Implemented effectively, these visual functions will convert a traditional enterprise that is at—or near—zero in terms of its current level of visual competency to full-on visuality, to which for the sake of discussion, I will assign a value of 100%. Let's take a walk….

The journey of this continuum starts on the far left, with a company struggling in a pre-5S/pre-visual work environment. It then crosses eight visual categories. The ultimate outcome or destination of this journey is an enterprise that is high-performing, stable, growing—and capable of driving. The visual conversion is comprehensive and complete.

Returning to the continuum, notice that *visual management* is located as the fourth function in the progression. I gauge its contribution to a fully-functional visual workplace at some 12%. You may consider that paltry, but it is not. Look at the contribution level of the other seven categories (pink bar at bottom). The contribution, for example, of the mighty *visual where* (aka, operator-led visuality/5S on steroids) is assessed at 14%, higher than that of VM but still a modest number.

The message is clear: the power of visuality is *not* in any single segment or function but in the synergies of their collective sum. Said another way, visual management can have substantial impact on operational effectiveness—but only when it is combined and aligned with its other functional partners.

Errors in Concept

Misunderstandings that currently surround visual management are largely errors in concept—the wrong idea about the definition, purpose, and scope of VM. These errors often lead us to believe that VM can do more than it is capable of doing. For example, VM cannot make the workplace speak. And when it doesn't, we blame the tool for failing us or blame ourselves for not using it correctly.

If, in this scenario, we equate visual management with the visual workplace, we may well declare them both a failure and turn our backs on all things visual. The truth is, however, we expected too much of visual management and not enough of workplace visuality. As a result, we often dismiss both as sad flavor-of-the-month examples. These are all errors in concept. Here's a closer look.

- **Errors in Definition:** Powerful though it is, visual management is only one element of fully-invested visuality at work. It is not all things to all visual needs. Because it has a specific scope and purpose, visual management is most effective when deployed with this understanding.

- **Errors in Purpose:** While an effective visual management deployment can create a very positive impact on the business, that impact will not be long-lasting if it is not combined with other categories of visual function. Visual management is a mechanism for defining, discerning, calibrating, and framing performance results—but it is *not* the performance itself.
- **Errors in Scope:** The third error is closely connected to the first. Because some companies do not realize that visual management is part of a larger construct, they wrongly assume it can achieve outcomes reserved for other functions in the visual workplace continuum. Though visual management makes no claim to omnipotence, if we think it is all-powerful, it will disappoint us.

The technologies of the visual workplace (which *include* the VM method) are powerful allies in every company's march to operational excellence. Unchecked, however, these conceptual errors will limit your use of visuality and your ability to reach your destination. Knowledge and logic are the natural antidotes.

Visual Management: Level by Level

In keeping with that, let's take a short walk through a representative array of visual management (VM) formats, level by level. In my lexicon, visual management has four step-down levels and a fifth that is all-encompassing:

Goal 1: Make the corporate intent visually understandable and appealing

Goal 2: Visually assess and align business results on the site-level

Goal 3: Visually assess and align process results on the department-level

Goal 4: Visually assess and align process results on the value-add level

Goal 5: Visually integrating priorities and results in a single location

Examples follow. As you will see, you can tailor any to the specifics of your company.

Goal 1: The Corporate Intent

When your company gets clear about its direction and wants to rally popular support, making the corporate intent visible is an early and very useful next step.

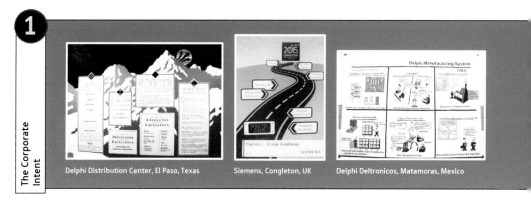

The Corporate Intent

Delphi Distribution Center, El Paso, Texas | Siemens, Congleton, UK | Delphi Deltronicos, Matamoras, Mexico

FIGURE 10.2:
These three VM formats capture a high-level of vision of where the corporation and its growth are aimed.

Here we enter the vision-/mission-sharing realm of visual management.

The three examples in Figure 10.2 reflect the executive view of the future—enterprise growth and the inspired journey to get there. As with any visionary statement, these 2-dimension visual formats convey more than words alone. Mountains signify challenge; but, because we are climbing them together, we'll reach the top. The roadway image strongly suggests not just progress but a plan: Follow us and we'll get there together. Example three shows a grid, evoking order, structure, and stability; we immediately have more confidence in what's in each of the six cells because we intuitively understand that they are connected. As a result, we also are connected, a part of something greater than ourselves.

Useful? Almost beyond measure when we consider again the capability of the brain to find *and interpret* visual data. These images take us directly into the vision they represent—and with that come the beginnings of understanding, ownership, and alignment. We enroll—and that's exactly what the corporate intent requires and so emphatically seeks through these visual mechanisms.

Goal 2: Site-Level Results

Having shown us the view from the top of the mountain—where the corporation is going and why—visual management ratchets down a level and displays measures and results on the site level (Figure 10.3). Most frequently these are an array of key performance indicators (KPIs) that disclose how the enterprise is doing in quantifiable terms—and nearly always as points of comparison: first time quality (FTQ)

2

KPIs on the Site Level

Delphi Distribution Center, El Paso, Texas   Plymouth Tube, West Monroe, Louisiana   GM Powertrain, White Marsh, Maryland

FIGURE 10.3:

What site would not benefit from a VM board that overviews site performance against commonly-accepted KPIs. Our three examples support that (left to right): Delphi's Glass Wall (signifying data transparency); a large board for plant-wide KPIs; and gigantic LCD monitor at GM Powertrain, displaying real-time performance data for key operations across this vast plant.

versus defect levels; customer complaints versus customer satisfaction; scrap versus productivity; late delivery versus on-time delivery or linearity; and so on.

Often called *The Glass Wall*, site-level displays of KPIs present enormously powerful data. The highly visual format discloses and amplifies meaning because it visibly captures relationship, making the impact more compelling. These speak to us of results and the impact of our performance on the bottom line. We begin to grasp what is expected of us in a very precise way and to understand our performance contribution in a wider, more substantial context. Effectively presented, KPIs can connect up and organize. They are not powerful enough to illuminate cause or create alignment. But they certainly point to the need for both—something that in the pre-visual workplace is not only unknown but unknowable.

Goal 3: Department-Level Results

Next stop: visual management on the departmental level—the realm of dashboards. Before we look at dashboards, however, let's make sure we understand the purpose of KPIs on the area or departmental level: They disclose the result of performance, closer to cause. Figure 10.4 shows you three such VM arrays.

Site level KPIs are frequently referred to as tactical feedback or measures; and on the corporate level, they are often termed *strategic* in nature. No problem there. In fact, making such distinctions helps the rest of us see that different organizational levels need differing data bundles or roll ups. Typically, corporate is looking

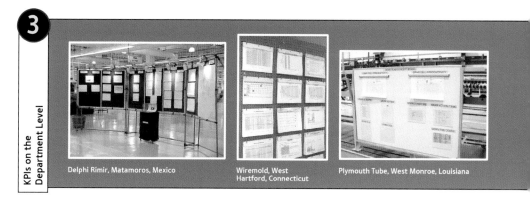

FIGURE 10.4:

KPI results on the area level bring us much closer to cause and therefore closer to understanding work, time, and performance factors on the value-add level. Sometimes called an "oasis," these centers of information help reveal the right and wrong of our systems and procedures. Visual problem-solving—which is not within VM's scope—is an obvious next step.

for evidence in the data that growth is needed or timely (or the reverse: better wait). On the site level, KPIs reveal the money- and time-eaters, conditions that need attention if the site is to make its required contribution to corporate mandates.

Departmental KPIs reveal where the bodies are buried—the casualties called cost, defects, accidents, long change-over times, excessive absenteeism, material shortages, and so on. The usual suspects. In this respect, visual management formats are superb communication tools. Cleverly and carefully configured, the best KPIs reveal the evidence—the result of people, machine, and system behaviors.

But be careful. KPIs are not powerful enough to change or improve those behaviors in any long-term or sustainable way. Area-level KPIs monitor only. Using them will not strengthen your operational outcomes, but they will make it clear when you need to do so. They sound the alarm. People will pay more attention, and this may well produce a temporary positive uptick in those very same KPIs.

Goal 4: Results on the Value-Add Level

There is a reason you hear practitioners declare that it "all happens at *gemba*." Gemba is the happening place, the source, the nexus of causality; and it exists exclusively on the value-add level. Interestingly, "Going to Gemba" was first used by detectives in Japan on their way to the scene of a crime—the site of primary evidence.

The formats of visual management on the value-add (or cellular) level track

KPIs on the Value-Add Level

Area-level KPI array on wheels at Kimray, Oklahoma City.   One of Kimray's many machining areas, with overhead VM monitors.   Real-time machine data are shared on this VM monitor.   This monitor connects operator, supervisor, and maintenance.

FIGURE 10.5:

With over 300 machines at the heart of its manufacturing process, Kimray installed an aggressive visual management system on the value-add level. Here a wide array of LCD monitors and shares mission-critical data, real-time, in support of production planning and machine utilization.

metrics from work's causal dimension, as well as local goals, targets, and cost drivers. In clever hands, they can also identify the minute contributors generated by the actual work. The value-add level is where data begins.

Figure 10.5 is a mini-album that illustrates this. We start with a KPI board on wheels that provides a performance snapshot in one of 300 machine centers. Then we capture real-time performance data in an airborne LCD monitor, electronically linked to the individual machine. Notice the OEE detail (overall equipment effectiveness). But be careful: These data only tell us the good or bad news related to machine and operator performance. It does not, as discussed in Chapter 7, illuminate or reveal cause and, therefore, does not position us to take immediate corrective action.

Still, even though more investigation is required before performance can improve, we are in a vastly more active position than we would be without these VM devices.

Goal 5: Integrating Priorities and Results in the Opex Room

A dashboard is an intense interface of priorities, measurements, and results in a narrow, highly-designed format. It typically addresses the big four KPIs: safety, quality, delivery, and cost. When integrated within an Opex or Obeya Room (Chapter 6), new connections, insights, and actions happen rapidly (Figure 10.6).

When dashboards link directly to live databases, you get to see the moving parts in real-time: the dynamic inputs that contribute to rolled-up results, with the line-of-sight easily switching between value-add, departmental, and site levels. As

5

Dashboards, Scheduling,
and the Opex Room

FIGURE 10.6:

From left to right: a) A mix of digital and manual dashboards in the Reliability Room of this machine-based facility; b) This company built an Opex Room right on its production floor; c) An array of physical scheduling boards help this aerospace manufacturer track and improve its site-wide scheduling.

a result, the entire enterprise (executives, managers, supervisors, operators, and support functions) can access up-to-the-minute information at a click. This makes results that were previously subject to lengthy preparation available instantly. Now add visual scheduling and enter the magical world of Opex Room capability. There is much to be said for—and done with—this heady level of visual management. Yet, however much VM helps you gain evidence and insight, it does not position you to improve results. Why? *Because you have still not entered the causal chain.*

Embedded-ness: Telling versus Making

As you have seen, the tools of visual management provide a quantity-based window on the behavior of people, machines, and systems. VM does this by monitoring, tracking, and displaying related information. The result is an array of priorities and KPIs that captures the current state.

Still, we must never forget that these spring from the performance of the work—*the causal chain.* They improve only when work performance improves. Visual functions other than VM are designed to help us do that by embedding the exact behavior needed for perfect performance. Because visual management is a subset of the visual workplace—it is *not* the same as *visual performance.*

As the following example at Holland's Schiphol Airport demonstrates, you don't have to prioritize, track, collect, and analyze KPIs when exact performance is

FIGURE 10.7:
VISUAL EMBEDDED-NESS

This embedded visual device has roots in Victorian England when Thomas Crapper, manufacturer of sanitary ware, embossed urinals with small bees to meet the splashback challenge. The bee was the symbol of the monarchy and Crapper was an arch anti-royalist. Later, cooler heads prevailed and the bee was exchanged for a fly.

embedded into the process itself.

Schiphol is the fourth largest airport in Europe, handling over 52 million passengers a year. Schiphol has another claim to fame: its sparkling men's rooms. In the early 1990s, the airport's cleaning department manager decided to ensure correct men's room usage by literally embedding that behavior into each urinal. The result was an estimated 50% reduction in the so-called "splashback" problem—and a parallel reduction in the need to clean airport men's rooms. In turn, this resulted in an estimated 20% reduction in cleaning costs. Figure 10.7 reveals the why and the how.

Yes, an image of a fly is etched in an *exact* location into the surface of each and every urinal—and the *exact*, correct behavior follows. Nearly 100% adherence is achieved without audits, checklists, supervision, training or KPIs—all without speaking a word. In-process visuality does all the work. Performance requirements are embedded, by design, and the men who enter Schiphol's lofty portals simply comply.

Let the Workplace Speak

Visual management is an important—and often dazzling—part of the improvement methodology known as the visual workplace. But it is only one part. VM can develop improved levels of awareness and therefore encourage improved performance. This improvement, however, is tied to people's exact understanding of what needs to be done. As that understanding fades, results will often also fade back to former wobbly levels. Engage the other dimensions of the visual workplace continuum to prevent backsliding. Create a robust array of all the categories of visual function—not just the numbers part—and let the workplace speak!

The single biggest problem in communication
is the illusion that it has taken place.
George Bernard Shaw

CHAPTER | **11**

Visual Thinking
Visual Transformation

The technologies of the visual workplace are capable of building precision and connectivity into the dynamic landscape of work we call operations. Whether a factory or office, a construction site or retail setting, a school or hospital, every operational landscape is grounded in information. Each work day consists of an unbroken series of transactions that are micro-informational—tiny bits of vital information that tell us what we need to know when we need to know it. Or so we hope.

In a pre-visual workplace, this happens hit or miss. When it doesn't happen, the company often declares that it has a problem in communication. Naming it as such, however, often leads us to a misdiagnosis—to the slippery slope where the effect of the problem is named as its cause. When that happens, we will seek to improve communications by increasing the number of meetings—or making the long ones even longer. All too often, a company with these so-called *communication* problems puts a ton of energy into getting us humans to do a better job in talking, conversing, discussing, and cataloguing. As a result, we focus on conversational clarity and binders of documentation, and better hand-offs between shifts, for example.

We are looking for the wrong solution to the wrong problem. George Bernard Shaw, that famous Irish playwright, had it right when he said: *The single biggest problem in communication is the illusion that it has taken place.*

Workplace visuality makes a radically different diagnosis. When it sees informational drops and mishaps, runaway defects, re-work, scrap, missed deadlines and late deliveries—as well as endless emails and long, fruitless meetings—it looks to the physical landscape of work for answers. To what extent is operational stability and flexibility grounded in a partnership between the world of attributes and behaviors and the items of the physical work environment—the desks, benches, equipment, tools, material, and so forth? To what extent are the physical things at work used as vehicles of information? To what extent does the workplace speak?

Throughout the chapters of this book, I have built the case for a fully-functioning visual workplace, mapping out a new *why* and a new *how* for transforming the enterprise. The Ten-Doorway Model contains the answers to both. First, it is the blueprint for visual transformation. And its utility does not end there. The model is also an assessment tool for diagnosing where to begin that journey.

The Distance Traveled

Achieving a visual workplace is no small task. It doesn't happen overnight. Yet, the rewards of doing so are remarkable: vast improvements in quality, on-time delivery, safety, cost, employee morale, customer satisfaction—and a splendid functional and cosmetic transformation of your operations, physically and conceptually. You may ask: "Who wouldn't want these outcomes?" But I ask a different question: "Why would you stop before you get them?"

You have doubtlessly seen what I have seen. Strangely, some companies make tremendous progress and yet decide to stop their forward march to visuality. Why do they stop? Have they decided that their operations have improved *enough*? Is it impolite to want too much of a good thing? Do they not want to appear greedy? Do they not want the piles of money that are still lying on the floor?

Other companies underestimate the distance they must cover—or overestimate their progress thus far. Sometimes both. There is no harm in valuing one's efforts highly. Yes, it is important to celebrate victories. It is equally important, however, to understand the distance to the goal—and, as crucially, to see the goal itself, vividly, comprehensively, and in detail. Vision is indispensable to the visual journey, but achieving a visual workplace is not an act of faith. It is verifiable. It is quantifiable. It is a known outcome.

Have You Fully Utilized Visuality?

Companies regularly invite us onsite to assess their current level of visual competency and measure the degree of completion they have achieved thus far on their way to a fully-functioning visual workplace. Typically, they fall into one of two categories:

1. Companies new to visuality that want to know the way to a visual workplace, why it is important to them, and what specific benefits will accrue to them when they do.

2. Companies already on their way to visuality that want an accurate diagnosis of their current level of visual competency, along with recommendations on the next steps that are right for them.

Though not treated here, there is a third type of company that benefits greatly from a visual assessment: greenfield sites—brand-spanking new facilities (or ones under construction) that want to build visual principles and practices into the building and layout design. An effective, early assessment can provide developers with a blueprint for building visual capability into the start-up architecture.

In all three cases, my team and I use the Ten-Doorway Model as the key diagnostic tool (Figure 11.1). Because we value self-sufficiency, we

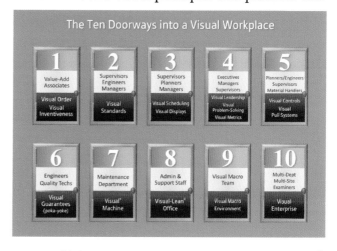

FIGURE 11.1: WHICH DOOR SHOULD YOU OPEN FIRST?

always offer to teach client companies how to assess themselves, giving them copies of our 13-page assessment instrument and providing feedback on their findings. Though they may lack the expertise to do a thorough diagnosis, having them put on their first pair of "visual" eyes invariably educates the wearer, thereby building resources within the company to keep visual improvement going and growing.

We use a plain scale of 1–10 (10 = high); and self-made company scores can reveal a lot about people's eyesight. For example, many facilities may proclaim themselves at a level eight or nine while we may assess them closer to a level three or two—and sometimes even those scores are generous. I make sure to announce that I have seen some sites at a level seven or eight but have yet to see a nine (yes, including Toyota, Milliken, Parker Hannifin, Virginia Mason, and Porsche).

Still, companies usually rank themselves significantly higher than we do. Interesting discussions ensue; and that in itself is important. Progress is always (and only) made through a meeting of the minds—and, in visuality, also through the eyes. Companies have to learn to see and learn to see differently, not just what's there but what is not there—and the meaning of each. Understandably, companies value the validation of outside experts. Next steps are mapped from there.

One of the key lessons learned through the assessment is that the visual workplace cannot be accomplished merely by tacking it onto to another powerful strategy—lean, six sigma, theory of constraints or what have you—even if the company has already implemented that other process successfully. Would you award a gold medal in figure skating to the winner of the decathlon just because he is a fine athlete and has a pair of figure skates in his closet?

We look for comprehensive outcomes when we calibrate using the Ten-Doorway Model. Strength in one doorway (or even three) is commendable, even exciting. Strength in seven of them signifies a complete enterprise transformation, often encompassing the supply chain. The result is embedded transparency and a workplace that speaks. The assessment instrument helps us see that and in detail.

Using the Doorways to Diagnose

The assessment begins with a discussion of the site's business case and what the company wants visuality to contribute to that case. Usually, this entails one of two target outcomes: stability or growth.

If stability, then visuality will be used to clarify, embed, and stabilize the organization's current operational capability. If the company is interested in growth, then visuality will be used to build flexibility and responsiveness into the operational landscape. But the savvy reader knows that stability and growth are closely, if not inseparably, linked. You cannot grow your company without the stability of attributes, processes, and behaviors at its foundation. By the same token, you cannot stabilize your company without growing, a lot. Comprehensive methodologies produce comprehensive outcomes.

A successful visual site assessment requires a new category of eyesight. Steeped in your knowledge of the ten doorways and the visual workplace principles and practices that support them, you must learn to see what is there—and, even more importantly, what is *not* there. Here, I am describing two very different levels of seeing. In the first case, you must see what is there and understand what that means. In the second case, you must see what is not there and understand what that means. In each case, the meaning is importantly different. And that is the point.

This ability to see and derive meaning from what you see is one of the keys to a successful visual assessment. It is also one of the prized outcomes that internal and external trainers and consultants achieve when they study at our educational arm, the Visual-Lean® Institute.

Figure 11.2 shows the scoring page of our assessment tool, along with the steps for using it. As you examine it, you'll notice that it maps closely to the Ten-Doorway Model—but is not an exact match. For example, Doorway 10 (Visual Enterprise) is not included; and Doorway 9 (Visual Macro Environment) is a mechanism for uniting all previous doorways into a single improvement process that aligns visuality within and across the organization, including multiple sites and the supply chain.

Even as a solo reader, you can put the instrument to use by assessing your own work area, and then checking your thinking against the knowledge shared in the chapters in this book. This will confirm or add to your understanding of workplace visuality and the technologies represented by the ten doorways. Either way, it is good learning and a way to check your visual thinking.

I also encourage you to visit our website (www.visualworkplace.com) where we have several avenues for going further, including training and certification systems, in-person visual site assessments, at-a-distance visual site assessments, and the Shingo Institute's online course on the Ten-Doorway Model.

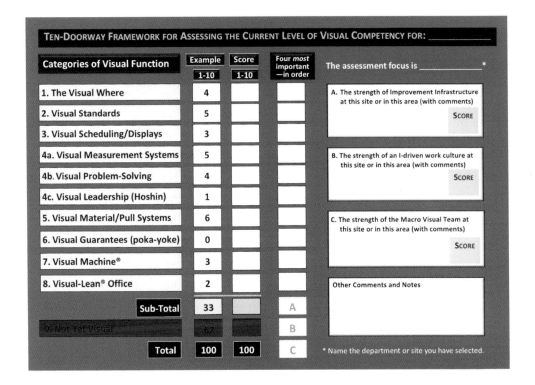

FIGURE 11.2: TEN-DOORWAY ASSESSMENT STEPS

1. Choose your assessment focus. It can be the entire site or a single department or work area. Note it in the upper right.
2. Considering each of the categories of visual function, look for evidence of the extent to which each is functionally in place and capable. Does that category measurably contribute to the performance outcomes of your assessment focus? Does it have discernible impact?
3. Based on your assessment, score the impact and completeness of each category, using a scale of 1-10 (with 10=high). Write in your score.
4. Do the same for boxes A, B, and C, based on your current level of understanding.*
5. When you complete your scores, consider them in light of the business case of the site (or area).
6. Select the four most important categories of visual function for the stability and/or growth of the site (or area).
7. Rank-order your selection, with #1 signifying the most important. You can include A, B, and C in the top four or rank them separately.

* The elements of a viable improvement infrastructure are treated in good detail in my book on operator-led visuality, *Work That Makes Sense*.

The Doorways at Work: Royal Nooteboom Trailers

Workplace visuality is a language—precise, comprehensive, and practical. That language is the details of your operational systems, embedded into the physical landscape of work as visual devices and visual mini-systems. Our operational intelligence, our knowledge and know-how, is made physical and manifest.

Move away from the notion that visuality is an inanimate collection of visual devices. Move towards visuality as the *language of performance*. It is your operational vocabulary in action.

In a visual workplace, the *power* in an *empowered* workforce is generated when information is reliably and repeatedly shared through visual solutions. When information is made visual by design, it becomes a concrete and indispensable part of your operations and therefore your company's business case.

I have cited the name of Royal Nooteboom Trailers (RNT) repeatedly throughout this book. Over the several years of our work together, owner and president Henk Nooteboom (and, later, GM Marc de Leuuw) decided to open the doors in the Ten-Doorway Model (Figure 11.3). But what exactly does that mean?

For RNT, it meant teaching people how to think *systematically*. When I arrived, the RNT workforce was already an accomplished population of skilled contributors. Innovative and independent, RNT welders and assemblers knew what they were doing, on a mastery level. Forklift drivers were clever and efficient. Supervisors tracked down mis-laid or mis-ordered raw material with the smarts that only veteran insiders possess. Engineers feverishly sought to stop the glut of ECNs (Engineering Change Notices) that flooded production every week. People were clever. They made the company work. Product got shipped on-time or near enough. And the quality stood up nicely.

When we started, the goal was to get operators

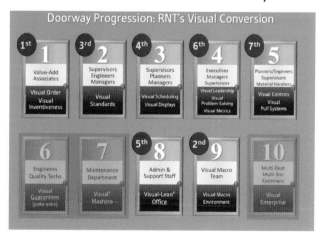

FIGURE 11.3:
THE ORDER IN WHICH RNT OPENED THE DOORS

involved and break down the silos between operational functions. People were not exactly fighting with each other. By the same token, they were not aligned. RNT's business case suffered, as a result.

We began. What happened next is a perfect example of using the Ten-Doorway Model as both an organizing logic and a diagnosis tool. What unfolded was a compelling enterprise-wide transformation of a company as it converted to visuality as the next step in its journey to operational excellence. Here's the snapshot.

Through operator-led visuality and the visual where (Doorway 1), many production-level work areas were transformed within the first 18 months, and with them, the people who worked there. Department-level productivity grew by a measurable 13% to 27%. The work culture of RNT's shop floor transformed from crafts-based contribution to a well-connected empowered team. I-driven visuality had begun to work its magic on the value-add level.

During the same 18 months, RNT organized its Visual Macro Team (Doorway 9), a group of ace visual thinkers, conducting projects to visually link departments and functions. Their job was to bring visual precision, adherence, and alignment across the company's macro-operational environment.

During this time and in quick parallel, visual standards (Doorway 2) made their contribution. For example, blueprints moved out of the engineering office and were posted in a color-coded array at the workstations themselves. In addition, dozens of SOPs were visually documented with specs and photographs and formatted onto laminated cards. Still other laminated cards revealed the tricky bits in achieving quality and process precision.

Visual scheduling and displays (Doorway 3) gave supervisors a sense of control and clarity over their corner of the world. The production schedule began to stabilize. Behind-the-scenes, the visual implementation team (Doorway 1/Infrastructure) started to make important inroads into building an improvement framework within the company that would grow to hold, support, and troubleshoot systematic improvement on an organization-wide scale. The Visual Macro Team was creating visual linkages between functions. Flow took hold, with the promise of pull not far off.

Those first 18 months saw the rewards of the first conversion cycle. The company had built the habit of thinking—visual thinking on the production floor. The exact same operators who had been in silos of work at the launch had become spirited, engaged, and aligned. A large measure of motion vanished, replaced by their visual devices, local inventions that solved and connected. RNT's transformation, born of progressive, systematic change, had taken root through four of the ten doorways—the technologies—of the visual workplace.

The Visual-Lean® Alliance

That conversion to visuality then stabilized and plateaued. The principles and practices of the visual where continued to spread, area-based productivity continued to achieve a double-digit improvement, and supervisors gained increasingly greater control over their line schedules. But there were no breakthroughs. And I knew why: Visual now needed lean.

The noise in the macro environment was absorbing the benefits that visuality had produced on the cell level. Those benefits would not—could not—hit the bottom line until that noise was removed. The critical path that materials followed at RNT had to be cleared, streamlined, and leveled through a thorough application of lean principles and practices.

Like the two wings of a bird, visual and lean share a single, grand purpose: to help the enterprise achieve, sustain, and grow operational excellence. Lean addresses the technical side of this challenge, focusing on the surgical excision of macro-level waste in the relentless pursuit of the least-cost means. The result is a nearly predictable 60% to 80% reduction in overall lead time and the footprint of production—even more in many cases—and for productivity to improve as dramatically.

Visual targets a different operational world, the world of information and its users—people and the health and flexibility of the company's work culture. This focus is on the micro-, even microscopic, level—the spaces within and between the elements of the critical path.

Visuality's first challenge, as repeatedly described throughout this book, is to find the enemy— missing information—and root it out. In translating information deficits into visual devices and systems, the technologies of the visual workplace enable employees to execute the standards formulated

PHOTO 11.1: THE VISUAL-LEAN®
ALLIANCE—TWO WINGS OF A BIRD

by lean into performance that is safe, precise, complete, and on-time. In a visual conversion, an aligned and engaged work culture is a by-product of tremendous bottom-line results. A 15% to 30% increase in productivity is nearly always a given, along with the stability that comes from reliable performance, no matter the venue, even in high-volume/low-mix production—and even if lean has never (and will never) be implemented.

Visuality is a gigantic adherence mechanism. It creates stability in the enterprise, from health care to discrete manufacturing, from offices to continuous process flow, from retail spaces to open-pit mines. Even Grandma's cupcake business will grow and prosper when housed within the architecture of a visual workplace. The path is identical in all work settings: Build the operational dynamic of visual information sharing into the living landscape of work. Learn how to think and apply visually and teach others to do the same.

Anchored in this platform of knowledge and know-how, the organization moves from strength to strength. Its excellence is sustained and sustainable, deeply rooted in visuality's ability to continually engage the creativity of the workforce and capture it in concrete, functional form—liberating information and in the process, the human will. This is a workforce of visual thinkers.

Visual takes on central business and cultural outcomes that lean does not *and cannot* address. Thus is the partnership between the two formed. The result of this alliance is an organization of rigor, focus, and longevity.

A Lean Stopover

Although it took some time for me to convince him, Henk Nooteboom finally secured the services of a lean group, based in the US. Putting my quarterly visits on pause, I waited to watch the US group work its magic. For the next 18 months, the organization put basic lean in place: standard work and the beginning of pull. Progress was made, but it was also unmade.

As with many lean practitioners, the US team did not understand workplace visuality, nor its powerful natural partnership with lean outcomes. As a result, they let visuality slide and with it the cultural and performance muscle we had worked so hard to put in place, focusing RNT's now-considerable improvement power on a comparatively light-weight lean agenda. But I digress; and so I will skip past, at least for this book's purposes, the many juicy issues and learnings of this period.

Visual Returns and Visual-Lean Begins

Suffice it to say that, when I returned, RNT was ready to open more doorways. But first we revisited Doorways 1 and 3, recovering and then strengthening the visual contributions of operators and supervisors. After another round of training in visual scheduling and displays, RNT supervisors developed the glorious display boards that became the backbone of production scheduling as the company transitioned into pull systems.

Operator training also gained strength. Working with the RNT implementation team, we turned the *Work That Makes Sense* materials into one-point lessons (less than 45 minutes each) and had them translated into Dutch. The result was a nearly complete training of all line employees across all five RNT sites that was fast and effective. Visual inventions began to pour out of the minds of RNT's visual thinkers and onto the shop floor.

About this time, Doorway 8/Visual-Lean® Office was opened and the hunt for motion in non-production work environments was underway.

By then, we had also opened Doorway 4/Visual Leadership. Engineering got serious about visual problem-solving, using the ScoreBoard methodology described in Chapter 7. Through it, they attacked the causes of ECNs. Within three months, the staggering number of 78 ECNs per week was reduced to 7 or less *per month*. This was mighty work—chronic, complex, and costly—and the ScoreBoard Diagram was up to the challenge. A cheer went up that could be heard all over Wichen, Holland (RNT's home town), when the new level had stabilized.

Senior leadership got on board with the X-Type matrix and other Hoshin tools. This was a revolution in the board room that not only made executive leadership more effective but allowed the enterprise to expand to other EU countries. It was a heady achievement.

Lean was never far from our awareness. Everyone understood that the company needed to go further into lean. Back in the driver's seat, I worked with the local team to pick up where the US team had left off and mapped out a visual-lean® conversion template (Doorway 5). That template became key in allowing the parallel implementation of lean and visual, area by area. As we braided the elements of time and information into each work area, productivity, reliability, and cost began to improve. Flow morphed into pull. This visual-lean transformation moved along the template's paced timeline of required milestones.

Interestingly, one of the most dramatic milestone moments was the installation of a simple school clock in each of the work areas targeted for visual-lean conversion. Though I carefully explained their importance for takt-time driven production, management exhibited massive resistance. Once the clocks were on the wall, however, value-add associates were visibly energized by the challenge and precision their *kleine klokken* imposed. Terrific progress was made.

By the end of my engagement at RNT, seven of the ten doorways had been opened, entered, and, in large part, achieved. The reins were passed to the local team, who had already gained tremendous strength in knowledge and know-how and were fully capable of continuing the journey on their own. They had become self-sufficient in workplace visuality, always the goal of my work. Indeed, small groups of employees were in the process of bringing visual thinking to their churches and schools, spreading the word and the benefits in an ever-widening circle of remarkable tangible and intangible results.

See Albums 24 and 25 for a wide array of visual solutions RNT employees invented, from value-add associates, to engineers, supervisors, material handlers, and Henk Nooteboom himself. Remember what the RNT workforce knows by heart: Workplace visuality is a system of thinking first; the devices flow from that.

I trust this description of RNT's visual conversion helps you better understand how and why the Ten-Doorway Model works, and the six levels of the Visual Workplace Implementation Pathway. Now it's time to ask if you are ready to respond to the call for visual thinking in your enterprise.

The Liberation of the Human Will

Information is power. If you are old enough, you learned that in the 1960s. The revolution that exploded during that period is still playing itself out. When we liberate information, we liberate the human will. That single sentence pinpoints one of visuality's core purposes: to liberate the power within—within me, you, and the person next to us, whoever he or she is.

The principles and practices of workplace visuality teach us to think and, through that thinking, to gain control over our corner of the world. Whether a CEO or value-add associate, engineer or purchasing agent, forklift driver or physician, each of us is confronted with an undifferentiated wall of information, *every day*.

Not only do we live in a world flooded with information and informational tidbits, some information is *always* more important than the rest. Some has more meaning, more importance and more relevance—however temporarily. Herein lies the catch: The specific information that we find meaningful, important, and relevant can change dynamically, not just every day but from moment to moment.

Madness!—unless you have a way to identify and control that informational flood and bend it to your will. Your sanity, happiness, and prosperity—and those of your business—depend on that.

The technologies of the visual workplace are specifically designed to give you that control—whoever you are. Because workplace visuality is an I-driven paradigm, each of us always starts the journey to a workplace that speaks, *solo*. While a large part of what we, as individuals, need to know is held in common with others, we rarely understand that at the outset. Instead, most of us make our escape solo because the struggle and stricture we suffer is, at the beginning, far too personal to share. We are caught in a world without answers. Things will stay that way forever, unless new knowledge and a new paradigm are inserted—the visual workplace.

Workplace visuality teaches and we learn. We learn the name and the nature of the enemy. We learn why it's been so hard to wipe that enemy out: It's invisible. We are struggling to find answers that are literally not there. The only way you can tell that it exists is to learn to detect its footprint, its telltale trace: motion/moving without working. That's when you realize that this invisible foe has been running your life—running you—for a very long time. And you decide to hunt it down and eradicate it because now you can.

You decide to follow the trail of motion and hunt down information deficits—thousands of missing answers that plague your work life every day. You replace them with solutions that are visual. Inventive solutions and plain ones. Innovative devices and ordinary ones. Ones that map to methodology and others that simply leap out of your brain, your magnificent, gorgeous mind—and solve. This is your journey from victim to invincible warrior. This is the journey of the visual thinker.

In Its Fullness

In its fullness, an implementation of the visual workplace changes everything. Everything. In its fullness, it represents the creation of an entirely new set of competencies for people, process, and leadership.

To tell by looking. To tell everything by looking. To put an end to motion

Photo Album 24

RNT gets Visual

The Doorways Opened

As the workforce at Royal Nooteboom Trailers (RNT) opened doorway after doorway into the visual workplace, dozens upon dozens of visual solutions flooded operations, lending the transparency and flexibility that make RNT a fierce competitor.

◀ ▲ Visual Displays Coordinator, Kees Smeeman, works with supervisors at—and directly after—the displays training

Victor Geertruida and his colleague, Jean, created a double-border function never seen before on the planet ▶

▲ RNT's all-associate Steering Team, with Roy and me visiting

▲ A high-precision visual scheduling board and Arnoud and Willem, its two proud owners (who refused the offer of an LCD monitor upgrade) ▶

Doorways 1, 2, 3, 4, and 8

Don't confuse visual management with a full-blown visual workplace. The first helps managers, the second helps everyone. Let the workplace speak!

RNT visual standard: the tricky bits ➤

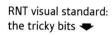

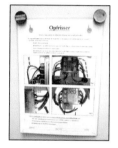

➤ RNT's GM, Marc de Leeuw, walked the talk when he brought visual order to his credenza

➤ Borders were impractical in small part storage so RNT's visual thinkers turned their borders into flexible walls

RNT's Operations Roadmap built alignment on the shop floor ▶

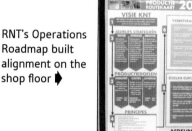

➤ Line supervisor, Pascal Winckers, found a dozen ways to use the strengths of displays

Production chief, Frits Foekens, gained control over his corner of the world through this display ▶

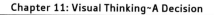

Photo Album 25

Go further/Going wider

The Doorways Opened

As the visual conversion continued, it expanded to include offices and many elements of lean. At the time, many companies, including RNT, were competing with China for steel, copper, and markets.

⬆ Supervisor Standard Work made visual

Supervisor and visual thinker, Wim ⬇

Purchasing gets visual ⬇

⬆ GPS for Coby Hermens, Executive Assistant

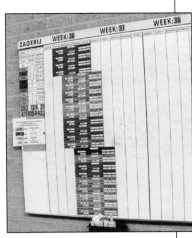

⬆ Visual scheduling for fabricated parts

The Lead Team plan and deploy improvement ⬇

⬆ Don discovers the door to Purchasing is locked....

Doorways 1, 3, 4, 5, 8, and 9

The more doorways that RNT opened, the more competitive it became. Visuality was directly responsible for far greater workforce alignment, increasingly effective leaders, and high levels of complex problem-solving.

◀ Roy coaches, VP/Engineering, Hans, in the ScoreBoarding method ➡ ▶

➡ Visual-lean conversion template (page 1)

◀ Highly-empowered and full of good humor, RNT associates pursue causality ➡

Takt
06:33
Gepland Werkelijk   Achterstand
5 : 4

◀ ⬆ *Time* enters the RNT production equation in stages: first analog and then digital

◀ Aboud contributes

by liberating information that has long been imprisoned in the binders, reports, books, computer files, and data systems of the company—and in the hearts and minds of the workforce. And, in the process, to liberate the human will.

Lean inherited its need for speed and precision from Toyota. But operational excellence is about more than speed and precision—as is TPS. In any genuinely world-class enterprise, adding value quickly (least-cost means) is always inextricably linked to safety, quality, and work culture.

In operational excellence, these are continually addressed in strong and equal measure, none taking precedence over the other. Those who already understand this will implement visual and lean in close alliance—information and the critical path, adherence and pull. Two wings of a bird—both are needed for flight.

To think or do otherwise is to shrink the possibility of tremendous profit, alignment, community, and human development that is the promise of every journey to operational excellence.

Many companies in the world know this and organize their conversion pathways accordingly. Many have yet to learn that the technologies of the visual workplace are *profit makers*. They turn thinking into money, setting up in the company a new core competency for stability and growth.

Visuality is the ground upon which the future of every enterprise rests. Let your visual transformation begin.

RESOURCES

VISUAL THINKING INC.
& THE VISUAL-LEAN® INSTITUTE

Gwendolyn Galsworth began developing the field of workplace visuality in 1983, as she discovered a set of core principles and practices during her client implementations. Over time, she codified her discoveries into a single, robust system of visual workplace methodolgies and outcomes. In 2005, she formed the Visual-Lean® Institute in order to train, certify, and support internal and external trainers and coaches in these. Her company, Visual Thinking Inc. (formerly Quality Methods International) sets the pace for the industry.

Our licensed affiliates are found in North and South America, Europe, China, India, Australia, and in parts of Africa. With over 70,000 visual solutions in our collection, we are continually refining and expanding what and how we share visual workplace knowledge and know-how with you.

We offer a full range of onsite and public services in our nine core visual workplace methodologies, including seminars, workshops, train-the-trainer, master certifications, site assessments, leadership training, trainer and supervisor coaching, and troubleshooting. Our goal is to help you achieve the transformative cultural and bottom-line results that a fully-functioning visual workplace provides. We are honored to count the Shingo Institute, APICS, SME, ASQ, the MEP Network, and AME among our many sponsors and supporters.

Visit our website (www.visualworkplace.com) to see our line of books, tools, training tools, complete online training packages, and onsite services. Customized training and complete visual conversions are our specialty.

Whether yours is a factory, forge, truck fleet, open-pit mine, hospital, school, office, agency or bank—we are here to help you transform your organization into a fully-functioning visual enterprise, the foundation of operational excellence.

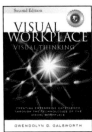

Visual Workplace-Visual Order DVD Training System (Spanish subtitles)

Training of Trainers

Track	Track Content • Courses	
Track 1	Visual Workplace/Visual Thinking Briefing + Pre-Launch Planning	
Track 2	Visual Order/Visual Inventiveness Implementation Suite	
Track 3	Work That Makes Sense: Operator-Led Visuality	
Track 4	Becoming a Leader of Improvement (1): New Role for Supervisors & Managers	Management by Sight: Visual Displays/Control Boards
Track 5	Visual Machine™ Implementation Suite	Machine Lubrication: Visual & Effective
Track 6	Becoming a Leader of Improvement (2): Creating a Business Systems Template	Policy Deployment + Operations Road Map
Track 7	Visual-Lean® Office Implementation Suite	
Track 8	Becoming a Leader of Improvement (3): Visual Metrics/Visual Results	Visual Problem-Solving Visual Standard-Making
Track 9	Visual Adherence: Visual Standards/Visual Controls	Achieving Zero Defects: Visual Guarantees (Poka-Yoke)

Visual Thinking : The Visual-Lean® Institute Curriculum

Online Training

Keynotes

Conferences

Public Seminars

Visual Benchmarking Tours

Work That Makes Sense Operator-Led Visuality
12 Modules of Knowledge and Know-How for Value Add Associates

Complete Online Training Systems

On-Site Assessments and Implementations

English & Spanish

Mistake Proofing for Perfect Quality
a Methodology for Engineers

I N D E X